Indian Ethos in Indian English Fictions

Dr. Samjy Vadakkedom C.M.I.

ATLANTIC
PUBLISHERS & DISTRIBUTORS (P) LTD

Published by
ATLANTIC
PUBLISHERS & DISTRIBUTORS (P) LTD
7/22, Ansari Road, Darya Ganj, New Delhi-110002
Phones : +91-11-40775252, 40775214, 23273880, 23275880
Fax : +91-11-23285873
Web : www.atlanticbooks.com
E-mail : orders@atlanticbooks.com

Branch Office: Chennai
Phones : +91-44-48531784, 28291383
E-mail : chennai@atlanticbooks.com

Printed & bound in India by Atlantic Print Services

Foreword

At a time when Indian writing in English has come of age and made its impact significantly in different parts of the world, and doctoral dissertations on this vast world of creative literature churned out from English departments across Indian universities and colleges are aplenty, a new book in the same area of scholarship may sound redundant. But this book fills some crucial gaps and mends the misreadings in the gamut of research in Indian writing in English, especially in long fiction. The author addresses an issue that is relevant not only to Indian English literature but also to the whole Indian nation, its people and their collective entity, namely, the Indian ethos. The vision that propels the narrative, facilitates the plot, and conceives characters in Indian literature in English is analyzed and placed in an organized frame of research parameters and testimonies that emerge from objective and well-focused study.

The Indian ethos has always been a puzzle and a fascinating subject of study for all Indologists. The diversity of our social, cultural and geographical milieu, the hugeness of Indian population and the length of our history from prehistoric times pose challenges to an exhaustive study on the topic. But the author has pursued this effort diligently in two ways:

(1) By identifying and explaining specific concepts in order to analyze the complex phenomenon of Indian ethos.

(2) By choosing eight novels as case studies in order to apply the concepts and to relate them to what transpires in the selected works.

Perhaps, this book is the best way to know Indian ethos and also to appreciate these novels from a broad ambience—a welcome lens to see into the world of Indian novels in English in relation with the history, culture, philosophy and politics of this country.

The book starts with a comprehensive presentation of Indian ethos as supported on eight pillars of cultural, spiritual and aesthetic principles. The interesting aspect of this book is the placing of a pair each of the eight selected novels within corresponding historical/political period of history. Thus, the ethos of Mulk Raj Anand's *Untouchables* and Raja Rao's *Kanthapura* is attributed to the social and political awakening and nationalist upsurge of the pre-independence period. The novels are analyzed identifying the literary reflection of the conflict between powers of imperialism and struggle for release from it to "build a unified nation on the foundation of Indian ethos". The subaltern voices heard in these novels are linked to the attempt to rehistoricize Indian past from alternative sources.

The literary representation of Indian ethos in the post-independence period is illustrated in R.K. Narayan's *Waiting for the Mahatma* and Kushwant Singh's *Train to Pakistan* which reflect efforts for decolonization, the plea for an egalitarian society and the search for an identity in tune with Indian ethos. Both novels are written after independence; but each one re-presents the issues during the formation of the independent nation, relating them to the principles which were held high for obtaining the political and social liberation of the nation from the external/colonial powers as well as the internal pressure of conflicting ideologies. An Indianness that is the fulfilled form of the promises heard in the freedom struggle is sought in these works, candidly admitting the disillusionment that set in soon after the independence. *Train to Pakistan*, though set in the backdrop of partition, pleads for reconciliation, restoration of peace, tolerance and harmony.

The period between 1975 and 1990 is presented as the phase of de/re-democratization during which time India witnessed the fall of democracy, under the pretext of emergency, and the return of democracy through an unprecedented shift of regime. Writers voiced their dissent against this dark period of Indian history when corruption and communalism darkened the face of Indian polity and autocratic forces crippled the democratic systems in the country. Shashi Tharoor's *The Great Indian Novel* and Salman Rushdie's *Midnight's Children* satirically lamented the failure of *dharma*—the greatest component of Indian ethos—and the consequent enactment of hypocritical display of principles and values.

The neo-liberal period from the 90's onwards inspired the composition of Arundhati Roy's *God of Small Things* and Aravind Adiga's *The White Tiger*. The huge change over to a way of life and vision that compromises with all moral values for making money and for social recognition and the massive transformation in human relationships that occurred as the outcome of liberalization, privatization and globalization provide the themes of these two works in different ways. The imbalance of *purusharthas* and restoration of *dharma* in *The White Tiger* make it an appropriate period piece.

This book, gives the experience of a cultural tour through the long corridor of Indian history, greeted frequently by the political milestones which echo the social transformation in each period with eight literary landmarks mirroring, interrogating and criticizing the mighty phenomenon of Indian ethos that sustained and failed the nation, intermitantly, in the past and yet ultimately maintains its relevance and inseparability in the Indians' individual and collective identity.

This book deserves special credit for the quantum, quality and extensive nature of the research undertaken for its preparation. As a reference book, it supplements existing critical discourses on Indian writing in English and excels them by providing an all-inclusive conceptual frame for similar pursuits.

Prof. Dr. Jancy James

Director, Cardinal Cleemis School of Management Studies, Mar Ivanios Vidya Nagar, Trivandrum

Former Vice Chancellor, Central University of Kerala, Kasaragod and Mahatma Gandhi University, Kottayam

Professor (Retd), Institute of English, Former Director, Centre for Comparative Literature, Kerala University

President, Association of British Scholars, Trivandrum Chapter

Preface

The research on the refurbishment of Indian ethos in selected fiction of some Indian English writers was undertaken to know whether Indian English novels take birth from the ethos of India. They should have the cultural rootedness in Indianness because a group of people who live in a locality, find meaning in a novel only when it foregrounds their culture, history and challenges. Especially in the neo-liberal period where hegemonic cultures imperialize the native cultures, identity of the people should be based on the indigenous culture. For the reason, it is crucial to make a study on the reflection of Indian ethos in Indian English novels. The major objectives of the research were the following:

- To find and review the features of Indian ethos, the unifying spirit of the nation in the light of different periods such as the pre-independence, post-independence, de/re-democratization (emergency and its aftermath), and neo-liberal.
- To explore different characteristics in the selected novels through which Indian ethos, including socio-cultural, religious, and linguistic features are expressed.
- To identify the growth or feel of national identity in the selected novels, which highlight the Indianness and nurture the spirit of unity and integrity.

In order to attain the objectives, I used a descriptive method of study which looked into the deeper aspect of the research work. For a systematic study I divided the modern phases into four periods: pre-independence, post-independence, de/re-democratization (emergency and its aftermath), and neo-liberal. Two novels were selected from each period for the analysis, such as *Untouchable*, *Kanthapura, Waiting for the Mahatma,Train to Pakistan, The Great Indian Novel, Midnight's Children*, *The God of Small Things* and *The White Tiger*. Cultural elements such as language, religion, myths, values and social system as portrayed in the selected novels were undertaken for the analysis for authenticating the nature of Indianness in Indian English novels.

The book is organized in eight chapters. The first chapter is devoted to the statement, objectives, relevance, limitations, and organization of the contents. The second chapter attempts to define the concept 'ethos', one of the key words of the study and to explain the nature of Indian ethos. The next four chapters offer the major incidents and spirit of each period, and examine how the selected novels reflect these ethos in Indian history and the present time. I have explored the Indian cultural elements in the novels. The seventh chapter attempts to make a comparative study among the novels of various periods to know how they cherish elements of Indian ethos like nationalism and pluralism according to the signs of the time. Nation building, identity formation, fostering pluralism, social awakening and economic reformations are the major concerns of Indian English novels throughout these periods. The novels also approach Gandhism from different perspectives and give re-interpretations to fight various challenges of each period. The interrogation reveals that Indian English novels are embedded with the socio-political and cultural situation of India.

The eighth chapter is a conclusion that sums up the findings of the study. It reveals that the novels facilitated the processes of de-colonization and expressed Indianness in its core. Even though the novels take English language which is the tool of the colonizer as a medium, they reflect the aroma of the local soil. The work is a rewarding endeavour to observe how the Indian authors attempted to Indianize the Indian English novels. First of all, the analysis revealed that the selected novels are deeply rooted in Indian ethos and they made the English language as an Indian language which can express the sensibility of Indians. Indian English novels facilitated the re-visioning of Indian ethos according to the historical development of the nation like *bhasha* novels and the selected novels ardently pursue to Indianize the imperial nature of English.

Secondly, Indian English novels also contributed much in the promotion of the national spirit. During the pre-independence period, they became a tool to nurture nationalism and after independence they interrogated the political climate which controlled the existence of India. The political deterioration of the Indian democracy was unveiled in the novels so the reader coheres the reality in its wholeness. Thirdly, the close reading of the selected novels reveals a common phenomenon that the novels give high regards to multiculturalism and secularism. They uphold the noble values of Indian ethos and resist chauvinistic tendencies such as regionalism and fundamentalism. Fourthly, the novels became a tool for the social awakening and facilitated to improve the quality of life, especially of the woman and the untouchable. These novels as the representatives of the respective age highlight the trivialization of the noble values of India and promulgate humanism. The gap between the rich and the poor is well depicted in the novels. Fifthly, the rapidly evolving Indian society in the neo-liberal period is depicted in the novels with its pros and cons. In the absence of subjectivity and identity, globalization can produce nothing. Hence, the novels re-conceptualize the vital need to be rooted in Indianness. Nevertheless, they try to formulate a new consciousness to resist the homogenization of the world culture and attempt to attain space for Indianness in the global cultural map.

Though the study covers a period of more than seven decades, it was observed that the very substratum on which Indian English novels are built up, remains almost the same, namely the "Indian ethos." The novels have the quest to express authentically the ethos and to nurture Indianness. They have succeeded in the indigenization of English with Indianness and decolonization of the minds by appropriating English according to the sensibility of the local culture. In short, the novels are the lighthouse to guide the Indians through the channel of Indian ethos. Thus they can be called native novels.

The book will be useful for the students and teachers of Indian English literature, especially Indian English fiction and researchers in these fields.

Dr. Samjy Vadakkedom C.M.I.
Phone No. 08281548126
E-mail: samjyveyahoo.com

Acknowledgements

With inestimable gratitude and boundless devotion, I praise and thank God Almighty for the abundant grace and immense blessing bestowed upon me for the completion of my research work.

I express my profound gratitude to emeritus Bishop Rt. Rev. Dr. Isidore Fernandes of Allahabad, for his noble advice throughout the research work. I also acknowledge my gratefulness to all the priests of the Diocese of Allahabad.

I am indebted to the honorable Vice Chancellor Rev. Prof. Dr. Rajendra B. Lal for having given me an opportunity to seek admission in the programme of Ph.D. in English.

With unbound gratitude I would like to express my deep respect to my advisor, Dr. Mrs. Shivani S. Verma, Asst. Professor, Department of English and Foreign Language for her able guidance. I am also indebted to my former advisor Dr. Ritu Shepherd for her cooperation at the initial stage of my research work.

I convey my profound thanks to Prof. Dr. Sr Marion Mathew CJ, Head and Dean, School of Education, SHIATS for her valuable support in providing all possible facilities for smooth pursuit of the work. I also express my thanks to all the Rev. Sisters of St. Mary's Convent, Allahabad.

I would like to express my deep appreciation to Mrs. Leena Dominie, Prof. George Thomas Ampttu,

Dr. Meenakshy Ramachandran, Mr. Thomas K. Mathew, and Mr. Thomas T.T. Thundiyil, for their professional guidance and timely help. I express my thanks to Sr Shaini SRA, Fr Jose Majail CST, Fr Francis Xavier and Mr. Francis Jose for their support and encouragement.

I owe a lot to my CMI Congregation, especially the communities in Carmel Vidhya Bhavan, Pune (2011-13) and S.H. Monastery, Chethipuzha (2014-15) for their valuable support and positive attitude that really encouraged me to make this work a reality.

I would be failing in my duty if I do not pay my respect and homage to my late father Mr. Mathen Mathew (Joychen). I am also indebted to my mother Smt. Marikutty Mathew for her love and affection throughout my life. I also express my sincere thanks to my brothers, relatives and friends from the depth of my heart for their personal care and concern.

Dr. Samjy Vadakkedom C.M.I.

Contents

List of Abbreviations

CWMG	–	*The Collected Works of Mahatma Gandhi*
GIN	–	*The Great Indian Novel*
GST	–	*The God of Small Things*
HC	–	Horizontal collectivist
HI	–	Horizontal individualist
KA	–	*Kanthapura*
MC	–	*Midnight's Children*
PWA	–	The Progressive Writers' Association
SIT	–	The Social identity theory
TP	–	*Train to Pakistan*
UN	–	*Untouchable*
VC	–	Vertical collectivist
VI	–	Vertical individualist
WM	–	*Waiting for the Mahatma*
WT	–	*The White Tiger*

1

Introduction

India is a nation of diversity with an underlying unity. In the journey from Kanyakumari to the Himalayas, one may encounter a variety of languages, lifestyles, climate, and landscape. Beneath these diversities, however, the resemblance and unity are remarkable. The unification of the subcontinent is designed by nature itself. India is sharply divided by the Himalayan mountain ranges in the north, the Indian Ocean in the south, the Arabian Sea in the southwest and desert and mountains in the west. Southeast is marked by the Bay of Bengal and rest of the east—by tightly grouped mountain ranges extending up to Burma. Interestingly, the same classics, *Puranas*, philosophical thoughts, and traditions are found from one end to the other with regional variations and they form the underlying distinctive spirit which can be called 'Indian ethos.' It reveals a deeper principle of integration and like-mindedness. "India, with its internalised multicultural and sub-regional diversity, subsumes an identity that tends to combine and assimilate an ethos, however unstable or precarious it may tend to be in terms of religious, cultural, linguistic and historical distinctiveness."[1] Indian ethos expresses the life of Indians in its wholeness: his/her past and present, conscious and unconscious; formed by the Indian environment, tradition, philosophy, etc.

To be an Indian is a matter of challenge in the neo-liberal age. On one hand, globalization and imperialism are encroaching over the subaltern ethnic natives and on the other hand, regionalism and decolonization are responding to establish the identity of the local aborigines. The two streams may pull one to the extreme opposite poles of intellectual and cultural climate. The over influence of the hegemonic cultures in the attractive labels of global cultural neutralization, disembedding, and deterritorialization on ethnic groups may uproot the indigenous from the native ethos. “If immediate and urgent attention is not paid, we shall again have the situation of unconnected culture islands being washed down as flotsam in a mighty river of globalization.”[2] On the contrary, the narrow chauvinistic thinking may resist the progress and lead to isolation. Rootlessness terminates one from existence, while narrowness dissolves into darkness. The fight between *desi* and *videshi* is not only a burning cognitive and mental issue but also aesthetic and existential issue too.

The literary and artistic sensibility of each society is born out of its ethos and manifests in the approach to life, problem, the means for amelioration, and self-actualization. Similarly, Indian aesthetics is formed out of Indian ethos and articulates Indianness. The Indian literature upholds the rich heritage, promotes the value system, brings refinement, and reforms society in accordance with current trends.

> National literature has traditionally been understood as reflections of the unique character and the experiences of the nation. That is, it is felt that the unique experience of national life generates a national, collective consciousness, or in some formulations a ‘Collective Unconscious’ marked by a distinctive set of values, tensions, myths, and psychological foci, that produces in turn a certain readily identifiable national character [...]. Thus, the distinctiveness of a national literature is seen as the natural embodiment of the distinctive national character.[3]

National identity greatly depends on cultural elements including both material and non-material elements. The ethos behind the cultural elements is fundamental in unifying the nation and for building a healthy society. Hence, identifying the major and common ethos of India is essential for nation building and being an Indian in the midst of cultural dislocation.

In the neo-liberal period, the space of India is occupied by the multinational companies and their products. The imperialists try to reduce the gap between the *desi* and *videshi*. Due to their efforts, the 'Indianness' is losing its grip in the selection of all types of products in the market. Aesthetic consciousness is also influenced by the global-market and cosmopolitanism. The politics of hegemonic powers behind these transnational apparatus which promote Western imperialism and subaltern cultural amnesia (ignore the aborigine) behind the globalism is not critically evaluated. As a counter discourse in its miniature form, *bhasha* consciousness gives prominence to reterritorialization and re-reads the *swadeshi* movement not as a finished crusade but as a continuous dynamic process which is a call to evolve a nationalistic lifestyle based on Indian ethos. In the modern age, it is not a cry for political independence but a call to be rooted deeply in Indianness. As a process of cultural centralization, the *swadeshi* movement may be suppressed more cognitively than physically.

At this juncture, a vital question arises about the nature of Indianness in Indian English novels since English is the tool of the colonizer. It is a critical and radical question which all Indians should ask themselves to form a personal identity based on Indianness. The English language arrived in India with the East India Company to make a group of people who could mimic their masters and represent the British Empire. It was a language that was meant for mind-training. In spite of that, the Indians used English with a different agenda, which was opposed to the intention of the colonizer. Thus, the English language was stripped of its Queen's culture and in the course of time it was absorbed as another tongue in the Great Indian language bazaar. When the world is shrinking and becoming a global village, English acts as a bridge for people around the world as a lingua franca. As a result of the globalization of English, the very character of the language is changing. During the nineteenth century and the first half of the twentieth, English denoted more of a culture, race, and class-marked phenomenon. Whereas today, it is slowly shedding its colonial nature since English is used all over the world and people in different countries have made it a medium to express their own culture. Presently English has become a necessary tool for proclaiming the regional ethos to the world. Indian writers too are adopting it and Indian English novels have been getting a prominent space in the global market.

In the case of novels, reading or writing them is not a mere act of entertainment but through them one is defining and expressing one's identity and culture. Novels should be born from the living conditions and aspirations of the natives to throw light on the way the future. Here, the question arises as to how far the nature of Indian English novels which are written in the 'colonizer's language' penetrate into the core of Indianness related to the selection of theme, setting, language construction, and above all 'the Indian spirit'. Therefore Indian English novels should portray the core of Indian ethos. For this reason, it is high time to ask whether they could be able to promote Indianness in the global scenario. Hence, the present research namely, 'Refurbishment of Indian ethos in selected fiction of some Indian English writers' is highly relevant in the global cultural economy. The research is an attempt to throw light into the upcoming questions about the Indianness in Indian English writings. Hence, the study is significant according to the signs of the times. The major objectives of the research are the following:

- To find and review the features of Indian ethos, the unifying spirit of the nation, in the light of different periods such as the pre-independent, post-independent, de/re-democratization (emergency and its aftermath), and neo-liberal.
- To explore different characteristics in the selected novels through which Indian ethos including socio-cultural, religious, and linguistic features are expressed.
- To identify the growth or feel of national identity in the selected novels, which highlight the Indianness and nurture national spirit.

Based on the politico-cultural space, the evolution of the Indian ethos in modern era can be divided into four stages: pre-independent period, post-independent period, de/re-democratization (emergency and its aftermath) period, and neo-liberal period. The rationale behind the division is related to the major political events which strongly influenced all the spheres of life including art and literature in India. These decisive political shifts had their impact on Indian English novels too.

> Drawing on this relation between nation and literature, especially fiction, one can explore India's coming into being as a system of cultural signification within the complex and discursive field of the 'nation'. Much Indian fiction in English has tried to elicit the material disparities and instabilities of nation-formation.[4]

The political developments have influenced Indian English novels and vice versa. The novels are selected for the study on the basis of the prominence of the author, acceptance of the novel within the particular period and relation to the research theme.

The thesis is organized in eight chapters where the first and eighth chapters are set apart for introducing and concluding the research respectively. The second chapter is incorporated to explain one of the major words of the study namely 'ethos' and various elements of Indian ethos. This chapter is essential to have sufficient knowledge for analysing Indianness in the novels. The four chapters that follow are dedicated to have a historical survey and to analyse novels of each politico-cultural periods which are mentioned above. The seventh chapter becomes relevant as it gives a comprehensive view about the Indianness in the novels covering five periods.

The first chapter is an introduction to the whole thesis. It gives the thesis statement, relevance, objectives and formulation of the thesis. The second chapter attempts to define the term 'ethos,' one of the key concepts of the study. It is the underlined and guiding principle of a person or a group. The chapter also focuses on the major features of Indian ethos. India has a diversified and rich ethno-cultural context which facilitates

Indians to nurture a firm ethos of their own. The third chapter discusses the pre-independent influences on the Indian ethos. The colonization, social awakening, nationalism, Gandhism, fundamentalism and freedom struggle are the main subject matters of study. *Untouchable* and *Kanthapura* which carry the Indian sensibility of the period are selected from the India English novels for analysis. *Untouchable* which carries realistic picture of society is written by Mulk Raj Anand who was a leading socially committed novelist. *Kanthapura* which follows the oral tradition of India is a *sthalapurana*. Many consider it as the first major Indian novel written in English. The fourth chapter deals with the pan-Indian identity of post-independent period. The aspirations of the independent India to build-up a new nation on democratic values and its challenges are enquired into. *Waiting for the Mahatma* and *Train to Pakistan* are selected for the review. *Waiting for the Mahatma* is an unconventional perspective on freedom struggle with gentle comic style. *Train to Pakistan* is a historical novel against the backdrop of the partition of India in August 1947. They reflect secularism, spirit of nation building, fundamentalism, pan-subaltern spirit, socialism, and regionalism of the age.

The fifth chapter is about the State Emergency and its aftermath. These were the years of political despair about the unfulfilled dream of nation building. *The Great Indian Novel* and *Midnight's Children*, which are selected for the study, portray the drawbacks of the Indian democracy with an optimistic outlook. The elements of pessimism never over shadow hope for a better India. They give prominence to pluralism and the pre-eminence of India. The sixth chapter is about the Indian ethos of neo-liberal period which gave a positive image to India as an emerging super power. The economic development, disparity between the rich and the poor, corruption, empowerment of subaltern groups, etc., are the major determining factors of the era. *The God of Small Things* and *The White Tiger* are the novels chosen for investigation. The former novel is analyzed on the basis of individualism which is a growing phenomenon in the Indian society and the latter is examined with the background of *purusharthas* (*artha*, *kama*, *dharma*, and *moksha*). The seventh chapter makes a comparison between different Indian English novels of various ages and their expression of Indian ethos. It surveys, how the major themes of nation building, Gandhism, identity formation, pluralism, social reformation, and economic changes are diversified throughout the modern history of India. The eighth chapter is a conclusion that sums up the central themes and findings of the study. It shows that the novels facilitated the processes of de-colonization and expressed Indianness in its core.

As the research on Indian ethos in Indian English novels is a pertinent and complex study the researcher had certain limitations too. First of all, the ancient richness and diverse heritage made the study a herculean task to identify the various elements and influences of Indian ethos. "Admittedly, India's is the most complex case, and hence the link between citizenship and national identity is the most vexing."[5] Yet the study is not limited to any particular racial lineage but has tried to incorporate as many diverse ethnic groups as possible. It is impossible to speak about a single India and there is the risk of generalization so the research tried to be multi-voiced. Secondly, the mandatory restrictions like limitation of pages of the thesis and restricted time frame to complete the research also compelled the researcher to shorten the study. Thirdly, because of the vast area of Indian English novels, the number of novels are limited to two novels per period and altogether eight novels are analyzed.

The present research observes, how Indianness is reflected in Indian English novels. It is, also an attempt to re-discover the ethos of India to maintain a meaningful and progressive existence with one's identity of being an Indian. "In spite of many culture-conflicts, there has always been the residue of all the cultures, surviving, generation after generation. This has left an ethos which is recognizable in every Indian, whatever his race, religion, or colour. The paradox is as relevant today as it was in the past."[6] The Indian ethos is the unifying factor among all the Indians. Indian English novels, which carry the Indian sensibility, became a manifestation of the ethos. Thus, they become a medium to carry Indianness to various regions of India as well as to all over the world. The following chapters thoroughly investigate the nature of Indianness and its reflection in the selected Indian English novels.

Notes

1. Manjit Inder Singh, *The Critical Space: Studies in Literature, Theory, Nationalism and Deaspora* (New Delhi: National Publishing House, 2005), p. 5.
2. Kapila Vatsyayan, "Culture: The Crafting of institutions" Hiranmay Karlekar (ed.), *Independent India: The First Fifty Years* (Delhi: Oxford University Press, 1998), p. 503.
3. Sarah M. Corse, *Nationalism and Literature: The Politics of Culture in Canada and the United States* (Cambridge: Cambridge University Press, 1997), p. 1.
4. Manjit Inder Singh, *The Critical Space: Studies in Literature, Theory, Nationalism and Deaspora* (New Delhi: National Publishing House, 2005), p. 46.
5. T.K. Oommen, "Citizenship and National Identity in India: Towards a Feasible Linkage" T.K. Oommen ed., *Citizenship and National Identity from Colonialism to Globalism* (New Delhi: Sage Publication, 1997), p. 1493.
6. Mulk Raj Anand, "Afterword: Cultural Self-Comprehension of Nations" Gobinda Prasad Sarma ed., *Nationalism in Indio-Anglian Fiction* (New Delhi: Sterling Publishers, 1978), p. 345.

2

Ethos and Its Reflection in Indian Culture

CHAPTER OUTLINE

2.1. Nature of Ethos

The attempt to understand 'ethos,' takes one to the classical traditions—Greek and Roman—where the term was discussed in depth by great thinkers like Isocrates, Plato, Aristotle, Cicero, and Quintilian. The word is derived from the Greek word *ethikos* and its etymological meanings are "moral character, nature, disposition, habit and custom."[1] 'Ethos' can be analyzed from two perspectives: individualistic and collective. In relation to the individualistic aspect, ethos is the character or credibility of a speaker or writer. Aristotle used the term in the *Rhetoric* as one of the components of argument or modes of persuasion along with logos and pathos. Here, ethos refers to the character or trustworthiness of the rhetor, logos to the internal logical appeal or clarity of the claim, and pathos to the emotional appeal or sensory details of the rhetoric. Ethos, the persona of the person plays a vital role in influencing the audience. It is the authenticity or the moral competence of the rhetor which influences the audience in persuasion. It is formed not at the time of performance but through habits, which become the character of an individual. Ethos, habit, and act form a correlated cycle and each influences and shapes the other. "Human beings, as they live, realize acts, the repetition of which generates habits that in turn will produce attitudes. In this view, man, through living, makes himself."[2] The word ethos, thus, is used to signify the attitudes of individuals which guide them in all their endeavours and is formed through practice, habit, everyday rituals, and fashions.

The collective perspective of ethos is that the actions and motives a person acquires to repeat similar activities, which lead to habits, are from the society. Along with the individual characters, the communal aspect of ethos was emphasized in the Greek tradition. This angle is emphasized in the Greek—English Lexicon of the New Testament and other Early Christian Literature which defines ethos as "a usual or customary manner of behaviour, habit usage or long—established usage or practice common to a group."[3] Ethos is used to denote the guiding ideals, views, values, convictions, and beliefs of a group, community, or nation. Even in the individual dimension, the communal aspect is implicit. While judging the ethos of a rhetor, the audience, which is the miniature form of the society, reflects the accepted ethos of the society. As part of socialization the individual assimilates and internalizes ethos of the society and later the individual tries to modify the social ethos. The society becomes the soil for the individual to root and to nurture and in turn, the individual contributes to the betterment of society. The process intertwines the society and individual. Once the individual assimilates the ethos, s/he feels at home in the society and moves with the collective psyche. The word 'ethos' also carries the meaning the 'comfortable space of a person in the community'. From the moment s/he is born, each individual is moulded in accordance with the life philosophy of the society s/he lives in. Therefore, personal ethos is formed along with the social ethos. The authentic persona is the result of the understanding of and adapting to the ethos of the society. Community consciousness is the part of social existence. The unity of a community depends on how deeply individuals currently identify with the community's ethos. Thus, ethos helps in the standardizing process and there by helps to establish solidarity. The communal ethos fosters interpersonal relationships and a sense of belongingness and security.

Ethos cannot be merely understood as the ethics or character of an individual or society. More than that, it is the cardinal spirit of all the basic assumptions which prevail in the society. In other words, the habitual gathering place of rhetoric (i.e. the society) is the basis of understanding the present uniqueness of individual and collective thinking pattern. Thus, it defines the identity of a person and a society. Ethos is an essential part of a social identity since it gives meaning to the collective behaviour. The society is founded on certain socially accepted or objective truths which create a common platform. In the case of sciences such as Mathematics, and Physics the pre-established scientific theories and laws give foundation for further development. In a similar manner, in society a set of principles based on culture, frames the foundation of synchronization. Here ethos plays a decisive role in creating a common identity. "It [ethos] constitutes one of the bases of social identity, by providing a common societal viewpoint that underlies the sense of belonging and identification."[4] This identity gives meaning and opportunity to identify with the 'significant others' for the individuals who form the society. The process of developing the personal identity depends on the social identity, which links one to the past ancestry, inter-relates with the present fellow beings and foresees a future descendant with a feeling of oneness.

Identity of persons, groups, organizations, or nations is the manifestation of ethos and it is essential for the very existence of the society.

> A fundamental condition for the evolvement of any society is the development of social identity, which confers a sense of belonging and identification. The meaning of social identity is influenced by the ethos that members of a society share. The ethos consists of shared, central societal beliefs that give the society a dominant orientation and characterize it.[5]

The holistic personality is moulded in the unique ethos of each society and it has not only cognitive orientation but also has affective orientation. It is a part of the psyche of the community. Ethos of different groups can be in opposition to one another and it may lead to conflict, for example, the hostility between Israeli Jews and the Palestinians. The ethos of each nation upholds the goals of each one and is in direct conflict with that of the others. In short, ethos is a relatively perceptual framework or underlying spirit which shapes and influences the identity of the individual and the society.

The evolution of ethos is a continuous and dynamic process. "The societal beliefs that underlie ethos can be changed as a result of new, prolonged experiences of the society. Israeli society presents an example of such a process."[6] Its progress depends upon various factors such as politics, philosophy, science, and religion which affect the successive generations and may cause conflict. The content of ethos is evolved from the social psyche which includes the collective unconscious and collective conscious. The collective unconscious is the inherent asset of the society—the archetype. It is the collective experience of the previous generations and is given to the present generation as archetypes. The collective conscious is the knowledge gained by the present generation through the encounter with the current environment. Here the different experiences of the individuals in the community have been put together to form the collective experience. Sometimes conservatives may debate with progressives and may arouse antipathy in the society. Thus through continuous effort of coherence and cohesion the collective ethos is formed. The collective experience gives meaning to the societal life of the people.

2.2. Ethos of India

The glorious past and the age-old culture facilitate a nation to develop and be rooted in its own ethos which is essential for its integrity and continuity. India, which has a recorded history of more than 5000 years, has been nurturing its own ethos from the historical events of ups and downs. Even though India possessed diversity of language, dress, festival, religion, etc., and was divided into different cultures and princely states, it is a wonder that the antique and rich civilization of India has been prospering for centuries with its unique dynamism and evolving through time to nourish a better society without losing its spirit of unity. Ancient writings testify to the unity of India; the Cankam classics, the earliest writings in the Tamil language, consider India as one unit in literature, culture, art and geography. Out of the cultural heritage, the elements of Indian ethos are formed and the ethos leads the nation with the like-minded citizens. The ethos of India coalesces the people and produces a strongly unified nation with a colourful mosaic of varieties of cultures by transforming diversities. To analyze the ethos of Indian English fiction, it is worthwhile to identify some of the peculiar features of the ethos of India.

2.2.1. *Oneness of Life*

Wholeness in outlook is the hallmark of Indian ethos. Each element in the universe is analysed not as a separate entity but in its relation with others. So integrity in coherence and holistic approach are part of Indianness. Human life cannot be separated from the rest of the universe and Indian culture gives due importance to integrity. Octavio Paz narrates the essence of Indian ethos in its true sense:

> The Indian genius is a love for abstraction and, at the same time, a passion for the concrete image. At times it is rich, at others, prolix. [...] It is abstract and realistic, sexual and intellectual, pedantic and sublime. It lives between extremes, it embraces the extremes, rooted in the earth and drawn to an invisible beyond. On the one hand, a repetition of forms, a superimposition of concepts, a syncretism. On the other, the desire for totality and unity. And in its highest moments; the incarnation of a totality that is plenitude and emptiness, the transfiguration of the body into form that, without abandoning sensation and the flesh, is spiritual.[7]

In the Indian tradition, religion, philosophy, spirituality, science, and astronomy cannot be separated from one another and from daily human life. They search together for outer beings and inner human consciousness. Integrated inward and outward (godward and humanward) pilgrimage is the soul of Indian *vijnana*. Descendence of Being and ascendance of beings are complimentary. Both reason and intuition are means of knowledge. The word as well as silence is significant in Indian *sastras*. "[that] language can become less and less insistently present in consciousness suggests the possibility of there being a state where it (consciousness) is bereft of language altogether and perhaps even of thought which seems to be essentially wedded to it."[8] The integral outlook about the finite, which is born out of infinity, is the core of the vision in life of Indian ethos. Physical, mental, and emotional well-being of a person should be simultaneously taken care of along with the spiritual growth. Yoga is an example for such a comprehension. According to the *Kosha* theory a person consists of five sheaths (*pancha-kosas*): *Annamayakosha* (food-apparent-sheath), *Pranamayakosha* (air-apparent-sheath), *Manomayakosha* (mind-apparent-sheath), *Vijnanamayakosha* (wisdom-apparent-sheath), and

Anandamayakosha (bliss-apparent-sheath) which also, gives holistic understanding of the human being.

The Indian's frame of mind cannot be understood only by reading the *Vedas* or the *Upanishads*, the books like *Inna Narpatu* (100-500 AD) of Putham Sernthanar, *Arthasastra* (400 BC) of Kautilya, *Kamasutra* (AD 200) of Vatsyayana, *Yoga sutra* (AD 400) by Patañjali, *Ganitasara-sangraha* (AD 850) of Mahavira, *Ganitatilaka* (AD 999) of Sripati, *Panca-siddhantika* (AD 550) of Varahamihira, and *Kuttanimatam* (AD 800) of Damodaragupta must also taken into account. Rishi Markandeya, Buddha, and Ashok the emperor were not the sole makers but Chandragupta Maurya, Rajendra Chola, Shivaji Bhosale, and Tipu Sultan also were there. "Upinder Singh, [...] says [...]. The ideas of Buddha and Ahimsa notwithstanding, it is evident that violence was an integral part of Indian history [...]. We are not a tolerant society at all. We are very violent."[9] However, violence is also controlled by dharma, to restore righteousness. Not only do *brahmacharya*, *ahimsa*, and *nirvana* explain Indian ethos but *kama*, *varna* and *artha* are also part of it. For Dharmasastras and Manu, spirituality does not mean to move away from one's duty towards the family and society. "The *dharmasastras* dominated by the householders' code of the reproduction of the people at its core, were given to glorifying the status of the *grhastha*."[10]

Out of the 'white man's burden' some of the writers over projected the mysticism and passivism of Indian philosophy.

> Nor is there any good reason to suppose that men and women in India were by nature inclined to be more religious than their counterparts in the western world. No historical data are available for holding the view that either the Indians or the ancient Greeks and Romans and/or medieval Europeans were more God-fearing, virtuous and religious relatively to one another.[11]

Even though the ultimate aim of *jeevatma* is *moksha* or *Nirvana*, the union with *paramatma*, reasonable significance is given to both material and spiritual realms in the Indian ethos. Each moment of life is interconnected and all activities have spiritual and material dimensions.

> The life of the Vedic Aryans was every moment of it a ceaseless effort to live up to the ideal of sacrifice, to think of it, to prepare for it and then to make it in an effective manner. Indeed it was their sole concern, the dominant idea behind all their activities and nothing existed for them which had no connection with this supreme work of life.[12]

In short, Indian ethos promotes a harmonious whole and comprehensive outlook to the universe.

2.2.2. *Spirit of Enquiry*

The unlimited power generated from the quest for knowledge has been the driving force of the Indian minds throughout the ages. People of India moved by the spirit of enquiry contributed a lot to the world, both in the physical and spiritual realms. This can be seen from the Indus Valley Civilization, one of the earliest civilizations on earth. Sir John Marshall expressed his wonder when he saw the art work of Indus Valley Civilization: "When I first saw them I found it difficult to believe that they are prehistoric; they seemed to completely upset all established ideas about early art, and culture.... Modeling such as this was unknown in the ancient world up to the Hellenistic age of Greece."[13] From the Vedic period onwards, Geometry (*Sulva*) and Astronomy (*Jyotisa*) were studied in India. The science of stars was named as *Naksatra-Vidya.* The priest and *rishies* contributed greatly to the development of knowledge. For example,

> Jaina priests showed remarkable interest in the study and development of mathematics. They devoted one of the four branches of *Anuyoga* (religious literature) to the elucidation of *Ganitanuyoga* (mathematical principles) and prescribed proficiency in S*amkhyana* (science of calculation) and *Jyotisa* (astronomy) as an important prerequisite of the Jaina priest.[14]

The basic steps in algebra, geometry, and decimals were initiated from 400 AD to 1600 AD. Aryabhata (AD 476-500) of Pataliputra was an outstanding genius in Mathematics and his contributions in the area of the notation system, the decimal system and the use of zero were profound.[15] Brahmagupta in the sixth century, Mahavira in the ninth century, Bhaskara in the twelfth century, and others, reflect the spirit of inquiry inherent in the native Indians. Charaka (BC 175) and Susruta (BC 600) were well-known even abroad for their scholarship in Ayurveda. Chess is a unique contribution of India to sports.[16] Military-powered rockets were used for the first time in the world at Seringapattam, in South India by Tippu's Soldiers.[17] In spirituality, philosophy, poetry, grammar, chemistry, astronomy, sex education, politics, and language, Indians made a lot of contributions. The number of universities and numerous study centres show the quest for knowledge of Indians. The universities like Takshashila Nalanda, Pushpagiri, Valabhi, Odantapuri, and Vikramashila were great centres which moulded the Indian ethos. The long tradition of education has contributed in forming a unified ethos which is very much rooted in the people of this great nation.

The *smriti* (oral) tradition has also contributed a great deal in building up Indian ethos. The *guru-shishyaparampara* (teacher-student tradition), where the student acquires knowledge from the *guru-mukhd,* had a unique role in forming the personality of the younger generation. Since the student lived with the guru in the *gurukul* system, the learning was not limited to a particular subject but was holistic and had an environment conducive for learning. "There is enough evidence to indicate that from ancient times India had developed a system of conferences and free discussions to which specialists came from all over the country. The summaries of those conferences were known as *samhitas*, the compilers being editors, not authors."[18]

Myths, folklores, sayings, and legends are part of the oral tradition. They carry the seeds of the Indian ethos and keep them for the coming generation. Thus, metaphysically each generation takes seeds from the previous generation and contributes to the next. In C.G. Jung's terminology, it can be called archetypes. "Myth is not mythic at all but a reality in life that is still being carried forward to some unknown destiny."[19] The rich mythological tradition plays a vital role in carrying the Indian ethos to the next generation unconsciously and smoothly.

2.2.3. *Multi-Culturalism*

Indian culture, which is pluralistic and complex, is like a banyan tree, which has aerial roots that grow and prop the tree. The tree has a complex structure where the original trunk cannot be distinguished from the rest. Similarly, Indian ethos is always open to the truth and goodness of other cultures. It shows a readiness to borrow and adapt to them without losing its own identity. Thus, the complexity and vastness become the nature of Indian culture. India is the mother for many schools of thought and foster mother of various ideologies, yet it remains 'one.'

By its very nature, India is pluralistic since the origins (the first factor of diversity) of Indians are from different sources. Indians immigrated from various places in different periods of history. The earliest inhabitants were Pre-Dravidian Munda. Then the Dravidians came in and built their shelters. The Indus Valley Civilization (3300-1300 BC) is known as the first developed urban civilization in the north-western region of the Indian subcontinent and had a population of over five million. The prehistoric invasion (1500 BC) of Aryans in the northwest of the Indian subcontinent is considered as the first large scale immigration which led to the interaction of a newfangled culture. In course of time, many minor invasions of people as well as ideologies took place in India. From the very beginning of the first century (AD 52), itself Christianity came to the southern part of India. Due to Muslim persecution a group of Zoroastrians immigrated to western India (Gujarat) from Persia in the 8th or 10th century AD and a new hybrid culture along with a new language (Urdu) was formed. Even though in the 7th century AD Islam came to the Malabar Coast on account of trade, the major invasion happened in the 12th century and it led to the second major cultural and religious fusion in the history of India. Another major cultural fraternization happened with the colonizers of the west, especially with the British for two centuries. "Today, whatever is Indian—whether it be an idea, a word, a form of art, a political institution, or a social custom—is a blend of all these and many other strains and elements. Indian culture includes little pieces of all and is a product of chemical reaction."[20] Indians belong to different race and origin however, these different life views were incorporated harmoniously and are flowing together even to this day.

The second major diversity is in faith and religious practices. As the ancestors of Indians are manifold, their faiths and beliefs are also multiple. The pluralistic nature of religion includes intra-religious and inter-religious differences. Religious harmony was the spirit of India. Rig Veda says: '*Ekam Sad Vipra Bahudh Vadanti*' (the Real is one, the learned speak of it variously). This spirit of acceptance continued even in the midst of Islamic conversion. Sufism stressed liberal reform movement and preached the love of God and humanity. Akbar believed in the coexistence of religions and promoted the love above the religious dogmas. During the medieval period, the Bhakti movement also facilitated the promotion of religious harmony. It originated in Tamil Nadu where the Nayanmars and the Alvars were the forerunners. Later the movement had its influence on the other parts of the country. Ramanuja, Ramananda, Tulsidas, Kabir, Namdeva, Chaitanya Mahaprabhu, Mirabai and others were moved by its spirit and promoted religious harmony among different sects of people especially among Hindus and Muslims. Tulsidas, the poet, saint and reformer, taught all to surrender to the perfect love for purifying oneself and to love all creatures. Kabir, the mystic, proclaimed the idea of the fundamental one in his work 'the Bijak' (the Seedling) and teaching of universal view of spirituality attracted many Hindus and Muslims as disciples. "The song of love and devotion sung by Kabir is a symphony of the deepest notes of religious feeling of the common people of India—Hindus, Muslims and others. Kabir's concept of God is a purely mystical one."[21] The mystical life of the great saints of India promoted religious harmony among people.

Thirdly India is multi-lingual. "According to the 2001 Census of India, 30 languages are spoken by more than a million native speakers, 122 by more than 10,000. Three millennia of language contact has led to significant mutual influence among the four language families in India and South Asia."[22] Sanskrit, Pali, and Prakrit were formed at the same age. However, Sanskrit was spoken by the upper caste minority whereas the other two languages were used by the masses. Though almost a dead language, Sanskrit, one of the oldest and classical languages is beyond doubt the prestige of India. Tamil is the earliest Dravidian language. The ancient Tamil literature is known as Sangam and was composed between 500 BC and 200 AD.

Fourthly, India is multi-ethnic. Forms of worship, music, folklore, dance, architecture, agricultural practices, dress, medicine, food, and handicraft are different from region to region. It is like a beautiful garden with a wide variety of flowers.

> A recent survey has indicated that 4,653 communities live in India (that include all major religions of the world in a predominantly Hindu society with sizeable Muslim population), professing different faiths, practising diverse forms of worship, entertaining different notions about migration of soul, speaking several languages and dialects. Each group has its own distinct folklores, industry and handicrafts. But India is more than a sum of these.[23]

Indian culture has a receptive nature and has assimilated many streams of ideologies without losing its essence. The eclectic approach facilitates the culture to grow in its comprehensiveness and inclusiveness. This characteristic of the culture also gives space to many creeds to exist harmoniously and many systematic attempts were made to combine the best from many religions. For example, Akbar the Great, the Mughal Emperor, during his reign showed respect and tolerance towards other religions, and celebrated various religious festivals like Diwali. He had discussions with Jain scholars and invited Christian priests to stay with him in the palace. This practice of Akbar was highlighted by the Indian Supreme Court as an example for the co-existence of Jain and Mughal architecture, calling Akbar 'the architect of modern India.'[24]

Multi-religious, multi-lingual, and multi-ethnic are common treats of India. However, the ethos of India is not 'multi' but one of 'synthesizing.' The very core of India is pluralism: heterodoxy in opinion but homogeneity in spirit. Since there is no concept of unity in diversity or having a state with multi-lingual community, for the west it is impossible to imagine a nation with multiple cultures. "Many observers have been astonished by India's survival as a pluralist state. But India could hardly have survived as anything else. Pluralism is a reality that emerges from the very nature of the country; it is a choice made inevitable by India's geography and reaffirmed by its history."[25]

It is impossible to define the national identity in terms of language, religion, caste, or tribe because defining these categories is difficult. Therefore, the only possible way to define India is by its plurality. Holism and synergy are the working principle of India. "[...] the only possible idea of India is that of a nation greater than the sum of its parts. An India that denies itself to some Indians could end up being denied to all Indians."[26] This diversity has enabled Indians to work as a team with mutual respect.

2.2.4. *Deep Relationship*

The deep relationship with fellow beings, culture, nature and God is a prominent element in Indian ethos. The famous usage *athithi-satkar* reveals the same. The hymns of the Rig and the Atharva Vedas emphasize in a more subjective sense the need and importance of unity in the community life. They fervently exhort human beings to be united with all, in heart, in aim and in work, to be friendly with all and to pray so that all may be friendly with him/her.[27] Since the relationship is so intimate, the members hesitate to move away from the tribe or the ethnic group. Such a deep spirit of relationship is the force behind the social unity and identity. "India is not a welfare state—the government provides little to its unfortunates—but it is a welfare society in which people constantly help each other out, provided they feel a connection that justifies their help."[28] People have not only horizontal relationship with their age group but also have vertical relationship, which includes ancestors and the coming generations. The ancestral home is named as *tharavad* and each family (kinship) has their own Kuladevata/Kuladev (family deity).

> The first conscious or pre-conscious thought in the Indian mind is, 'How happy and proud my family will be!' This is why Indians tend to idealize their families and ancestral background, why there is such prevalence of family myths and of family pride, and why role models for the young are almost exclusively members of the family, very frequently a parent, rather than movie stars, sporting heroes, or other public figures favoured by Western youth.[29]

In the midst of great social, philosophical, economic and political changes over centuries, India has the long heritage of a stable family life. The spirit of family solidarity which provides meaning to the daily lives of the Indians is still the core of Indian society. Hence, the children of India are brought up with love and care of parents and relatives.

Next to family, individuals are linked with kinship, which is the extension of the family in a wider sense. The behaviour of individuals in the society operates within the framework of kinship structure. The elders of the kinship settle the conflicts, contract marriages, and take decisions. One of such kinships is Singimari in Assam which operates very powerfully.

> Among the Singimari Muslims the *chubas* are not merely geographical divisions—they constitute kin groups as well. The heads of all households in any *chuba* are patrilineally related to one another. [...]. The residents of a *chuba* feel that they are like one big family which is demonstrated by frequent inter-household interaction and economic cooperation in agriculture or at times of crises. This feeling of kinship is quite strong.[30]

Another example for the deeper relationship is the corporative life of the tribe. Family, marriage, kinship, intra-family relationship and inter family relationship are important among tribes like Asur, Birjia, Kisan, Munda and Oraon and their social relationship is very high.[31] The tribal community was administered by a *samiti* which was formed by the member of the territory and it is the preliminary form of democracy.

The relationship was maintained with the backup of philosophy and religion. Another feature of Indian conservatism was sublimation to higher values. "The social hierarchy is intentionally established on the moral virtues required by the persons who have to be faithful to their duty."[32] *Danda, Dharma*, and *Svadharma* are the three doctrines that facilitate the society to maintain the social structure. *Danda* is the principle of just administration and it is related to rulers or kings. *Dharma* is interpreted as that which upholds or sustains the positive order in oneself, family, society, nation, and ultimately in the universe. Every individual has a particular dharma according to his or her stage in life. *Svadharma* (*Varnasrama Dharma*) is attached to one's castes. The *Sanatana Dharma* (the eternal religion) guided the relationship with love. The incorporation of *Dharma Chakra* (Wheel of Law) in the national flag shows its deep rootedness in the national history. The metaphysical doctrine of *Karma* also paid a powerful rationalization for inequalities in the society. *Karma*, which says that the present life situation is the result of the past life, which is the driving force to accept the life as it is, without revolting against the fellow beings. "He can improve the prospects for his later births only by adhering to, and performing well, the role proper to the stratum into which he is born."[33] However, the abstract metaphysical thoughts sometimes gave way to ritualism in a concrete form.

One of the great drawbacks of the deep relationship is that social change cannot take place easily as society is too conservative. Different types of *Vyavastha*, the word used for division in the society, prevail in the society with its injustice. One such division is *varna* system and without any exception it influenced all the Indians. The deep affiliation to one's group made it difficult to change the *varna* system. Another group which suffered because of the deep relationship based on patriarchal system and joint family was 'women'. The condition of women in the society was very difficult to be changed because the affiliation between people was very high and the society clung to the traditional practices. Deviants had to face the aversion of the society. Hence, people preferred to go with the society without challenging the unfair social norms and regulations. Even though, Lord Mahavira (599-52 BC) and Lord Buddha (566-486 BC) challenged the exclusive social order, which neglected the outcaste and women, they could not bring about a total change in the society. Instead of accepting the renewal, the newly enlightened were rejected from the society. Hence, the acceptance of the society was a basic factor to bring changes in the Indian community.

2.2.5. *Unity in Aesthetic Consciousness*

'A unifying artistic sense' is one of the elements of Indian tradition which unites everything even that which appears different and distant. Here art is defined in a broad sense. It means all the expression or application of human creative skill and imagination which includes not only visual forms such as painting or sculpture but also literature, dramas, poems, epics, architectures, paintings, and dances.

> Kavya or literature is only one of the forms in which aesthetic consciousness of a people tend to express and embody itself. That consciousness finds even more concrete expression in music, dance and dramatic performance. There is overwhelming evidence, literary as well as of other kinds, to show that the above-mentioned arts were cultivated in India from the earliest times.[34]

Even before 2000 BC the economic and cultural exchange between north and south India led to a close relationship. The comparative archaeological studies in various places in South India, Mohenjo Daro and Harappa reveal that a lot of cultural exchanges happened among the people all over India. It can be conformed from the similar objects such as burial urns, earthen pots, shells, and pearls found in different places of India. The presence of nearly fifty per cent Dravidian words in the Brauhi language spoken in some parts of Baluchistan is a strong evidence that there was a close and frequent communication between the Indus Valley and South India from pre-historic time onwards.[35]

It says that *Agthiam,* the first Tamil grammar text, was written by Agastya, an Aryan Preacher and *Tolkappiam*, early Tamil grammar and literature, by one of his disciples.[36]

The *Ramayana* and the *Mahabharata*, the classical epics of India, were accepted throughout the country and translated into different languages with their own changes. They are formed out of collective Indian consciousness and comprehend the Indian ethos. "The Mahabharata is the creation and expression not of a single individual mind, but of the mind of a nation; it is the poem written by a whole people."[37] The epics were studied thoroughly in southern schools and translated into Tamil, the first among Indian languages. The Vedas, theory of *Karma*, and the *Dharmasastras* are part of the life of the people of the whole of India.[38] The Puranas are also part of the culture and enable Indians to comprehend the ethos of India. "The Puranas relate to the whole of India so far as the historical portion therein is concerned and the whole world so far as their ethical, philosophical and religious portions are concerned."[39]

Visual art is another creative expression of Indian ethos and its unity. The Ajanta and Ellora caves have been built by generations and they have been influenced by the artistic and philosophical outlook of the whole country. These also reveal the close relation between the various ethnic groups of India. The Dravidian culture of South India, the Sind Valley Civilization, etc., influenced the Buddhist culture and they adopted them without any discrepancy because along with the Aryan ones, non-Aryan figures like the Nagars, are also seen in their works.[40] The artists of India were not sectarians, so they drew ideas from all religions and ethnic groups. Art played a vital role in concretizing the abstract Indian ethos.

Art also fostered religious harmony. The art which had a lot of restrictions in Arab countries flourished well in India under the Muslim rule. 'Khayal/Khayal the musical genre invented by Sultan Hussain Sharqui of Jaunpur was popular among different religious followers. "Dhurpad" the classical Hindu genre, another example, was very much liked by Muslims of refined taste.[41] Thus, the aesthetic consciousness united people and they moved together with the rhythm of Indian ethos. The

Muslim rulers were influenced by the architecture of India and they employed Hindu architects and artisans to build palaces and Masjids. The design of Juma Masjid in Ajmer influenced by the Jain temple on Mount Abu and Quwatul-Islam mosque near Delhi were modelled by the art of the Gupta era and the Shikhars of the medieval periods.[42]

Not only the art forms but also their meaning and aim were a unifying factor in the country. According to the Indian ethos art is not for art's sake but a means of self-realization. Art is not merely a source of entertainment but an overt expression of human feelings both spiritual and emotional. The ultimate aim of all the classical art forms of India is to take the *jeevatma* to *paramatma*. Through the aesthetic performance, the performer as well as the audience experience *rasa* which is the aesthetic counterpart of *moksha*. For example, Meerabai, the mystic, composed around 1300 *bhajans* and invoked the ultimate. The alwar/azhwars, the Tamil emotional devotees of Vishnu, sung songs for long time to please the God. The Indian artist lives in what s/he performs and has a mystic experience.

2.2.6. *Eco-friendly Attitude*

Eco-friendly means having an affectionate or loving attitude towards the environment, earth and ultimately to all the living and non-living beings in the universe. In Indic ethos, cosmic matter (*prakrti*) which is made of *panchamahabhuta* (the five great elements: space/*akasa*, air/*vayu*, fire/*tejas* water/*ap*, and earth/*prthvi*) is revered. The indwelling God (Atman) in all beings including human beings is the basis of the ecological view of Indian ethos and it attributes divinity to all.

> Indian spiritual culture 'Opens up a hundred ways to arrive at the truth of our religious being, but its consummation is to see God in man and man in God, God in Nature and Nature in God, God in all things and all things in God, and to go beyond them to their origin in the supracosmic Absolute, Eternal and Infinite.[43]

The universe is an expression of the transcendental creative nature and it is named as *vasudevasarvam* (the Supreme Being resides in all beings). "Only after taking many births is a wise person able to comprehend the basic philosophy of the creation; which is: Vasudeva. If anyone understands this fundamental, such a person is indeed a Mahatma."[44] Even after all research done, nature still remains a wonder for human beings.

The life and faith of Indians are linked to the environment. Quite a number of myths related to nature show that Indians have been leading an eco-centred life. The land was precious to them. For Indians the land, on which they live, is sacred and they are attached to it.

> The forest also plays a dominant role in terms of culture, domestic well-being and spirituality, as they [Dongaria: one among the 63 tribes in Orissa and they live in the remote Niyamgiri hill range] believe it is the home of many of their deities. Before they fell a large tree, for instance, the Dogaria Kondh propitiates and entreats the gods for permission to do so.[45]

Nature is not to satisfy the selfishness of human beings but for survival. "How can we cut the trees of the God?" These are the words of the people at a Bhil temple in Banswara district, Rajasthan.[46] Bhils who originated in Dravidian-speaking southern part of India and moved to the north and central forests of India, have deep rooted value system among them to protect some of the natural resources. They are the largest caste-group of Rajasthan and the third largest in India. They were one of the first communities, which protested against the Indian Forest Act of 1878 which denied the rights of indigenous people over the forest.[47] This is a typical attitude of Indians who respect nature and they learned this not from the modern classrooms but from their ancestors.

One of the greatest contributions to ecology by the ancestors to the present generation is the sacred groves, which have a rare and endemic species of plants. From time immemorial, Indian villagers were active in protecting the natural resources and were against greedy exploitation. "While my research with rural communities had little, if any, evidence of their ecological practices being influenced by modern scientific researches about global warming, the modern organizations, on the other hand, seem to be largely responding in their own ways to save the planet."[48]

The land is one of the primary unifying factors of the society especially in an agricultural society and the territory where people stay together is the homeland which differentiates them from others. According to the nature of the geographical area, people build-up an eco-friendly lifestyle. So nature is part of life. "For them, their 'way of life' implicitly includes environmentalism. They revere nature not for saving biodiversity but because this is how they practice their traditions and their dharma, or dharam, as they describe it in vernacular Indian languages."[49] The entire law functions under the law of dharma and human beings should not disturb the rhythm of the cosmos. "[...] men had to respect the natural regulations of the universe by paying homage to the supervising powers of nature personified by the gods. This was one of the main motives of the Vedic sacrifice."[50] For Indians, nature is the compassionate mother.

2.2.7. *Self-realization*

The goal of life is to attain self-realization through fulfilling both material and spiritual duties. The life principles such as matter, life and mind are connected with the spiritual principles. They are the lower planes which derive from the spiritual principles 'sachchidananda' (sat = existence, truth, real; chit = consciousness; ananda = bliss). Mind derives from light of the consciousness and truth, life from the energy of consciousness (force) and matter from the primal substance of existence.

> [...] the real implication of the Vedic teaching, life with all its powers is affirmed as a field for the gods' adventure, for a divine efflorescence. If man is of the earth, he is also of heaven; and his godhead will be reborn in him when 'Heaven and Earth equalized join hands in the bliss of the Supreme.[51]

Human beings must be striving for fulfilling their *karma* based on *dharma* aspiring for the heavenly bliss. Indian ethos always promotes each one to attain individual identity. The ultimate aim of life is *Moksha*, which literally means freedom. The Indian basic way of life is guided by the philosophy of supremacy of the spirit over matter. "Even an ordinary illiterate peasant has almost a philosophical attitude about the transitoriness of life, about the reality of another world hereafter, about good deeds bearing their fruits in an afterlife, and even a certain spirit of resignation and renunciation."[52] This liberation theory succeeded in giving hope to the Indians and they are ready to accept the events of life as the will of God but it does not keep them away, from doing the *karma*.

Along with the ultimate liberation, *artha*, *kama* and *dharma* should be accomplished. The priority of Purusartha's changed from time to time and it shows that all are important. In the Rigveda *kama* is linked to the divine action of creation, sacrificial rituals, etc., and regarded as high. "Kama is considered as the principle of enjoyment and aesthetic consciousness is characterized by a peculiar sense of enjoyment. [...] In actual life, enjoyment is closely related to the activity of the senses."[53] At the period of the *Mahabharata* and the *Ramayana* the priority was determined and *dharma* (the ethical virtues), and *artha* (the wealth) were placed higher.[54] *Mahabharata* clearly states "wise man tries to secure all the three but if all three cannot be attained he secures *dharma* or *artha* or only *dharma* if he has a choice of only one."[55]

To attain the goal each person's life is divided into four stages (*ashram*): *brahmacharya* (student life, age: till 24), *grihastha* (household life, age: between 24-48), *vanaprastha* (retired life, age: 48-72) and *sannyasa* (renounced life, age: 72-onwards). Each person has to fulfill his/her dharma according to the stages of life. Ashram is a way of life which portrays a life of discipline and simplicity. To attain the goal, everyone needs a disciplined life. In a broader sense, all sacrifices and efforts one makes to attain a particular goal can be called *Tapasya*. It is needed in all the stages of life to fulfill the duties of each stage. "Indian authors, on both ethics and polity, lay great emphasis on the need of exercising control over the mind and the senses. Both Manu and Kautilya advocate the desirability of self-control. Sankara makes the attainment of such control a pre-requisite for the study of the Vedanta."[56] Simplicity is another virtue which is essential to attain the goal and Indian ethos gives due importance to simplicity in all spheres of life. "Another characteristic of these [the Ajanta] paintings, as of all Buddhist art, is simplicity and restraint that is the avoidance of elaborate decoration."[57] To attain the goal of each stage of life it has its own virtues to follow.

Life always moves towards the ultimate objective. Since each person is unique, s/he has to follow a path, which is suitable for him/her. In general, there are three paths: the way of knowledge, the way of devotion and the way of action. To select the way, the ultimate objectives should be personalized through continuous reflections. Irrespective of the way, all endeavours should be performed with the attitude of *Nishkama Karma*. Detachment enables one to renounce everything and it is the most purified attitude. Detachment is a philosophical and psychological concept which liberates human beings from all sufferings. "A certain spirit of renunciation is not only wise but is conducive to happiness, happiness born of inner harmony, not happiness which is simply based on material comforts."[58] Detachment is a means for transcending the whole life of a person which helps the person to enjoy the inner peace/*shanti*. "Finally, the great message of India throughout the ages has been the emphasis on and yearning for peace and harmony. All our ceremonies end with *shanti*, *shanti*, *om shanti*."[59] The state of infinite peace is *nirvana* and that is the final realization of human life.

In the journey of life, human beings are not deserted but God's providence is always with them. The indwelling spirit guides them to the truth, the light, and the life. For instance, the saving power of God is expressed in the concept of *Avathar* who restores dharma in the midst of *adharma*. According to Sri Aurobindo the process is called involution. Here *Sachchidananda*, the divine being and the creative power, by reason of delight descends into the realm of the inconscient.[60] The descent brings transformation and integration of the whole being. Involution initiates the process of evolution that is the reunion of matter to spirit. The ultimate purpose of all the activities including spiritual ones is to discover and strengthen the soul's relationship with the Infinite. In short, the whole beings are in a journey towards the supermind, the eternal goal.

2.2.8. *The Cosmic Coherence*

Indian ethos is inclusive and tries to encompass all. Its outlook on human existence has global and regional dimensions but are complementary. Each part is interpreted not as a separate entity but in relation to the cosmic order. Even the concept of God which is narrated as *satyam* (truth), *shivam* (bliss), and *sundaram* (beauty) has a universal outlook. A person from any culture and religion can accept such a comprehensive reflection. The global consciousness of Indian ethos, also, can be seen in extending love towards the whole humanity. The phrases *vasudhaiva Kutumbakam* (the whole world is one family/the family of mother earth), *sarvabhutahita* (the welfare of all beings/ devotion to the good of all creatures) and *loka-hits* (devotion to the good of humanity/kindness to one's species) are examples of the wider perspectives. In Indian ethos, the brotherhood is not limited to any boundaries; neither geographical nor man made boundaries. "Indian culture is not racially exclusive, but has affected men of all races. It is international in feeling and intention."[61] There is no isolated existence for anything but all elements in the universe move together in harmony.

For instance Buddhism, born out of Indian ethos, teaches the concept of peace to all beings. The Lion Capital, which is erected by Emperor Asoka at Sarnath symbolizes the proclamation of peace by Buddha to "The Four Quarters of the World." India adopted it as the State Emblem. Buddha said: "to pervade the world with kindness, pity, sympathy, and equable feeling—that is the way to union with Brahma."[62] Along the lines of Buddhism, Bhakthi movement also preached love, compassion and human brotherhood which are the core of Indian ethos. "The saints of middle ages sang the unity of existence and taught the universality of love. They evinced a remarkable breadth of vision and proclaimed that all religions are essentially one."[63]

Since all human beings are brothers and sisters, the Indian ethos teaches all to show *Karuna* (compassion) to all beings. "The other significant attribute of the spirit of India, is compassion, what we call *karuna*, compassion for all creatures, compassion for those afflicted in any way."[64] A holy person is one who shows compassion. There is a heart touching prayer by a disciple in Bhagwata, one of the ancient religious books: "I beg not for kingdom nor for paradise, nor immortality, but only that the sorrows of the afflicted ones of this world should be assuaged."[65] This is the high-water mark of the spiritual longing of man. Compassion urges humanity to be non-violent. *Ahimsa* is considered as one of the fundamental values in Indian ethos. Along with other schools of thoughts, Jainism strongly lays emphasis on *ahimsa*. "Jainism is ahimsa and conversely also ahimsa is Jainism!"[66] Ahimsa is not passive or indifferent to the challenges but is constructive and creative. The Kural, the Tamil text considers ahimsa as the highest virtue and advocates absolute non-injury. Its advice consists of the abstention from doing harm to others, even in thought, at all times, without exception, and without making the slightest distinctions.[67]

To be compassionate and non-violent, one should have the virtue of tolerance, which enables people to have a graceful acceptance of various viewpoints, even the contradictory, and does not impose one's ideologies on others. Tolerance facilitates approaching people and perceives their outlook without prejudice. It provides the means to have a better understanding about others. The complex reality of the universe cannot be interpreted by a single dogma or an image, so humanity needs a variety of symbolic languages to understand the reality. A uniform standard teaching which is acceptable to all is impossible. Hence, for the existence of India, which is a pluralistic nation, tolerance is necessary and from the ancient times, it is added to the ethos of India. "Nothing is more dear to Indian life and thought than the spirit of tolerance."[68] India is unified in the midst of plurality with the virtue of tolerance. "The other characteristic of this spirit of India, and I say it in all humility, is tolerance."[69] Harmony among different sects is created through respecting the faith and values of others. While having one's identity, everyone should assimilate the spirit of all other's culture and it is the law of harmony. "Love without attachment, strength without malice, non-violence without inaction, tolerance without fear, peace without being cowardly, and a life devoid of all extremes of passions like anger, enmity, pleasure and pain make up the ideal of ahimsa. It is earthly, at the same time intensely spiritual. It is a way of life, an Indian way of living."[70] The continuous reflection widens the cosmic coherence and purifies the egoism with altruism. The Indian ethos guides human beings to attain the highest form of love.

In short, the above-mentioned eight characteristics are the pillars of Indian ethos which gives orientation to the nation. India is like a piece of beautifully designed fabric. Its variety and harmony in composition gives beauty. The Indic civilization has unique and unifying ethos which is simple and complex; local and global; terrestrial and celestial; personal and philosophical; active and passive. Indians celebrate the plurality that is its charm. The ethos of India has continuity and it influences the people. The whole course of recorded history witnesses for the unbreakable cultural unity of India with its strongly built foundation of ethos. The remarkable ethos of India continues to form new horizons.

Notes

1. Douglas Harper, "Ethic" Web page 2001, Accessed: 2nd April 2012. <http://www.etymonline.com/ indexphp? allowed in frame=0&search=ethos&searchmode=none>.
2. Maria Goicoechea, "The Post Human Ethos in Cyberpunk Science Fiction," CLC Web 10.4 (2008), Accessed 2nd April 2012. <http://docs.lib.purdue.Education/clcweb/vol10/iss4/9> p. 2.
3. Frederick William Danker (ed.), *Greek-English Lexicon of the New Testament and other Early Christian Literature* 3rd ed. (Chicago: The University of Chicago Press, 2000), p. 277.
4. Neta Oren and Daniel Bar-Ta, "Ethos and Identity: Expressions and Changes in the Israeli Jewish Society," *Estudios de Psicología* 27.3 (2006), p. 3.
5. *Ibid.*, p. 1.
6. *Ibid.*, p. 1.

7. Octavio Paz, *In Light of India* (United States of America: Rediff Books, 1998), p. 185. http://books.google.co.in
8. Daya Krishna, "India's Intellectual Tradition: An Overview" Daya Krishna, (ed.), *India's Intellectual Tradition: Attempts at Conceptual Reconstructions* (New Delhi: Indian Council of Philosophical Research, 2003), p. 215.
9. Subhro Niyogi, "Violence, not Ahimsa, Integral to Indian Culture: Upinder," *The Times of India,* ed. Kolkata, 28 Jan 2012, http://articles.timesofindia.indiatimes.com
10. Shalini Shah, *Love, Eroticism and Female Sexuality in Classical Sanskrit Literature: Seventh-Thirteenth Centuries* (New Delhi: Manohar, 2009), p. 56.
11. N.K. Devaraja, *The Mind and Spirit of India* (Delhi: Motilal Banarsidass, 1967), p. 1.
12. Sisirkumar Mitra, *The Vision of India* (Calcutta: Culture Publishers, 1947), pp. 6-7.
13. L.K. Singh, *Indian Cultural Heritage Perspective for Tourism* (Delhi: ISHA Books, 2008), pp. 11-12.
14. Bibhutibhusan Datta, "Vedic Mathematics" Priyadaranjan Ray & S.N Sensibilityed, (eds.), *The Cultural Heritage of India* (Calcutta: The Ramakrishna Mission Institute of Culture, 1986), p. 36.
15. R.S. Sharma, *India's Ancient Past* (New Delhi: Oxford University Press, 2005), p. 311.
16. Balmiki Prasad Singh, *India's Culture: The State, the Arts, and Beyond* (India: Oxford University Press, 2011), p. lii.
17. A.P.J. Abdul Kalam, *India 2020: A Vision for the New Millennium,* Y.S. Rajan (ed.), (New Delhi: Penguin Books, 1998), pp. 27-28.
18. Balmiki Prasad Singh, *India's Culture: The State, the Arts, and Beyond* (India: Oxford University Press, 2011), p. 1.
19. Staff Ananda, *Myth, Symbol and Language: A Modern Perspective with Reference to India and her Religions* (New Delhi: Aryan Books International, 1998), p. viii.
20. Balmiki Prasad Singh, *India's Culture: The State, the Arts, and Beyond* (India: Oxford University Press, 2011), pp. 178-79.
21. S. Abid Husain, *The National Culture of India* (India: Asia Publishing House, 1961), p. 92.

22. "Languages of India." Web page. *Wikipedia: the Free Encyclopedia*. Accessed: 28th August 2012 <http://en.wikipedia.org/wiki/Languages_of_India>.

23. Balmiki Prasad Singh, *India's Culture: The State, the Arts, and Beyond* (India: Oxford University Press, 2011), p. xlix.

24. Ashish Vashi, "Ahmedabad turned Akbar Veggie" *The Times of India,* Ahmedabad ed. 23 Nov. 2009. Accessed 2nd September 2012 <http://articles.timesofindia.indiatimes.com/2009-11-23/ahmedabad/28111782_1_mughal-emperor-akbar-jainism-architecture>.

25. Shashi Tharoor, *From Midnight to the Millennium* (India: Penguin Books, 1997), p. 9.

26. *Ibid*., p. 5.

27. Sisirkumar Mitra, *The Vision of India* (Calcutta: Culture Publishers, 1947), p. 65.

28. Shashi Tharoor, *From Midnight to the Millennium* (India: Penguin Books, 1997), p. 289.

29. Sudhir Kakar, "Indian-ness: So what really makes Indians Indian?" Web 2nd April 2007. Accessed 4th September 2013. <http://www.littleindia.com/nri/1730-indian-ness.html>.

30. A.N.M. Irshad Ali, "Kinship and Marriage among the Assamese Muslims" Imtiza Ahmad (ed.), *Family, Kinship and Marriage among Muslims in India* (New Delhi: Manohar, 1976), p. 144.

31. Ajit K. Singh, Gaya Pandey, and Prabhat K. Singh, *Forest and Fribals in India* (New Delhi: B.K. Taneja, 1998), p. 77.

32. Stefano De Santis, *Nature and Man: The Hindu Perspective* Vol. 2 (Delhi: Sociecos & Dilip Kumar Publishers, 1995), p. 294.

33. Indra Deva and Shrirama, *Society and Culture in India* (New Delhi: Rawat Publications, 1999), p. 62.

34. N.K. Devaraja, *The Mind and Spirit of India* (Delhi: Motilal Banarsidass, 1967), p. 72.

35. S. Abid Husain, *The National Culture of India* (India: Asia Publishing House, 1961), p. 32.

36. *Ibid*., pp. 32-33.

37. Sisirkumar Mitra, *The Vision of India* (Calcutta: Culture Publishers, 1947), p. 64.

38. N. Subbu Reddiar, "Emotional Integration and Ancient Tamil Literature." Indira Gandhi Abinandan Samiti, *The Spirit of*

India. Vol: II (New York: Asia Publishing House, 1976), p. 473.

39. Diwan Bahadur and K.S. Ramaswami Sastri, "The Puranas" Suniti Kumar Chatterjied, *The Cultural Heritage of India: Language and Literatures,* Vol. 5 (Calcutta: The Ramakrishna Mission, 1978), p. 64.
40. S. Abid Husain, *The National Culture of India* (India: Asia Publishing House, 1961), p. 60.
41. *Ibid.*, p. 94.
42. *Ibid.*, p. 95.
43. Sisirkumar Mitra, *The Vision of India* (Calcutta: Culture Publishers, 1947), p. 62.
44. *The Bhagavad Gita* 7.9. Trans. O.P. Dwivedi "Dharmic Ecology" Christopher Key Chapple and Mary Evelyn Tucker eds, *Hinduism and Ecology* (Harvard: Harvard University Press, 2000), p. 12.
45. Klaus Seeland and Franz Schmithusen, *Man and Forest Series* (New Delhi: D.K. Printworld, 2002), p. 106.
46. Pankaj Jain, *Dharma and Ecology of Hindu Communities* (USA: Ashgate Publishing Company, 2011), p. 79.
47. *Ibid.*, pp. 82-84.
48. *Ibid.*, p. 3.
49. *Ibid.*, p. 15.
50. Stefano De Santis, *Nature and Man: The Hindu Perspective* Vol. 2 (Delhi: Sociecos & Dilip Kumar Publishers, 1995), p. 276.
51. Sisirkumar Mitra, *The Vision of India* (Calcutta: Culture Publishers, 1947), p. 9.
52. G.L. Mehta, *Understanding India* (New York: Asia Publishing House, 1959), p. 7.
53. N.K. Devaraja, *The Mind and Spirit of India* (Delhi: Motilal Banarsidass, 1967), pp. 80-81.
54. Shalini Shah, *Love, Eroticism and Female Sexuality in Classical Sanskrit Literature: Seventh-Thirteenth Centuries* (New Delhi: Manohar, 2009), p. 56.
55. *Mahabharata*, Uddyogaparva, 124, 34-38. Urmila Sharma & S.K. Sharma (Trans.) *Indian Political Thought* (New Delhi: Atlantic Publishers and Distributors, 1996), p. 20.

56. N.K. Devaraja, *The Mind and Spirit of India* (Delhi: Motilal Banarsidass, 1967), p. 9.
57. S. Abid Husain, *The National Culture of India* (India: Asia Publishing House, 1961), p. 60.
58. G.L. Mehta, *Understanding India* (New York: Asia Publishing House, 1959), p. 8.
59. *Ibid*., p. 12.
60. L. Thomas O'Neil, *Towards the Life Divine: Sri Aurobindo's Vision* (New Delhi: Manohar, 1979), p. 60.
61. S. Radhakrishnan, *Religion and Society* (London: George Allen and Unwin Ltd, 1947), p. 43.
62. George Kotturan, *Ahimsa: Gautama to Gandhi* (New Delhi: Sterling Publishers, 1973), pp. 29-30.
63. Sisirkumar Mitra, *The Vision of India* (Calcutta: Culture Publishers, 1947), p. 101.
64. G.L. Mehta, *Understanding India* (New York: Asia Publishing House, 1959), p. 9.
65. *Ibid*., p. 10.
66. Bansidhar Bhatt, *Ahimsa: In the Early Religious Traditions of India* (Rome: Centre for Indian and Inter-religious Studies, 1994), p. 81.
67. *The KuralI*, 32.317. "Tahtinen Unto," *Ahimsa: Non-Violence in Indian Tradition* (London: Rider and Company, 1976), p. 53.
68. George Kotturan, *Ahimsa: Gautama to Gandhi* (New Delhi: Sterling Publishers, 1973), p. 3.
69. G.L. Mehta, *Understanding India* (New York: Asia Publishing House, 1959), p. 10.
70. George Kotturan, *Ahimsa: Gautama to Gandhi* (New Delhi: Sterling Publishers, 1973), p. 6.

3

Literary Representation of the Indian Ethos in Pre-independent Period

CHAPTER OUTLINE

3.1. Pre-independence Period

The Indian ethos during the pre-independence period was formed around a threefold fight: against the colonialism, social decadence, and narrow chauvinism such as caste system, religious fundamentalism, regionalism, etc. India struggled through various uncertain situations, which empowered Indians to reflect deeply on their own identity and in turn led to various reformations related to political, cultural, social, and religious factors. Ultimately, during the pre-independence period, the self-consciousness of Indians reached its peak.

3.1.1. *Colonization*

The ethos of the pre-independence India should be analyzed against the background of colonialism which had not only political but also cultural implications. It deeply influenced the Indian ethos in all its dimensions due to its overt and covert nature. External acts of colonization such as economic, political, and territorial conquest can be called overt colonization. That which was dangerous and difficult to decolonize was covert hegemony which included the colonization of spiritual, emotional, intellectual, and cultural richness of the natives. Here the colonizers tried to define themselves against the colonized and presented them as the 'other' or the binary. It might create a superiority complex in the colonizer and an inferiority complex in the colonized. It is evident that covert colonization was a hidden agenda of the British in India.

> Lord Thomas Macaulay saw such high moral values and calibre in Indians that he came to the conclusion that the British colonialists would never ever conquer the country if they did not break the backbone of the nation, her spiritual and cultural heritage. So he recognised in Indianness various qualities such as spirituality, cultural heritage and enlightenment and started on a project to make Indians think that all that is foreign and English was good and greater than their own.[1]

The colonizer attempted to destroy the very nature of India's identity. They claimed that even the word 'India' which denotes the whole subcontinent, itself was formed during the British rule. "In denying such an identity for the people of the subcontinent, the British wished to take credit for the formation of the modern political nation state called India and perhaps more to the point, to deny an independent civilizational status to the Indics."[2] The distorted views and interpretations of history altered the true nature of Indian ethos. The colonizer could never understand the mind of the native because they approached the colonized with prejudice and forcefully started the 'civilizing mission.' Thus, it was not the savagery of the native but prejudice of the colonizer that created problems.

Indians, who considered the culture of the colonizer as superior, fell in the trap of the persuasion of the colonizer and felt inferiority about their culture; so they wholeheartedly mimicked the colonizer's culture. English education was not completely a project of the colonizer but Indians also took initiative to start English education. In 1823, Ram Mohan Roy strongly wrote to Lord Amberst about the need for modern education in India. "The Samgscrit system of education would be best calculated to keep this country in darkness, if such had been the policy of the British Legislature. But as the improvement of the native population is the objective of the Government, it will consequently promote a more liberal and enlightened system of instruction [...]."[3] Only in 1835 did Macaulay's Minute on Education came into force. Sympathetically, the colonizer formed the mental framework of the intelligentsia among the colonized.

3.1.2. *Social Awakening and Nationalism*

Decolonization is a more complex process than colonization since the colonized themselves are divided in their views. The decolonization process in India was marked by the uprising of 1857 not by the elite but by the *sepoys*, who did not have England education. A series of civil localized rebellions arose against the foreign rule. Even though such revolts lacked long-term goals, sense of national freedom, concept about colonialism, etc., they sowed the seed for a new decolonization age. From the thirties of the nineteenth century onwards, the Western education spread widely in India, which led to progressive thinking and formed a new elite class. The so-called elites failed to know the soul of India. "While fighting for the creation of a nation, these leaders realized they did not know the 80 percent people of the country who lived in the villages and on whose behalf they were fighting to gain independence."[4] However, the education enlightened them to re-examine the social system that prevailed in India and to re-discover its identity.

The Indian renaissance and nationalism went hand in hand and both complimented to build-up national identity on the ethos of India.

> Modern India's renaissance and the anti-colonial struggle were both expressions of the people's search for a national identity. [...] They were deeply involved in the social challenges of their time. The anti-colonial struggle at its best assumed the form of a cultural movement and the cultural movement grew as an anti-colonial mobilization in the realm of consciousness.[5]

The need for social awakening in India was an unquestionable issue during the pre-independence period but the approaches were different even though they overlapped each other. Bhikhu Parekh distinguishes four types of approaches: traditionalism, modernism, critical modernism, and critical traditionalism.[6] The traditionalists found a little change so they were not much worried about the British rule. On the contrary, the modernists stood for radical transformation. Critical modernists like, Ram Mohan Roy, Gopal Krishna Gokhale, and others tried to synthesise modern developments of the west and of the Indian culture. Bankim Chandra Chatterjee, Aurobindo, Vivekananda, and so on despised the Western influence and stood for self-renovation. Apart from the gap between the elite class and common people, the conflict between Indian education and English education, and disagreement between various approaches, in course of time all came together against colonization and for social reformations.

The social upheaval was the need of the time and the visionaries of India focused on it with great enthusiasm. As

Tagore says: "Our real problem in India is not political. It is social."[7] The Indian renaissance had an effect on all spheres of life—social, religious, cultural, economical, political, and literary. It contributed to develop high national consciousness and the upliftment of various oppressed groups. Many leaders including Gandhiji and B.R. Ambedkar toiled a lot for the promotion of the untouchables. Even though many social evils could not be eradicated completely, Indian society achieved a lot. In the words of Annie Besant, "it is not a plant of mushroom growth but a giant of the forest with millennia behind it."[8] The Indian renaissance prepared the way for the regeneration of the Indian ethos, and a new spirit of nationalism began to grow in the minds of people. "The inner spirit of this renaissance penetrated into our political life and generated a tremendously powerful force which boldly challenged the very basis of alien domination and imperialism."[9]

In the period, along with the social upheaval, nationalism also grew and Indians began to visualize a unified and glorious *Bharat Mata*. For national integration, the nationalists began to re-interpret history from a wider perspective. They tried to avoid the emphasis on racialism in Indian history that was interpretation of the British historians who were influenced by the German racial theories. The Aryan-Dravidian controversy is an outcome of the distorted interpretation of Indian culture as Aryan culture is equated with a race of people who had come into India a long-time back. Indian historians interpreted 'Arya' in a wider perspective. The word 'Arya' was interpreted as a collective ethos developed by different races. Another example for the re-reading of the ethos of India is that the nationalists attempted to break away from the British point of view of India as a land of spiritualism and tried to establish the Indian approach as holistic understanding. During the independence struggle the self-consciousness of Indians was aroused and attempts were made to rediscover India from various perspectives. The works of A.L. Basham (*The Wonder that was India*, 1953), Jawaharlal Nehru (*The Discovery of India*, 1946), Rabindranath Tagore and others authenticated the ethos of India and encouraged the process of rediscovery of Indianness. Even though the people of the land cherished the concept of one nation, physically it never materialized. Only in the pre-independence period was the idea of unified India crystallized. To rebuild the unified identity, leaders romanticized the Indian glorious past. "Indeed, the rediscovery of India's past, through the dedication and unceasing efforts of scholars, poets and social or religious reformers, proved to be a highly inspiring force."[10] The emotional writings touched the common people. The nationalists glorified Indianness to instil unity and patriotism in the masses. It created strong anti-colonial feelings in them and the motivation to practice Indian culture.

3.1.3. *Influence of Gandhiji*

Even though Gandhiji returned to India in 1915, he did not enter into the nation-wide freedom struggle but moved among the common people to understand them and the ethos of the land. Until the emergence of Gandhiji, the freedom movement was in the hands of the elite and there was a gap between the world of the intelligentsia and the peasants. "Gandhi was one of the few nationalist leaders to make a heroic effort to close this gap. He succeeded by involving the peasant masses in the freedom struggle through symbolic and highly effusive issues."[11] Through the ideologies and policies, Gandhiji was able to attain the confidence of the elite along with the upper class, middle class and above all the lower class who constituted the majority. Even the poor participated in the freedom struggle not only through physical efforts but also by contributing money. Nehru shares his experience: "Crowds come and fill the air with their slogans. They [the Assamese people] are mostly tea-garden coolies. In their poverty they give us money for Swaraj."[12] Gandhiji's influence on the people, including the literate and the illiterate, colonizer and colonized, was immense and he was able to move the hearts of even the opponents by the mantra of 'love.' The greatest contribution of Gandhiji is that he mobilized the common people of India. Thus, India's freedom movement became a mass movement and part of the Indian ethos.

Gandhiji was not a mere leader of the independence struggle but an icon of the Indian ethos. He followed a set of principles and the two most important values among them were truth and *ahimsa*. His weapon to fight against the colonial power was *satyagraha*, which is an active means to win over oneself and persuade others in love. "During the national imagining of identity, Gandhi forms the locus of identity because he stands for a pan-Indian symbol of India's peacekeeping and non-violent heritage: the whole of India, with its thousands of years of tradition, comes to identify itself with this frail figure."[13] Internationally, Gandhiji is acclaimed as the epitome of nobility. Gandhiji synchronized political and spiritual life; active and contemplative life which is the real ethos of India. He used the soul force, the mastery of oneself, for freedom. Many consider him as a saviour or *avathar*.

3.1.4. *Sectarianism*

Nation building is a herculean enterprise. When the challenges are more and the resources to resolve them are less, certain traumatic incidents may occur in the society. For India, the pre-independence period was a time of *agni-pariksha*. To a certain extent, Indians won through it but in a few areas, Indians surrendered themselves to a disgraceful failure especially in relation with narrow chauvinism like regionalism and sectarianism. When the regional elements get undue importance at the cost of wider vision of the nation, it weakens the uniting threads.

To rule the Indian subcontinent which promotes pluralism, the British framed the policy of divide and rule after the 'mutiny' of 1857 where all the people from different faiths and regions came together to fight against them. The colonizers began to sow disunity in the name of caste, religion, language, etc., and it gave way to sectarianism. The narrow-minded Indian leaders with various selfish motives, also, used regionalism.

> Central to the growth of regionalism in modern India has been the rise of regional elites that embody and sustain the distinctive values of the area and shape its political life. Formed from those who successfully grasped the limited but still substantial opportunities

> for power and influence made available by the British, these elites gained positions of dominance during the nineteenth century.[14]

Cultural regionalism, in other words, communalism based on religion, which is expressed in gods, rituals, myths, festivals, etc., dominated in the pre-independent India.

The major religious fundamental forces were Hindutva or Hindu nationalism and Muslim fundamentalism. Hindutva movement is based on three views. Firstly, it presents a mono Hindu philosophy based on Brahminic tradition instead of the pluralistic ethos of Hinduism. Secondly, it attempts to identify Hinduism with nationalism. Thirdly, it tries to establish a hegemony and regimentation over others. The Hindu fundamentalism began to flourish in the country. Getting the recognition of a separate representation for Muslims in 1909 was the major achievement of the Muslim fundamentalists. As a prophecy, Iqbal wrote in 1923: "It is pity that in the Punjab the jealousy, no, rather enmity of Hindus and Muslims is growing. If it remains like that, then life will become difficult for both the communities during the next 30 years."[15] Things went in the same way and religious communalism had begun to rule the country. The Muslim League passed the famous resolution of a 'North West Indian Muslim State' at Lahore in 1940 and Jinnah openly declared that to have a nation is the right of Muslims.

The country was caught between secular and communal forces. In 1946, Nehru said that Pakistan could not exist in the age of atom bomb and Patel visualized a united India. However, in April 1947 Patel said, 'no alternative but to divide' and in June 1947, the letter sent by the Congress President to the Viceroy, drafted by Nehru stated 'in order to achieve a final settlement' accepted the proposals.[16] On April 1947, Gandhiji said, "No one listens to me anymore. I am a small man."[17] The growth of communalism reached its climax on 3 June 1947 when Mountbatten announced it. India moved to post-independent period on 15 August 1947, along with the traumatic experience of partition and many other challenges.

3.1.5. *Fictional Representation*

The writings of pre-independent India can be classified as the nationalist phase of literature. The creative works reflect the Indian renaissance, struggle for freedom, Gandhism, the spirit of nationalism, etc. Along with regional novels, Indian English novels portray the ethos of pre-independent India. Bal Krishna's *The Love of Kusuma* (1912?) is a love story that aims at social reformation. The fictions of Mulk Raj Anand like, *Coolie* (1936), *Two Leaves and a Bud* (1937), *The Village* (1939) are stories based on sufferings of the subalterns. Another novel of Anand, *The Big Heart* (1945) also reflects humanism and unfolds the problems of the working class. R.K. Narayan's *The Dark Room* (1938) is a story about the suffering women in the Indian patriarchal society.

During the period, there were many novels written about the freedom struggle and about the influence of Gandhiji. For example, K.S. Venkataramani Murugan's *The Tiller* (1927) reflects the freedom movement under Gandhiji. The fiction of K.A. Abbas like *Tomorrow is Ours* (1943) and *Defeat for Death* (1944) speaks about the freedom struggle. Further, Aamir Ali's *Conflict* (1947) is a narration about participation of students and rural people in freedom struggle. S. Subrahmanya's *Indira Devi* (1930) gives an account of the political and social events of the Indian community. For the present analysis, Mulk Raj Anand's *Untouchable* (1935), and Raja Rao's *Kanthapura* (1936) are selected because the novels as well as the novelists were famous in the period. The novels reflect the spirit of the pre-independent India in various dimensions.

3.2. Analysis of *Untouchable* in the Light of the Pre-independent Ethos

To hold together the virtue of unity and diversity is hectic; most probably either of them may be sacrificed. However, India made an effort to hold together both of them. It tried to accommodate different races by the principle of tolerance and promoted heterogeneity. Hence, India became rich in diversity and plurality. At the same time, the challenge before Indians was to unify different people with diverse identities. One of the solutions evolved was the caste system that smoothed way for the harmonious relationship between the whole. For Tagore, "her [India's] caste system is the outcome of this spirit of toleration."[18] Caste system was the by-product of the attempt to create homogeneity within heterogeneity. Dumont says, "The caste, unified from the outside, is divided within. More generally, a particular caste is a complex group, a successive inclusion of groups of diverse orders or levels, in which different functions (profession, endogamy, etc.) are attached to different levels."[19] The various groups were assigned with different missions to serve the society and to find livelihood. Thus, unhealthy competitions between different ethnic groups were avoided and unity of the society was attained. The caste system could be seen all over India without any religious or racial differences. The system became a part of Indian ethos.

India attained a unified and diversified society but she lost the flow of people from one stratum to the other. India accommodated all but failed to incorporate them like a rainbow. Some took more advantages and became privileged ones. The *Untouchable* (1935) by Mulk Raj Anand (1905-2004) narrates the sufferings and the aspirations of the underprivileged ones in the caste system. With his pen that is mightier than the sword, Anand fought against the caste system that caused trauma and torment for many in the traditional Indian society. The time-honoured custom of caste system was criticized severely by him and the novel can be called 'the epic of misery'.[20] It is an eye opening novel that fights against social evils arising from the caste system, which is the weak side of the Indian ethos. It is a sociological novel which envisages social transformation. It portrays Indian ethos not only because of the narration of caste system but also expresses nationalism, Gandhism, regional culture, and suffering of the woman. Thus, the novel highlights certain elements of the Indian tradition.

3.2.1. *The Oppressed Untouchable*

The caste consciousness is deeply rooted in the minds of Indians. Bakha, the protagonist of the novel took an injured child to its mother. Instead of expressing gratitude, the mother used abusive words. "Oh, you eater of your masters! What have you done? You have killed my son! she wailed, flinging her hands across her breasts and turning blue and red with fear" (*UN* 106). A similar incident happened in the life of Anand. As a child, he was injured and a sweeper brought him to the house. Rather than offering a word of thanks, the mother scolded the sweeper for polluting the child and the purification ritual was done before applying medicine.[21] Purification is more important than anything else. It was believed that the purity from the untouchable might be needed for Moksha and it set forth the awful social statutes for the untouchable. "*Untouchable* stands as the most moving book in the entire corpus of Anand's writing."[22] The 'six thousand years of racial and class superiority' (*UN* 8-9) is really an unimaginable victimization of a group of poor people.

The personal and social conditions of untouchables were very pathetic. Anand starts off his personal sharing about the suffering of Bakha with the narration of the outcast's colony that is separated from the rest of the world with an environment filled with all kinds of misery and wretchedness. The author narrates two separate worlds: of touchables and of untouchables. The world of gentleness includes cantonment and main town, and the world of the untouchable includes the colony of the outcastes. The untouchable, who cleans the whole town, stays in the most "uncongenial place to live in" (*UN* 1). The society exploited them without any human consideration. The untouchable was doubly colonized and their fight had two dimensions: the first against imperialism and the second against the high caste. The second colonization immediately affected the social, political, spiritual, religious, economical, professional areas of daily life. As a result, he tried to imitate the foreign imperialists to get a high status in the society.

All the incidents in the novel, which reveal the heartbreaking social condition of the outcaste, took place in the life of a sweeper boy named Bakha, within a short period of twenty-four hours and most of them are traumatic. The novel describes the physical and mental segregation of a group of downtrodden people who are the vital organs of the town, yet there is a great chasm between them and town dwellers. "[...] under the shadow both of the town and the cantonment, but outside their boundaries and separate, from them" (*UN* 1). The suffering continues day and night and the whole year. The oppression by the upper caste is well narrated in the road incident that happened to Bakha who had just started to enjoy the *Jalebis*, a cheap sweet but the highest dream of a lower-caste. On the way, he unintentionally touched an upper-caste man and the man began to harass him. "Keep to the side of the road, you, low-caste vermin!" (*UN* 38). The man was not ready to accept the apology of Bakha with folded hands. The upper caste considered the untouchable as unclean. The pain of their feelings echoed in the words of Bakha. "They think we are mere dirt because we clean their dirt" (*UN* 70). Not the service but caste matters. The untouchable toiled for others' welfare, yet they were oppressed.

The untouchables were deprived of their indispensable necessities of life like food, water and clothing. Food is used as imagery in the novel to show the intensity of the suffering of the untouchable. In the Indian culture, food is regarded with great reverence and *annadanam* (sharing of food) is a sacred act to attain *moksha*. After the hard work and toil of the morning, Bakha went to a house for food but the woman of the house for whom he took the pain for cleaning, harassed him in an inhuman manner and flung some *chapatti* at him. After this humiliation Bakha took the food and wrapped it in his duster. Whereas, the woman fed the *sadhu* lavishly and asked him to come on the next day. The real love does not degrade people in relation to their job and wealth but expresses concern and care. Another image used in the novel is water, which is the basic necessity of any living being. In the opening paragraph itself Anand obnoxiously painted the stream to show the pathetic condition of the untouchable. To have drinking water at somebody's mercy is atrocious. The untouchables were deprived of water. They did not have the permission to use the public well. They had to wait near the well until someone from the upper caste drew water for them. Each moment of Bakha's life was filled with hardships. "To Bakha, every second seemed an endless age of woe and suffering. His whole demeanour was concentrated in humility..." (*UN* 40). Bakha stands for the miserable life of each underdog in India.

3.2.2. *Religious Barriers*

Until the 5th century B.C., there was no political power to unify the diversified and nomadic groups in India. As a result, religion took the role of bringing social order with the tool of the caste system. Later the upper caste misused religion to sanction the caste system in such a manner as to get advantage of it. The strong philosophy of metempsychosis and karma theory supported the same. Even the gods were created by the upper caste and there was no place for the lower caste before the gods. The lower caste had no place of peace.

Many challenged the unjust system and even religions such as Buddhism and Jainism were formed for the upliftment of the common people. Buddha says about the real spirit of the caste system: "Not by birth does one become an outcaste, not by birth does one become a brahman. By [one's] action one becomes an outcaste, by [one's] action one became a Brahman."[23] Moreover, in the medieval period Bhakti Movement questioned the caste system. Since Brahmanism had an upper hand, the movements could not attain the goal envisaged by their leaders. It is not birth but one's actions that determine the status of a person in the society. The real ethos of India is that all human beings, including brahmins and shudras, are equals since all have the *atman* of the *Paramatman* that unites them in spirit.

Bakha challenges the theory of Karma. Bakha moved away from the theory of life after death and broke the religious force behind the unjust system. He defiled the temple premises and was ready to kill the priest to uphold the dignity of his sister. "He felt he could kill them all" (*UN* 54). The injustice could not be tolerated for long and the untouchables were in search of the inner spirit of religion. "For many Dalits, God is dead, and the universe empty and uncaring. Rejecting the idea of God, such Dalits often favour atheism. Their actions are oriented to a casteless society."[24] Many made use of religion as a tool for enslavement of others. Thus, the profession of religion became the root cause of discrimination and exploitation and Anand strives to renew the religion by exposing the existing evil practices. The priests and sadhus should become the real voice of the soul but they became the proponents of the evil system. Their participation and communication-operation turned it to the worst form. In the name of purity, they kept themselves away from the untouchable and indeed they sexually exploited the lower-caste women. The temple, the seat of love, also appears like an ogre that terrifies the low caste. Religion became a barrier for the progression of human beings and justice. "He could not overstep the barriers which the conventions of his superiors had built up to protect their weakness against him. He could not invade the magic circle which protects a priest from attack by anybody, especially by a low-caste man" (*UN* 56). It is very difficult to pull out the yokes created by religions.

Furthermore, the religious symbols are also used to highlight the purification process of religion. The image 'fire' that is a very common symbol in religion is used around thirty four times in the novel. "The spirit of fire which lay buried in the mass of his flesh had ignited this morning" (*UN* 109). It has the meaning of purification, renewal, change, rebirth, etc. The verb 'burn/t' is used about seventeen times in the novel and it stands for the destruction of the unjust system. "This burnt Bakha's soul" (*UN* 70). The idea of reformation is again emphasized by the word 'power' and it is seen around fifteen times in the novel. "The burning flame seemed to ally itself with him [Bakha]. It seemed to give him a sense of power, the power to destroy. [...] It seemed as if burning or destruction was for him a form of physical culture" (*UN* 13). So the transformation of the religion that has contributed a lot to build-up Indian ethos, is emphasized in the novel for the betterment of the downtrodden.

3.2.3. *Status of Women*

The exploitation of women is more heartbreaking than that of men in the society. There are several glimpses of the sufferings of women in the novel. They underwent three types of oppressions: the colonization of the White, the oppression by the upper caste, and the ill treatment from the male. Since the Indian society is patriarchal, women are subjugated by men. There are a lot of abusive words related to women. The author depicts the misery of the woman mainly through Sohini, the sister of Bakha. Since "Sohini being of the lowest caste among the outcastes" (*UN* 16), the society "naturally looked down upon" (*UN* 16) her. Not only in the society but also in the house there was no peace for the lower-caste woman. After her mother's death Sohini took care of the cooking in the family. She was even ill-treated by her father. Men always thrive for their comforts and have little concern for the women folk.

After completing her work "in the corner of the little mud-house which was her kitchen" (*UN* 23) she also had to go for sweeping. She, who is so beautiful, suffers a lot from the society. She exemplifies caste and sex exploitation, the representative of doubly exploited lower-caste women. The Pundit attempts to molest Sohini; she screams for help but no one turns up. To save himself, the pundit shouted "Polluted, polluted, polluted!" (*UN* 53). The crowd, who do not extend their hands to help the girl, sympathizes with the priest who is the culprit. The crowd moves against Bakha, who comes to rescue his sister. Anand unmasks the hypocrisy of the Brahman priests who are considered as the apex of the caste system and the social system which always found fault with the outcaste. As a consequence, the untouchable woman suffered many agonies in the family as well as in the society.

3.2.4. *Nationalism*

Even though, caste system has been prevailing in India for centuries it is not the same at every time and in every region. "Caste is not and never has been a fixed fact of Indian life."[25] Cultural variations, political systems, economic changes, power concentrations, philosophical shifts, and religious teachings made a lot of influence in constructing and deconstructing the caste system over ages. The more generalized and fixed caste system, which exists today, was formulated in the early 18th century by the colonial rule. "Under colonialism, caste was thus made out to be far more—far more pervasive, far more totalizing, and far more uniform—than it had ever been before, at the same time that it was defined as a fundamentally religious social order."[26] Since Indians themselves defined the society in hierarchy, it was easy for the foreigners to get into the system. They, who claimed to have more objective and scientific knowledge, defined themselves as the highest caste or the finest race and above Brahmins. The Indians accepted the Western supremacy without any resistance because they had the mental disposition to accept the supremacy of others. Hence, the colonizers did not feel a need to wipe out the native culture but they paraphrased it for their benefit. When the *Untouchable* was written, it was the need of the time, to build-up patriotism among Indians and to find out the true spirit of Indian culture apart from the orientalists.

Although, Anand bursts out against caste system in India, it was indirectly against the colonizers who promoted it. He had the national consciousness and had the self-confidence that India can solve her problems. *Untouchable* tries to put forward the philosophy of the revivalist for the progression of India. "[Revivalists] are disposed to primarily look at their sastras and the past history, and the traditions of their people and the ancient institutions of the land which were in vogue when the nation was at the zenith of its glory."[27] The poet in the novel says, "We know life. We know its secret flow. We have danced to its rhythms. We have loved it," (*UN* 143). For Anand, as a revivalist the advancement and growth should be with a nationalistic feeling. He also observes the misunderstanding of the orientalists about India, "The Victorians misinterpreted us" (*UN* 143). The imperialists interpreted the Indian philosophy in favour of their exploitation. "You don't believe in this world; to you all this is *maya*. Let us look after your country for you and you can dedicate yourself to achieving Nirvana" (*UN* 143). In turn, Anand denounces the materialistic attitude of westerners. The view that India is a land of mysticism and people are striving only for *moksha* is a misconception of the orientals. The Indian philosophy is an integrated one which gives equal importance to the material and spiritual worlds which are complementary to each other.

The Britishers came with the negative attitude of 'the white man's burden' that led to 'cultural imperialism.' The natives who attained English education also consciously or unconsciously assimilated the very nature of the colonizers and acted with superiority complex. 'The English-learned' constituted a new elite group within the colony who felt superior among the colonized like high caste among the lower caste. The elite group considered themselves as enlightened and they began to follow paternalism. Anand criticizes the Western thinking pattern which was based on binary and the folly of equality. Whoever learns from the west cannot acquire 'real love.' It is true that Tommies related with Bakha with dignity and he is better with Englishmen who "treated him as a human being" (*UN* 2) than Indians who consider him as outcaste. However, Bakha learnt how to feel superior and in turn gave up the dogma of equality. "He had learnt to think of himself as superior to his fellow-outcastes" (*UN* 2). Hence, the attitude of the colonizer is paradoxically narrated. "In the ideology of liberal humanism, the feeling of superiority to other human beings is not supposed to be the consequence of being treated like a human being. This semantic and logical abyss warns the reader from the very outset that the colonial promise of universalism is a lie, and is not a viable solution to the predicament of the untouchable. A good part of the novel is spent in unravelling this particular double bind through the narrative construction of Bakha's subjectivity."[28] Bakha's mind is colonized "by the glamour of the White man's life" (*UN* 2).

The novel fights against the imperial rule. "[Anand] hated imperialism and raised voice against it through his writing. Feudalism unleashed terror on the poor Indians. They sucked the blood of the poor like leech."[29] Against imperialism, *Untouchable* underlines the greatness of India. "It is India's genius to accept all things" (*UN* 143). Iqbal Nath Sarshar, the young poet who edits the *Nawan Jug*, expresses the opinion that "we are so acutely aware of our blood-stream" (*UN* 145). India does not lag behind in scientific knowledge than the west and 'the spirit of enquiry' is one of the major elements in the Indian ethos. Anand wants to uphold not only the Aryan culture, the so-called dominating civilization, but also other subaltern philosophies of the regional races. He critically evaluates the philosophy of Shankaracharya. “There has been only one man in India who believed this world to be illusory-Shankaracharya. But he was a consumptive and that made him neurotic” (*UN* 143). He attacks the brahminic tradition and moves to embrace the knowledge of the folklore. “Take a ploughman from the plough, wash off his dirt, and he is fit to rule a kingdom” (*UN* 145). Thus Anand concludes that “we can destroy our inequalities easily” (*UN* 145). Each folk adds beauty to Indian culture which is formed from a variety of ethnic cultures. If one is denied its proper place in the Indian map, then the Indianness will lose its symphony.

3.2.5. *Nobility of Human Life*

All nature is the manifestation of the eternal goodness, so everything carries the eternal truth. This is one of the basic ethos of Indianness. The core teaching of the Buddha is that all must come to understand that lives are ever changing and infinite yet universal and part of the totality.[30] Hence respecting all beings, both living and non-living beings, and moving with the rhythm of the universe is a part of the culture. The *atman* (the self), the innermost individual being with individual consciousness (*Chitta*), links beings with the *Paramatman,* the innermost universal being with pure consciousness (*Chit*). *Atman* dwells in body, life, mind and intellect, yet it goes beyond them. Since each person is the visualization of the Pure Consciousness, the good dwells in every person and all are blessed with various potencies. In the first sight, *Untouchable* seems to be a novel full of sufferings and oppressions of the lower caste especially Bakha who experienced unimaginable instances of rejection and rebuff. Yet the novel carefully upholds the basic goodness in human beings. It is not a pessimistic but an optimistic novel which acknowledges the eminence of each human being.

Bakha, himself is a noble person in mind and body. “It seemed to suit him, to give a homogeneity, a wonderful wholeness to his body, so that you could turn round and say: ‘Here is a man.’ And it seemed to give him a nobility...” (*UN*

12). After the death of his mother, he who was the breadwinner had to look after the members of the family. Though everybody abused him, he selflessly worked hard for others. He helped the little boy who was injured and loved his sister. Out of concern for his sister, he endangered his life and questioned the priest. At the end of the novel he did not want to revenge the upper caste who humiliates him but earnestly searches for an alternative for his work. He is sincere in life. His sister, Sohini, also is good in character. She has a heart to empathize with others in their sufferings. Moreover, Sohini is a true Indian woman who tries to understand others' hardships. Nature blesses everyone to fit in the cosmic order and no one is rejected.

Human goodness is also seen in Hutchinson, Gandhiji, and Iqbal Nath Sarshar, who offer their own way for the betterment of the untouchable. Their ideologies may not sometimes be acceptable, yet they toil for the humanity and aims to empower the downtrodden. Even though their means are different, their goals are constructive. The novel calls to accept the basic goodness in all beings and universal brotherhood. It is an embodiment of humanism, which is one of the cores of Indian ethos.

3.2.6. *Gandhism Depicted*

The early 20th century of India can be called the Gandhian epoch since he recasted the perceptive and style of the freedom struggle. It was not merely a power seeking activity but a search for truth and a pilgrimage for self-realization that touched the hearts of many. For Gandhiji, inner purification was more important than external activities. He incorporated both the outer world and the inner world that is the ethos of India. He nurtured healthy political consciousness and prepared the people for independence. In the 1920s, all felt that Gandhiji's leadership could not be substituted with anyone else's for independence. Gandhism became a part of Indian ethos.

Gandhiji did his best for the upliftment of the untouchable. In 1932, Gandhiji opposed the idea of separate electorates for the untouchable. Even though it was severely criticized, according to him the policy might not facilitate the total eradication of untouchability and could endanger the unity and nationalism of the country. It was on the Harijan cause that Gandhiji took a twenty-one day fast starting on 8 May 1933. And from 7 November 1933 to 29 July 1934, for nearly nine months, he conducted an all India 'Harijan tour' travelling over 12,500 miles and collected money for the Harijan Sevak Sangh.[31] He propagated the removal of untouchability in all its forms and introduced various programmes for the empowerment of the untouchable. Many nationalists and orthodox Hindus even within the Congress found fault with him for his utmost concern for the Harijans and for shifting the attention of people from the main issue of anti imperialist struggle to Harijan work.[32] Gandhian approach to untouchability was rejected by many of the fundamentalists. The workers and peasants were moved by the new socialist approach, opposing the non-violent struggle of Gandhiji against imperialism. The socialist ideology began to take root among the intellectuals as well as common folk and took an upper hand in the national movement. Lots of youth were attracted by the socialist ideology and they demanded a new leadership style other than Gandhiji's.

Untouchable was written in the backdrop of these historical events and as a result, the novel reflects the unenthusiastic attitude towards Gandhiji. It is not a complete adulation of Gandhiji; it contains critical views as well. The author never questions the integrity and authenticity of Gandhiji in *Untouchable*. Bakha says: "Surely he is a good man" (*UN* 140). The poet accepts the personal authenticity of Gandhiji. "He has his limitations but he is fundamentally sound" (*UN* 142). However, the tone of the novel is a denunciation of Gandhism and it is presented in a superficial and imprecise manner. Not only did Bakha disapproved the Gandhian ideology, but he also failed to understand the path of Gandhiji.

More than disapproval, Bakha could not understand the path of Gandhiji, for instance the meaning of 'fasting' (*UN* 131), and 'soul's salvation' (*UN* 147). At three different places, he mentioned that he could not follow Gandhism (*UN* 136-37, 147). Because of the communication gap, he felt that "the Mahatma is blaming us" (*UN* 139). Bakha was not aware of the internal purification or eternal life but he wanted a solution for present suffering. The last words of Bakha highlight the pragmatic philosophy. Bakha did not feel that Gandhiji offered a solution for him to come out of the suffering.

Contrary to criticism, the novel highly regards the teaching of Gandhiji, such as "true religion of God-love which is the best swaraj" (*UN* 129); his stand against the British policy of divide and rule (*UN* 136), etc. The novel states that Gandhiji was against untouchability 'I regard untouchability,' [...], 'as the greatest blot on Hinduism' (*UN* 137). However, he emphasized the true spirit of religion and did not want to blame Hindu religion, for instance, he says: "untouchability was not sanctioned by religion" (*UN* 137), and "they should understand that the fault does not lie in the Hindu religion, but in those who profess it" (*UN* 139). Gandhiji wanted the inner transformation of the upper caste. Gandhiji is against neither the orthodox Hindus nor the untouchables. For him 'All life is one'[33] and that is the real ethos of Gandhiji as well as of India.

3.2.7. *Vernacular Influence*

Narrating in the language of the common folk and retelling the truth about the suffering of the marginalized is a peculiar quality of Anand. Table 3.1 shows some of the regional words, including prefixes and suffixes used in *Untouchable* which make the novel lifelike. These regional words attest that the novel says a typical Indian story and it is a true picture of life in the country.

Table 3.1: The Regional Words used in the Novel with its Approximate Number of Usages

Regional Words	No. of Times Used	Regional Words	No. of Times Used	Regional Words	No. of Times Used
Aarti	2	Girjaghar	6	Nirvana	1
Adalat	1	Gulabjamans	1	Panchayat	4
Angrez log	1	Harijans	3	Pandal	2
Annas	5	Hookah	6	Pandit	2
Ashram	4	Huzoor	6	Parshad	1
Avatar	1	Izzat	1	Patloon	1

Regional Words	No. of Times Used	Regional Words	No. of Times Used	Regional Words	No. of Times Used
Babu	36	Jalebis	9	Pipal	1
Baksheesh	1	Jaydeva	1	Rasgulas	1
Bakshish	1	Kalijugs	1	Sahib logs	1
Bhai	1	Kara	1	Sahib/s	102
Bhangi/s	11	Karma	1	Sahid	1
Biris	2	Kheer	1	Salaam	7
Buk	2	Khuti	2	Sarkar (Sarkari)	6
Burfi	1	Kothi	1	Sepoy	17
Burra	2	Lallas	1	Shakti	1
Chamar/s	5	Langar	1	Swadeshi	3
Chandal	1	Lat	3	Swadharma	1
Chapatti/s	4	Ludus	2	Swaraj	2
Chilm	2	Maharaj	7	Tehmets	1
Chingri	1	Maidan	1	Thak	6
Dawaikhana	1	Matchint	1	Tintint	1
dharmic	2	Maya	3	Topee/s	9
Dilli	1	Mehrbani	1	Vardi	1
Fashun	4	Mukadamas	1	Vay	3
Ferungi	2	Mukti	1	Vilayat	3
				Wallah/s	8

Table 3.2 depicts some of the abusive words and phrases used against the untouchable and some are literal translations from the regional language. For example, Anand used: "For them I am a sweeper, sweeper-untouchable! Untouchable! Untouchable! That's the word! Untouchable! I am an Untouchable!" (*UN* 43). The language expresses the piteous cry of the lower caste and reveals the Indian sensibility.

Not only vernacular words but also English words and phrases with regional influences are used. Some of them appear repeatedly in the novel, for instance 'gentreman' is used seven times in the novel. They arouse Indian style of conversation in the readers and they are not imitations but remodeling the colonizer's language as an Indian language like any other regional language. Some more examples are: 'oheBakhya' (*UN* 8); 'fashun' (*UN* 11) 'natus' (*UN* 11) 'VayBakhia, vayRakhia' (*UN* 23); 'brahminee' (*UN* 44); 'Sadhuhood' (*UN* 62); 'Vay Bakhya' (*UN* 65); 'jernel' (*UN* 84); 'uncreased' (*UN* 90) 'Turn udas' (*UN* 113); and, 'blackies' (*UN* 122). To intensify the feeling of Indian culture, short sentences, religious usages, and slogans are also used. The phrases in the Table 3.3 are samples for such usages.

Table 3.2: Some of the Abusive Expressions from the Novel

Abusive words & Phrases used against Untouchables	Abusive words & Phrases used against Untouchables
you little dog!	Low caste vermin
You swine, you dog	Cock-eyed son of a bow legged scorpion
Formless	Swine
Greasy	Brute
dense	Dirty dog/dog
discoloured	Son of a bitch
Untouchable	Off spring of a pig
patched	The son of a dog
Filth	Careless, irresponsible swine
misery	You eater of dung and drinker of urine
Ugliness	You illegally begotten
you eater of your masters	May the vessel of your life never float in the sea of existence.
barrier	You illegally begotten! Dog! Pig!
Odour, stink	You son of a pig! You son of a dog
the bottom dog	Get down, get away, you dog!
You bitch! You prostitute! wanton!	This dirty dog bumped right into me! So unmindfully do these sons of bitches walk in the streets
Confirmed rogue	'Dirty dog! Son of a bitch! The offspring of a pig!'
Dirt	You eater of dung and drinker of urine! You bitch of a sweeper women!

Moreover, Anand makes use of the regional linguistic usages to add an Indian flavour to the novel, for example, "it is lucky to see a dead body when one is out in the streets" (*UN* 33). The fragments of Punjabi and other languages, make *Untouchable* a regional novel and they intimately manifest its Indianness. The reader may assimilate and live in the culture as well as the social system of the space and time of the Punjabi town where the story takes place.

Table 3.3: Regional Usages from the Novel

Regional Usages	Regional Usages
'Kala admizamin par hagnewala' (*UN* 10)	Don't bukbuk, O bey brother-in-law (*UN* 28)
Salaam, babuji (*UN* 29)	tish-mish, tish-mish (*UN* 30)
Tan-nana-nan-tan (the bells of a bullock-cart) (*UN* 33)	'Ram, Ram, Sri, Sri, Hari, Narayan, Sri Krishna' (*UN* 49)
'Baba pesa de' (*UN* 125)	'Om, Om, Shanti Deva' (*UN* 49, 51)
'Arti, Arti' (*UN* 51)	'Sri Ram Chandarki Jai' (*UN* 52)
'Bham, bham, bholeNath' (*UN* 62)	Shioh! Shioh! Shi! (*UN* 79)
'Acha, jaojaldikaro, surkabacha, kutekabacha' (*UN* 114).	'Ham desi sahib' (*UN* 141)
'Mahatma Gandhi ki-ji' (*UN* 132)	'Ham desi sahib' (*UN* 141)
Nawan Jug (*UN* 144)	

3.2.8. *Hope for Meaningful Life*

The pre-independent period can be called a holistic transitional phase in Indian history. The Freedom movement was not limited to the political realm alone but it touched all areas of the life of Indians. At that time, certain values had been concretized, such as the spirit of a united India, democracy, secularism, and socialism. Like any other field, the writers also joined the process of purification of Indian ethos and this effort took new dimensions in their writings. Mulk Raj Anand was one among the leading figures in the transition period. Along with many others such as Jyotirmaya Ghosh, Sajjad Zaheer and so on, Anand was instrumental in the founding of The Progressive Writers' Association (PWA) in 1935. PWA made a radical shift in the concept of art and they touched the life of colourless people and ferocious realities of the society. "The PWA set out to use literature and the arts to reshape society as well as give expression to people's lives. Its aspiration was, to use the terminology of Antonio Gramsci, 'hegemonic' and not merely 'literary', and its history has to be assessed in these terms."[34] They synthesized art including literature with politics where the power concentrated. Thus, modern art and literature became a means in search of identity and meaning in the life of the subjugated.

Untouchable can be considered as the inauguration of PWA for social change and emancipation of the oppressed classes. The untouchables began to ask themselves 'why was all this?' (*UN* 42). By taking their side, the novel attempts to build-up an identity in the new emerging India and a search to rediscover the real ethos of India in which everyone is respected. Bakha is not a character who succumbs to the oppression but continuously searches for identity and growth. This underlying but unseen thread connects all events in the novel. The events of life taught him about his social isolation. "There was an inseparable barrier between himself and the crowd, the barrier of caste. He was part of a consciousness which he could share and yet not understand" (*UN* 128). His journey continues as an effort to become a better human being.

Lakha, father of Bakha, hankers for food at any cost. But the priority of Bakha is different. Personal dignity is more important to him than the fulfilment of physical needs. Later he thinks: 'I shouldn't have picked up that bread from the pavement,' he said, and he sighed. That seemed to relax him (*UN* 65). His father dreams about food. "As he said so, the Jemadar's mouth watered and his mind travelled to the great big piles of cooked food which he had received on the occasion of marriages in the alleys of the city" (*UN* 68). However, Bakha dreams about education and high social status. Bakha's urge to build up a new identity can be seen in his attitude towards education. Bakha visualizes the merit of education. "How nice it must be to be able to read and write! One could read the papers after having been to school" (*UN* 30). Education, as a privilege of the upper caste, remains an unattainable dream for the oppressed. Denial of education is the cruellest part of untouchability.

Bakha's afternoon dream can be interpreted as his ambition to reach the top of the society. "He saw himself getting onto the top of one of these loads and sitting there, a bundle by his side, an umbrella with a carved silver handle in his hand, a solar topee on his head and the tube of his father's hookah in his mouth" (*UN* 60). In his search for identity, Bakha follows a pragmatic philosophy to find immediate result. When an upper caste boy 'hesitated to give [him] a lesson a day he added: "I shall pay you for it" (*UN* 31). Indirectly Anand says that economic growth may facilitate in the attainment of higher aims and social status. By pragmatic thinking Bakha is "removed in time and space" (*UN* 124). In his approach to machinery also, one can observe practical and realistic thinking. Thus, Anand brings pragmatism to attain a better life.

Bakha's efforts do not bring the desired reward at the end and his desires remain unfulfilled, "And yet there was a futility written on his face" (*UN* 56). In spite of this, the novel is powerful enough to touch the heart of every Indian to think of a better way of life. E.M. Forster in his preface to the *Untouchable* writes: "Avoiding rhetoric and circumlocution, it has gone straight to the heart of its subject and purified it. None of us is pure—we shouldn't be alive if we were. But to the straightforward, all things can become pure, and it is to the directness of his attack that Mr. Anand's success is probably due."[35] The author made every effort to find space for the lower caste in the emerging new democratic nation. Even though Bakha did not attain higher levels, there is unbeatable hope for higher meaning in life. During the pre-independence period, Indian ethos was filled with optimism.

In brief *Untouchable* has a medicinal effect to purify the age-old accumulated adulterations. It can be called a purification novel since it tries to refine Indian ethos by highlighting the dark side and attempts to kindle hope in the downtrodden. The novel ends with the call for "the transformations of space and time" (*UN* 148). The Indian ethos is eternal and cannot be destroyed. However, it may progress with proper renewal. It has been trying to remove all the barriers that stand as a hindrance to the self-realization of each Indian. No one should be isolated from the society and it is one's birthright to have fundamental human rights for the fulfillment of one's potential. The novel ends with: "And he proceeded homewards" (*UN*

148). Home which stands for love, care, and relationship is imagery. Bakha steps towards the home with enthusiasm. It shows the continuous journey to rediscover and revitalize the pre-eminent Indian ethos.

3.3. Analysis of *Kanthapura* in the Light of the Pre-independent Ethos

Raja Rao (1908-2006) who was born at Hassan in Mysore, was an ardent seeker of Indianness throughout his life and his writings are cantered on Indian sensibility. "Raja Rao's fictional corpus can be viewed as a bold, cultural and spiritual statement made through a medium that was considered Western, breaking down all accepted conventions and reaffirming the unique identity of Indian culture and philosophy that can survive any threat of globalization."[36] The writings are aimed to reassert the glory of India to nurture Indian identity in the midst of colonization. For him, India is not merely a political or geographical entity but an abstract vision. In his article "The Meaning of India," he defines India as a *darshan* and those who possess that vision can be called the 'Indian'. His works reflect the Indian ethos through the use of myths, native languages, and narration style.

> Of all Indian writers of fiction in English, it is Raja Rao whose work is, both in content and form, perhaps the most 'Indian', though he has not hesitated to draw freely upon the West. He has brought to Indian fiction in English many elements in which it has previously been deficient: an epic breadth or vision, metaphysical rigour and depth of thought, a symbolic richness, a lyrical fervour and an essential 'Indianness' or style.[37]

His search of Indian sensibility is profoundly expressed in *Kanthapura*. The major elements of Indian ethos found in the novel are analyzed here and they all are incorporated to promote the spirit of nationalism. It vividly fictionalizes the independence struggle from 1919 to 1931 with social, political, religious and economic point of views.

3.3.1. *Feeling of Nationalism*

The pre-independent period is a landmark in the evolution of the Indian ethos. New values related to nationalism and democracy became a predominant part of Indianness. The Revolt of 1857, the Swadeshi Movement (1903-08), the Home Rule Movement of 1915, the Non-Cooperation Movement (1920-22) and various other movements contributed to the growth of the spirit of nationalism. It stimulated the sentimental attachment to Bharat Mata and hatred towards colonial rule. Nationalism, indeed, led to deep identification with one's culture and aroused passionate love towards the nation. Ernest Renan, the nineteenth-century French scholar, argued that it is the 'will' which makes a nation. A nation is a 'moral consciousness,' a community with a common memory—a people which has suffered together.[38] To resist the colonial rule and to build a united nation with one identity, the Indian nationalists intentionally tried to inculcate in every citizen, the Indian nationalism. Indian English novels also dealt with the same in the most forceful manner. At the peak of nationalism, in 1938 *Kanthapura* was published with the strongest political consciousness of 'Indianness' to build a unified nation on the foundation of Indian ethos.

The novel is a fusion of traditional folk style and modern nationalism: it has traditional rhythms, beliefs, rituals, characters, caste system, spiritual system, etc., and modern colonial rule, feudal system, social revolution, political resistance, religious-interpretation of religion in relation with nationalism, etc. *Kanthapura* is a bastard for conservatives but a legend for progressives. It remained in the dark for a long time which is clear from the fact that the author had to approach sixteen publishers to publish it. For progressives, he made a hybrid style by expressing Indian sensibility through a foreign medium. He himself writes in the foreword: "One has to convey in a language that is not one's own the spirit that is one's own" (*KA* V). It narrates the ethos of India with an eagle eye, which views the pre-independence period from a puranic perspective and unfolds the incidents in the picturesque village which attracts the readers. He has made use of myths, sensibility of Indian villages, native idioms, native language styles, etc.

The novel is one of the best of its kind to study the dynamic nature of ethos of India from its pre-historic period incorporating political, social, and cultural ethos of the pre-independent period with the ancient history of India.

> You [Brahma] gave her the riches of gold and of diamonds, and you gave her kings such as the world has never seen! Asoka, who loved his enemies and killed no animal; Chandragupta, who had the nine jewels of Wisdom at his court; and Dharmaraya and Vikramaditya and Akbar, and many a noble king. And you gave her, too, sages radiating wisdom to the eight cardinal points of the earth, Krishna and Buddha, Sankara and Ramanuja. But, O Brahma! you who sent us the Prince propagators of the Holy Law and Sages that smote the darkness of Ignorance, you have forgotten us so long that men have come from across.... (*KA* 15)

The novel depicts the glorious past of India to instigate nationalism. In short, Rao transferred the historical mass movement of the independent struggle to a myth, so that it would never die away and the spirit of nationalism echoes through all coming generations.

Kanthapura is an attempt to nurture love and pride in the Indian ethos which is the foundation of Indian nationalism. Nationalism is not an accidental creation but should be cultivated with a well-planned agenda. The novel enhanced the cultural, mental and physical resistance against colonialism. "The entire novel speaks volumes for how a creative writer assimilates and transcends a contemporary political reality into the cultural consciousness of a tradition, race and people."[39] Repeatedly, the novel uses patriotic slogans and expressions to internalize the love towards the nation (Table 3.4). The novel acts as a powerful medium to inculcate nationalism in people. Because of the deep-rooted nationalism the entire people of the village stand for the national cause.

More than the feeling of hatred *Kanthapura* attempts to awaken the self-consciousness of Indians. Indian ethos upholds the wider concept of nationalism which is not restricted to the nation with political boundaries and depicting others as enemies.

For Tagore "Man will have to exert all his power of love and clarity of vision to make another great moral adjustment which will comprehend the whole world of men and not merely the fractional groups of nationality. [...] man shall discover his soul in the spiritual unity of all human beings."[40] According to the Indian ethos, not only this nation but all nations are sacred because the Mother Goddess dwells on the whole earth. Hence, a nation is a spiritual unit and it extends into the whole world.

Table 3.4: The Nationalistic Expressions along with its Number of Recurrent Use

Patriotic Usages	No. of Times Used	Patriotic Usages	No. of Times Used
Zindabad	18	Mataram Vande	4
Vande Mataram	21	Jai Mahatma	4
Inqualab	16	Mahatma Gandhi Ki Jai/Ji	50
		Satyanarayan Maharaj Ki Jai	8

A comprehensively and spiritually united world view is adopted in the novel. The novel describes the nation as a temple. "You know, brothers and sisters, we are here in a temple, and the temple is the temple of the one, and we are one with everything that is in the One..." (*KA* 169). For Rao, the nation is not only interpreted politically, but transcendentally too. Every citizen of the nation is important for its unity as the pillars of the temple help it to stand. "A cock does not make a morning, nor a single man a revolution, but we'll build a thousand-pillared temple, [...] and each one of you be the pillars in it, and when the temple is built, stone by stone, and man by man, [...] India then will live in a temple of our making" (*KA* 169). The Mother land is holy, like a temple. A temple is the stronghold of culture and unity. It becomes a social, religious and political meeting place. For example, Moorthy fasts and people sing *Bhajans* in the temple. Thus, Rao links religious ethos and national ethos with a wider perspective for the ultimate self-actualization of each person. Only through the cooperation of the nation and the religion, the material and non-material goals of human beings can be attained.

3.3.2. *Inclusive Relationship*

Kanthapura that represents the macro Indian society with its positive and negative ethos, is a fictionalized village, which can be identified as a remote village of Hassan, near Mysore, Karnataka. Hence, the novel can be called a *sthalapurana*. One of the greatest legacies of Indian culture is the Puranas, which is an integral element of literature, and Raja Rao was the pioneer to introduce it into the Indian English novel. They have a personal or social instructive purpose with short-term or long-term goals and are narrated with simple and attractive style. "Without this story-telling mode, Kanthapura would have lost, perhaps, much of its charm. 'Sthalapurana' is a traditional way of story-telling in rural India."[41] In *Sthalapurana* the mutual relationship between people and their attachment to nature including animals are very cordial. The use of 'our village' (*KA* 1) as the first phase of the novel shows the passion to the place. The all-inclusive relationship is one of the cardinal elements of Indian ethos. The beauty of relations, which is depicted in the novel, makes it more emotional and heart-touching.

The lives of Indians are very much attached to the land where they live and it is a part and parcel of their home. Indian mythology calls earth Prithvi Devi/Prithvi Mata, "the earth is your mother" (*KA* 223). The stories, beliefs, sayings, fables, and myths are formed in relation to their geographical nature. Kanthapurians' lives are wedded to nature. Rao creates a natural setting in the very beginning of the novel as a background to narrate the ethos of India which has a close relationship with nature. The second sentence goes like this: "High on the Ghats is it, high up the steep mountains that face the cool Arabian seas, up the Malabar coast is it, up Mangalore and Puttur and many a centre of cardamom and coffee, rice and sugarcane" (*KA* 1). The novel talks about the legendary history that includes beliefs, gods, festivals, castes, social customs, festivals, religious ceremonies, administrative systems, etc. of the village. C.D. Narasimhaiah writes, Kanthapura is 'a piece of life' not merely 'a picture of life', and it is probably the only novel of its kind in English, depicting with such authenticity, life in a village, in a land of villages.[42]

The rituals and celebrations are very much linked with nature. "[...] a mango-leaf garland of welcome hangs at each door and the courtyards are swept and washed and decorated" (*KA* 164). Kanthapurians draw a lot of images from nature in their conversation. It shows that life is completely blended with nature. Hills, water and river are sacred and have socio-religious importance; so there are a lot of mythical legends related to them. A river is necessary in the life cycle of a person. Many rituals are related to nature. After cremation, the ash of the body is scattered in the water of Himavathy and it helps the dead person to complete the samskara. Himavathy, the ever flowing divine spirit, is compared with the rivers in puranas, for example, Narmada in Matsya Purana. The animals are also respected in Indian culture. Moorthy is considered as holy bull, cow, and elephant.

The Indian society especially in the villages is built on relationships. For them, the home is not limited to one's property alone but the whole village territory is an extended part of their home. Therefore, the people of the village know each other personally as it is in the novel. Kanthapurians are identified with pretty sobriquets such as Waterfall Venkamma, Temple Rangappa, Front-house Akkamma, Postmaster Suryanarayana, Nose-scratching Nanjamma, Corner-House Moorthy, Pock-marked Sidda, and Street-corner Beadle Timmayya. Achakka, the old woman, narrates the personal and social life of Kanthapurians in a messianic manner and it reflects her attachment to the village. The people of the village are very affectionate to each other. More than individuality Indian ethos gives importance to collective identity and collective realization. The festivals, congregational devotions, mass rally, etc., reveals this. The broad-mindedness and inclusiveness are the very nature of the Indian community.

3.3.3. *Transcendental View of Life*

Indian ethos views human life in its 'oneness' instead of analyzing it as separate watertight compartments. The holistic outlook is necessary for the realization of the self as well as for the progression of the society. Rao portrays life in the village in its wholeness. Different levels such as ecological, physical, spiritual, political, and social are woven into one. In Indian ethos, every action of a person has a transcendental level. Therefore, even the struggle for national independence was not only political and social but spiritual too.

Rao narrates the story in the background of religion and glorifies the great religious ethos of India. It helps him to build-up nationalism in people who identify themselves with religion. The patriotic songs and religious *bhajans*; political slogans and pious prayers go hand in hand. Along with the slogan, '*Mahatma Gandhi ki jai!*' they also cried out 'Narayan! Narayan!' (*KA* 180-81) because both would contribute to the final destiny. The election of the members for the Congress committee happened only after *bhajan* and God's procession. The satyagraha of Murthy was like a *pooja* or sacrifice to god. Every act is spiritualized so that the religious life does not become passive and ritualistic but an active effort to transform in tune with the cosmic rhythm. *Kanthapura* is a story of *parinama* (परिणाम, transformation) from material to spiritual. The novel begins with the narration of the physical nature of Kanthapura, the village. But it ends with the spiritual ritual to attain eternity. Even though there was no material profit, the Kanthapurians participation in the freedom movement was out of desireless effort (निश्कामकार्म, *niskama karma*), which would help them attain self-realization and मोक्ष (*moksha*, liberation).

> At the end of the novel material gains for Kanthapurians are nil. But spiritually they are transformed totally and have become a bold, politically conscious, spiritually strengthened, and freedom-loving people. [...] for the spiritual gains narrated by her [Achakka] would be invisible in the eyes of a western historian or politician. [...] It is the ability to fictionalise this essential Indian cultural identity, the religiosity and spirituality that are part of the Indian ethos, that make Rao's writings different.[43]

Through political freedom, Raja Rao aims at the ultimate and eternal liberation. Indian ethos ultimately aims at *moksha*, the ultimate liberation of the *atman*. The personal and social lives are expressions of one's internal *atman* to attain *Paramatma*. Haydn describes Rao as the most 'ideological' of all the twentieth century Indian novelists and Kanthapura shows his intense preoccupation with Indian religiousness—the permeation of religion through society at all levels.[44] The author goes to such a high level that he presents India as the daughter of Brahma. "Far down on the Earth you chose as your chief daughter Bharatha, the goddess of wisdom and well-being" (*KA* 15). Hence for the author, to love India is parallel to the love of God and to undertake the pain for 'India' is a sacrifice to God. Brahma showered blessings in abundance on India and in her lamentation under the colonial powers, God would save her by sending a savoir. "My beloved daughter from her enforced slavery" (*KA* 16). The political and social life became a pilgrimage for self-realization. In Indian culture pilgrimage means a spiritual search. Rao gives much importance to pilgrimage and renunciation. Pilgrims (यात्रिकी: *yatriki*. Pilgrim) are regarded with great respect and others fulfill their needs. Spiritual life is a continuous conversion. In Indian tradition, the seeker of truth undergoes a constant rebirth into new values and God experience. Moorthy the protagonist undergoes continuous transformation each moment. At the moment of blissful union with the absolute, Moorthy recites Sankaracharaya's chant: "Sivoham, Sivoham. I am Siva. I am Siva. Siva am I" (*KA* 89). It is the ultimate aim of all human beings.

3.3.4. *The Gandhi Purana*

Kanthapura commences with *Sthalapurana*, and proceeds to narrate Gandhi purana. In the pre-independent struggle Gandhiji, who is considered as the icon of Indian ethos, was the 'soul force' who unified the diversified people of India to rise against the colonial powers in one voice. For Rao, Gandhiji was not just a human leader but an *avatar*, the incarnation of God who would liberate India from all evil and restore good. The incarnation of Gandhiji is related to the *Trimurti*. Thus,

Gandhiji became the continuation of the mythic tradition of India. The patriotic fire set by Gandhiji spread like anything. The brutality and inhuman activities of white men added fuel to the fire. Many became fervent supporters of Gandhiji and embraced nationalism enthusiastically.

Gandhi made the freedom struggle the fight of the masses: rich and the poor, literate and illiterate, urban and rural people. People moved with him. Raja Rao never brings Gandhiji directly to Kanthapura but his power wafts over the entire novel. He touches Moorthy not by his words but by the indefinable power formed out of his renunciation of the material world. "Moorthy looked from the audience to the Mahatma and from the Mahatma to the audience, and he said to himself, There is in it something of the silent communion of the ancient books..." (*KA* 47). A revamp occurs in Moorthy. By seeing his life Kanthapurians, the static and illiterate society is moved towards the path of Gandhiji. Following which the equation of the social and political structure of the village begins to change and they stand for attaining their rights by soul-force.

They followed the principles of Gandhiji such as *ahimsa*, *sathyagraha*, *swaraj*, etc. "And remember always, the path we follow is the path of the Spirit, and with truth and non-violence and love shall we add to the harmony of the world. For, brothers, we are not soldiers at arms, say I; we seek to be soldier saints" (*KA* 180). In positive terms, *ahimsa* means universal love, pure love, and practice of compassion. *Ahimsa*, one of the major pillars of Indian ethos, is upheld in *Kanthapura* even at the cost of life. 'Truth' is eternally enduring; so the whole life of Gandhiji is a search for truth. "Truth must you tell, he says, for Truth is God, and verily, it is the only God I know" (*KA* 17).

Gandhi played a crucial role in constructing a national identity. It happened in two ways. First, he was able to unify the diverse people of India and rejuvenate the Indian spirit in them. Secondly, through symbols like *charka*, *khaddar*, etc., and various other programs like *swadeshi* movement, the *Dandi March*, etc., he opposed westernization. Indians learned to be proud of their Indianness and rejected mimicking the West with Gandhiji. *Kanthapura* depicts this process. It narrates a group of people who willingly seek martyrdom for India, out of their nationalism. They are nurtured in Indianness by following the foot steps of Gandhiji. Gandhism is the thread that weaves the various personalities and incidents and sets the tone of the novel.

> The apotheosis of Gandhi into an avatar further turns contemporary politics into a religious saga in an attempt to build a national-popular movement in a society acutely divided by language, caste, and class. To present a unitary identity of the country was an important task in the face of colonial domination. Consequently, Kanthapura is securely mapped within an identity encapsulating the nation.[45]

Rao presents Gandhiji as a real Guru who does not compel the *shishya* to have blind belief in his philosophy but guides the *shishya* to truth and gives space for his/her personal experiments in the search for truth. At the end of the novel, the protagonist who is a faithful follower of Gandhiji and leads many to him, moves to Nehruism. "Jawaharlal will change it. You know Jawaharlal is like a Bharatha to the Mahatma, [...]. And he calls himself an 'equal-distributionist,' and I am with him and his men" (*KA* 258). However the Kanthapurians steadfastly follow Gandhiji. Rao deploys this shift in two ways: on the one hand, to glorify Gandhiji as a real Guru who helps everyone to investigate truth in one's own way. Every disciple of Gandhiji is free to take up a responsible search for truth and meaning. On the other hand, the poor and illiterate people trust Gandhiji and follow him even without a mediator. It shows that they wholeheartedly embraced Gandhism even when the initiator moved away from it. In short, Gandhiji becomes the symbol of the ethos of India and the consciousness of India. Gandhiji blends politics and spirituality, which are the real ethos of India. He uses the soul force, the mastery of oneself, for freedom.

3.3.5. *Indianized Style*

Not only the plot and story but the settings and style of *Kanthapura* are also typically Indian. Through the structure, characters, narration, tone, speech pattern, and usages, Rao expresses the Indian sensibility in the novel. Indian ethos incorporates that of the west linguistic idiosyncratice blending of English with Kannada. Kannadized English gives the regional slang. For instance, the word 'Sankar' is changed to 'Sankaru' by the influence of Kannada. The Indian words add Indian colour to the novel and in the Table 3.5 some of the words are listed.

Table 3.5: Indian Words Used in the Novel

Indian Words	No. of Times Used	Indian Words	No. of Times Used
Dhoti	13	Sari	47
Chutney	1	Khadi	17
Khir	1	Sankara	12
Jayanthi	5	Dasar	3
Patwari	10	Patel	13
Sankaru	10	Maharaja	16

Idioms and expressions from Kannada are also used freely with literal translation, like 'You are a traitor to your salt-givers' (*KA* 20); 'the Non't-touch-the-Government Campaign' (*KA* 86, 96, 177, 178); 'nobody will believe such a crow and sparrow story' (*KA* 22), 'Fig-tree-House people' (*KA* 6); 'Fig-Tree-House Ramu' (*KA* 36); 'Nine-beamed house of Patel Range Gowda' (*KA* 8); 'Seventh-month ceremony' (*KA* 25); 'if you are sons of your father' (*KA* 107); 'I touch your feet' (*KA* 124); 'I lick your feet' (*KA* 35, 81); 'stomach burn' (*KA* 3); etc.

The influence of Indian culture is very evident in similes like, 'as honest as an elephant' (*KA* 12-13), and 'as good as kitchen ashes' (*KA* 40). The ill-use is also expressed in Indian style, like 'You son of my woman' (*KA* 84, 118, 158); 'stitch up your mouth' (*KA* 84, 136); 'traitor to your salt-giver' (*KA* 20); 'sons of concubine' (*KA* 19, 84, 118); 'son of a widow' (*KA* 84); and 'I'll sleep with your wife' (*KA* 84). The colloquial nicknames are interesting, for example, Waterfall Venkamma. The regional resources are used without hesitation to express Indian ethos. To inculcate the Indianness in English, the author changes English into an Indian language just like any other regional language.

Rao tries to imitate even the speech pattern of Indians. In the preface of *Kanthapura* he says:

> We, in India, think quickly, we talk quickly, and when we move we move quickly. [...]. The *Mahabharatha* has 214,778 verses and the *Ramayana* 48,000. Puranas there are endless and innumerable. We have neither punctuation nor the treacherous 'ats' and 'ons' to bother us we tell one interminable tale. Episode follows episode, and when our thoughts stop our breath stops, and we move on to another thought. This was and still is the ordinary style of our story-telling. I have tried to follow it myself in this story. (*KA* vi)

Long sentences are framed with many phrases to capture the way of talking and rhythm of speech of the natives. In joint families, the grey haired women gather for a long-time for their intimate and personal conversations. This tempo of conversation is copied in the novel through repetition of phrases, clauses, changing the normal word-order, etc. Example: 'Is that why, Rangamma,' interrupts Bhatta angrily, Is that why the Mahatma has adopted a pariah girl as a daughter? He is a Vaisya and he may do what he likes.... But, Rama-Rama, really if we have to hang the sacred thread over the shoulders of every pariah... it's impossible, impossible..." (*KA* 38). *Kanthapura* is a fusion novel. Rao literally and culturally liberates India before political independence. "His style has the flavor of Kannada speech, and its rhythms are almost incantatory, the rhythms of Sanskrit, a language which is the source of Indian languages. This evolution of a suitable style for the expression of Indian sensibility is Rao's most significant contribution to the Indo-Anglian fiction."[46] He breaks all the literary conventions of the colonizers to a great extend. Such an act in politics may be judged as exceptional by the colonizer.

Apart from the linguistic means, the author adapts the Indian sensibility by taking resource from the oral tradition of the nation. The knowledge and wisdom are handed over to next generation by grandparents, gurus, elders and so on in the oral form. Oral tradition is a treasure house of knowledge in India. In the novel, Rao adapted the style of storytelling in which an Indian grandmother shares her experiences to the next generation. Oral tradition is reflected in the long rambling dialogues and narrations. In it, the pace of speech is rapid, it provides a detailed poetic picture of nature, and has a simple style. To *Kanthapura*, it is very evident as seen in the description of Kartik (*KA* 115).

Raja Rao follows the Harikatha style of storytelling and the word Harikatha is used 16 times in the novel. Harikatha, which means stories of the Lord composite of different art forms such as storytelling, folk songs, drama, dance, and poetry, is one of the great genres in Indian literature. It is used to convey religious and moral messages in relation with a saint or a great hero from epics. It is a great source for entertainment and is also instrumental in transmitting values, beliefs, ethics, and culture. In the novel, the story is narrated very emotionally. Through Harikatha the freedom struggle is internalized in the minds of generations. There is no gap between the national identity and religious identity. Both are complementary and become the part of the history. *Kanthapura* has the structure of Indian folk epics, for example, Kenchamma is narrated in the style of Vishnupurana (*KA* 2). The use of folk songs is another strong means to express Indian sensibility. Recitation of poetry during festivals, and community work is very common in the villages of India.

Raja Rao links the present history of India with that of the past to establish the ethos of present India as a continuation of ancient history. Such methodology can be called mythologizing historical events. The antique and vast history of India is embalmed as living through various myths. Indians have a great tradition of mythologizing the glorious past and handing it over to the next generation. They may have re-told them and thus the continuity of the community can be attained. Myths are fundamental to each society since they express worldviews, values, morals, lifestyle, etc. They explain how ancestors resolved their problems in life and idealized heroes were imitated by the next generation. It also helps to form collective unconscious mind and archetypes of the generations.

The novel tries to mythologize the freedom movement by likening it to the most celebrated myths. As M.K. Naik observes, Rao emerges as perhaps the finest painter of the Indian ethos and of East-West confrontation, the greatest symbolist and mythmaker and the only truly philosophical novelist in English that India has so far produced (1982: 214).[47] He envisages the freedom movement as the re-enactment of the *Ramayana*, the great epic of India. The epic is linked with the novel by saying 'Valmiki entered' (*KA* 15). Red man is portrayed as Ravana, who was the Rakshasa king of Lanka who kidnapped Sita the wife of Rama. As the word 'ravana' means one who anguishes the world or one who makes others scream out of fear or torment, the classical character in *Ramayana* is the embodiment of evil actions. He mythicises the political leaders. Gandhiji is the incarnation of Rama, the avatar of Vishnu, and Nehru as Bharata, the brother of Rama. The independent Indian is depicted as Sita, the avatar of Lakshmi.

The *ahimsa* and fasting of Gandhiji are compared to Parvati's *tapas* (तपस, asceticism) which is portrayed as the greatest abstinence than all others, to reunite with Shiva. Gandhiji's non-violence, the means to attain freedom, is glorified and spiritualized. His visit to Britain to take part in the Round Table Conference is compared to Ram's visit to Lanka. "He will bring us Swaraj, the Mahatma. And we shall all be happy. And Rama will come back from exile, and Sita will be with him, for Ravana will be slain and Sita freed, and he will come back with Sita on his right in a chariot of the air, and brother Bharatha will go to meet them with the worshipped sandal of the Master on his head" (*KA* 258).

In addition to the comparison to Rama, Gandhiji is also considered as Lord Krishna and his birth is legendary as the birth of Krishna. The narrator praises the birth of Gandhiji: "As soon as he came forth, the four wide walls began to shine like the Kingdom of the Sun, and hardly was he in the cradle than he began to lisp the language of wisdom" (*KA* 16). As Krishna fought against Kali and slew its head, Gandhiji fights against the foreign rule. Through the use of *harikatha* stories, and folk songs, Rao gives eternal life to the freedom struggle because generations have handed over these stories. Indians have painted Gandhiji as an archetype of God, Moorthy as the *avathar* and the white men as *asuras*. The firm faith in the timely intervention of the divine power in the life of each person and of society gives deep belief in moral and religious views. It gives assurance and stability to moral life. Rao mythologizes Gandhiji as the eternal light that illumines the Indian ethos.

3.3.6. *Subaltern: History of Independence*

Kanthapura is a re-reading of pre-independence history from a subaltern point of view. It is the vivid and electrifying narration of self-sacrificing nameless heroes of Indian independence struggle. "It [Kanthapura] can be read as a creative documentation of the other histories, or to put it in a more politically correct expression it is a literary recording of alternative sources to history; history of the subaltern classes."[48] *Kanthapura* is a historical book of freedom fighters, of women and untouchables and their struggles in the society. "Kanthapura is a brilliant attempt to prove the depths to which the nationalistic urge penetrated, showing how even in a remote village, the new upsurge fused completely with traditional religious faith, thus rediscovering the Indian soul."[49] Even though they lost physically, spiritually they gained: the eternal victory.

Kanthapura is an attempt to empower women. In the early Indian ethos, male and female aspects are two sides of one coin and it is reflected in all the aspects of life. For instance, the supreme divine concept envisages God or Devan which is the male part and Goddess or Devi is the female side. Without Devi, the Great Mother, the male aspect remains powerless. Later in the Medieval Period the status of women declined and could be called the dark age of women. *Sati*, *jauhar*, child marriage, *purdah* system, *devadasis*, restriction in girl education, and prohibition of widow's remarriage were introduced during the period. During the renaissance of pre-independent period, the pathetic condition of women was questioned. The feminine role performed in Indian nationalism was great and it is excellently portrayed in the novel. It is a breakthrough in giving voice to women's feelings and a recognition for their contribution to the nation.

Kanthapura is a subaltern history of Indian independence where women take part actively and selflessly. They draw power from Kenchamma, who is the goddess of folklore with tremendous power. She protects people from sickness, natural calamities, etc., and is involved even in the freedom movement. Through this fictional narration, the author attempts to restore the personal and social authority of women. At the same time, he also affirms that the Indian concept of motherhood is noble, self-sacrificing and heroic. Kenchamma, the goddess and central figure of the novel, is the protector, spiritual source and the mother for the villagers.

In the agrarian society, Kenchamma is presented as the primary breadwinner of the village through the involvement in ploughing, harvesting, etc. The narrator challenges the supremacy of men as the breadwinner and claim for equal rights. Through the identification of the women with Kenchamma, the novel accepts the dignity of women and their ability to perform. The novel criticizes the Indian concept that a woman ought to be meek, docile, humble, soft, quiet, lamblike and should remain within the four walls of the kitchen. Raja Rao uses the linguistic phrases like, 'next-house woman's kitchen' (*KA* 23) to show the enslavement of women in the house and protest against such exploitation of the women.

The patriarchal society regards Sita, the wife of Rama as the model for the women but in the novel, it is interesting that it not the epic Sita but Rani Lakshmi Bai of Jhansi who was killed in 1857 who is portrayed as the personification of an ideal Indian woman. "Rangamma calls the children and says, 'You will be Rani Lakshmi Bai once, and you will then put on a turban, and he will put on a kumkum mark on his face and he will be Rani Lakshmi Bai,' and the children were so happy at this that they went away puffy-cheeked and satisfied" (*KA* 152). Kamaladevi, Sarojini Naidu and Annie Besant and all other heroic daughters of India became the role models (*KA* 150). The oppressed 'Sita' of the patriarchal society is removed and the self-image of the woman is reestablished. In India, there have been incidents that husbands have torched their wives as punishment and women have lacked the freedom of movement and expression. "Radhamma's husband beat her on that day he returned from village inspection, though she was seven months pregnant" (*KA* 51). The incident shows the animistic attitude of the patriarchal society. The novel is a feminist history of Indian independence and the march can be seen as the march to a new life.

The living conditions of widows were intolerable. The Indian society denied them an identity. However Rao upholds their status. The three prominent females in the novel are Brahmin widows: Achakk, the narrator, Rangamma, the heroine and Ratna, the boyish. The novel is a promulgation of their rights. For the widows Rani Lakshmi Bai, who was a widow, became the role model. "King said, [...] the worthiest of them was Rani Lakshmi Bai of Jhansi. Why, she rode the horse like a Rajput, and held her army against the British, [...] fighting for her enslaved Mother" (*KA* 149). Achakka, who belongs to Veda Sastra Pravina Krishan Sastri family, is not a passive narrator but an active participant. It shows the prominent place given to women in the novel. Kanthapura itself is born out of the suffering of a widow. "Within her four-walled existence, she was allowed to occupy herself with the children of the family and her only form of engagement with them was an oral tradition of storytelling that encompasses mythological and legendary stories, folk tales and fairy tales. ...Raja Rao portrays the narrator Achakka with this concept of evoking the confined duties thwarted upon by the patriarchal orthodoxy."[50] Kanthapura is a true attempt to regain the glorious status of the woman through the voice of grandma.

Rangamma, the feminist leader, resembles the historical character Pandita Ramabai (1858-1922) who founded the Arya Mahila Samaj in 1882. Rangamma organized *Sevika Sangha* to empower women. "She says, Let us not call ourselves Volunteers-let us call ourselves Sevika Sangha,' and we were called Sevis..." (*KA* 150). She became the spokeswoman and reformer of women. Through Ratna, who became a widow at the age of ten and who saw her proposed husband only once, Rao shows how the modern Indian woman should be. She refused to cut her hair, wear black dress, etc., and questioned the rituals of the society.

As a subaltern novel, Kanthapura also gives voice to the underdogs and upholds equality, one of the major values of democracy. "...the novel is an attempt to deconstruct the hierarchical mind set of the people which underestimates human value in terms of tradition and culture. The violation that happens in the name of tradition and culture still continues to be a major threat for the human existence in India."[51] Indian nationalism redefined the ethos of the social system, which was earlier defined in terms of (वर्णक्रम) varnakrama (order of castes/Varnasram). *Kanthapura* aims at social transformation. The author makes use of the binaries of epic and folklore in narration to highlight the oppressed. In the epics, the gods and goddesses such as Brahma, Siva, Hari, Krishna, Rama, Valmiki, Sita, Parvathi, Sakunthala, Yasoda, and so on are from upper caste whereas in folklore gods and goddesses are from lower caste. Kenchamma, the goddess of the folklore is the central figure of the novel. Like folklore and oral discourse which are the treasure house of the real ethos of the land are part of Indian culture.

At the outset, the narrator describes the existing condition of the Indian society based on caste system. The life quality of the untouchable is pathetic. The individual identity of the untouchable is denied in the Kanthapura except Rachanna and his wife Rachi. However, during the pre-independence period, the Indian society was at the dawn of removing caste system. Moorthy, out of Gandhian influence, broke the unjust social system and proclaimed the human love. Following the Gandhian way of life, people rose above the caste system and they could indeed make a genuine success story. The force of Gandhism mobilized the people from all the cross sections of society and they marched towards independence. More than sacrificing their lives, they purified themselves of impurities of the mind.

Even, the so-called Gandhian progressive thinkers sometimes feel the difficulty of moving away from the orthodox system.

The resistance from the existing ethos is powerfully narrated in the novel. “Rangamma says only, ‘I shall at least give you a little Ganges water, and you can take a spoonful of it each time you’ve touched them, can’t you?’ [...] After all a brahmin is a brahmin, sister!” (*KA* 104-05). The novel does not reveal a complete eradication of caste system but a radical shift in the existing outlook which Kanthapurians achieved.

In a nutshell, *Kanthapura* is a museum of Indian ethos. It envisages a holistic liberation, including both the foreign colonizer and the native oppressor. For that, the novel brings a subaltern history of pre-independence. Thus, the novel encourages nationalism and empowers the doubly oppressed group such as the woman, and the untouchable. To be liberated culturally and mentally from the foreign superiority, the author attempts to bring out Indianness to the whole world through English, the language of the colonizer. He uses English of India, not English of the oppressor and it succeeds in developing a new way of articulation in English to treat thought, form and expression with an Indian sensibility to proclaim the Indian ethos. The narrator takes the reader from the present to the past for constructing a future with the sublime ethos of India, which is entrenched in the glorious traditions. The novel ends with the self-actualization, the real and everlasting victory of the Kanthapurians. The physical victory is not a criterion for satisfaction but an opportunity to live for a noble cause. Be a martyr rather than a colonizer.

Notes

1. “Is there something called Indianness?” Web page 30th January 2011, Accessed: 4th September 2011. <http://www.ghadar.in/gjh_html/?q=content/there-something-called-indianness>
2. “What’s in a name; ‘India’ and the ‘Indian’ Identity” Accessed: 3th September 2013. <http://vepa.us/dir8/identity.htm>
3. Rammohun Roy, “The need of modern education.” Ramachandra Guha (ed.) *Makers of Modern India*. (New Delhi: Penguin Books, 2010), p. 45.

4. Rafiq Dossani, *India Arriving: How this Economic Powerhouse is Redefining Global Business* (New Delhi: Amacom, 2008), p. 9.
5. P.C. Joshi, "Culture and Cultural Planning in India." *Economic and Political Weekly* 18.50 (1983), p. 2128 <http://www.jstor.org/stable/4372774>
6. Bhikhu Parekh, *Colonialism, Tradition and Reform: An Analysis of Gandhi's Political Discourse* (New Delhi: Sage Publications India Pvt Ltd., 1989), pp. 63-64.
7. Rabindranath Tagore, "Nationalism." Fred Dallmayer and G.N. Deny (ed.). *Between Tradition and Modernity: India's Search for Identity* (New Delhi: Sage Publications 1998), p. 77.
8. K.K. Datta, "Our Cultural Renaissance and Nationalism." Indira Gandhi Abinandan Samiti, *The Spirit of India*. Vol: II (New York: Asia Publishing House, 1976), 295-300, p. 295.
9. *Ibid.*
10. *Ibid.*
11. Javeed Alam, *India: Living with Modernity* (Delhi: Oxford University Press, 1999), p. 88.
12. Jawaharlal Nehru, "Letter to Indira Gandhi, dated 4th December, 1937." Sonia Gandhi (ed.). *Two Alone, Two Together: Letters between Indira Gandhi and Jawaharlal Nehru* (1922-1964) (New Delhi: Penguin Books, 2005), p. 185.
13. H.S. Komalesha, "History, Colony, Nation and Nationalism: Revisiting Raja Rao and His Kanthapura," Sarangi Jaydeep (ed.) *Raja Rao: The Master and His Moves* (New Delhi: Authors Press, 2007), p. 55.
14. J.H. Broomlfield, "The Regional Elites: A Theory of Modern Indian History." Thomas R. Metcalf (ed.) *Modern India: An Interpretive Anthology* (America: The MacMillan Company, 1971), p. 60.
15. Annemaire Schimmel, *Gabriel's Wing: A Study into the Religious Ideas of Sir Muhammad Iqba* (Netherlands: E.J. Brills, 1963), p. 31.
16. Sucheta Mahajan, *Independence and Partition: The Erosion of Colonial Power in India* (New Delhi: Sage Publications, 2000), pp. 333-38.
17. *The Collected Works of Mahatma Gandhi*, Vol. LXXXVII (New Delhi: The Publications Divisions: Ministry of Information and Broadcasting Government of India, 1983), p. 187.

18. Rabindranath Tagore, "Nationalism in India" (1917). Nalini Bhushan and Jay L. Garfield (eds.) *Indian Philosophy in English: From Renaissance to Independence* (Oxford: Oxford University Press, 2011), p. 30.

19. Louis Dumont, *Homo Hierarchicus: The Caste System and its Implications*. Mark Sainsbury (Trans.) (Great Britain: Vikas Publications, 1966), p. 43.

20. S. Sen and J.K. Chopra, *Untouchable: Mulk Raj Anand* (New Delhi: Unique Publishers, 2007), pp. 56-57.

21. P. Rajendra Karmarkar, "Reality and Realism: An Unorthodox Reading of Anand's *Untouchable*." *Journal of South Asian Literature*. 31.1 & 2 (1996), p. 116.

22. Suijit S. Dulai, "Practice before Ideology: Mulk Raj Anand's *Untouchable*." *Journal of South Asian Literature*, 27.2 (1992), pp. 187-207, p. 190. Accessed: 1st May 2013 <http://www.jstor.org/stable/40874125>.

23. Pali Text Society Translation. Series No. 45. *The Group of Discourses (Sutta-Nipata)* 2nd ed. Chapter 1:7 verse 136 (Great Britain: The Pali Text Society, 2006), pp. 16-17.

24. P. Rajendra Karmarkar, "Reality and Realism: An Unorthodox Reading of Anand's *Untouchable*." *Journal of South Asian Literature* 31.1 & 2 (1996) p. 114.

25. Susan Bayly, *Caste, Society and Politics in India from the Eighteenth Century to the Modern Age*. Vol. IV.3 (Cambridge: Cambridge University Press, 1999), p. 25.

26. Dirks Nicholas B., *Castes of Mind: Colonialism and the Making of Modern India* (New Delhi: Permanent Black, 2002), p. 13.

27. Lajpat Rai, "Reform or Revival (1904)" Nalini Bhushan and Jay L. Garfield (ed.) *Indian Philosophy in English: From Renaissance to Independence* (Oxford: Oxford University Press, 2011), p. 84.

28. Ben Conisbee Baer, "Shit Writing: Mulk Raj Anand's *Untouchable*, the Image of Gandhi, and the Progressive Writers." *Modernism/Modernity* 16.3 (2009), p. 578.

29. S. Sen and J.K. Chopra, *Untouchable: Mulk Raj Anand* (New Delhi: Unique Publishers, 2007), pp. 56-57.

30. C. Peter Bankart et al., "On the path of the Buddha: A Psychologists' Guide to the History of Buddhism." Kathleen H. Dockett & et al (ed.) *Psychology and Buddhism: From*

Individual to Global Community (New York: Klumer Academic/ Plenum Publishers, 2003), p. 19.

31. Choudhury Janmejay, "Gandhi's Padayatra in Orissa and Upliftment of Harijans." *Orissa Review*, January (2011), p. 51.
32. *Ibid.*
33. R.R. Diwakar, "*Satyagraha—Some Reflections.*" Indira Gandhi Abinandan Samiti. *The Spirit of India.* Vol: II (New York: Asia Publishing House, 1976), p. 335.
34. Talat Ahmed, *Literature and Politics in the Age of Nationalism: The Progressive Writers' Movement in South Asia, 1932-56* (New Delhi: Routledge, 2009), p. 5.
35. E.M. Forster, "Preface." Mulk Raj Anand *Untouchable.* 1935 (New Delhi: Penguin Books, 2001), p. V.
36. D. Maya."Raja Rao's Fiction: Cultural Reassertions in the Context of Globalisation." Jaydeep Sarangi (ed), *Raja Rao: The Master and His Moves* (New Delhi: Authors Press, 2007), p. 25.
37. K. Ratna Shiela Mani. "A Critique of Raja Rao's Art." Jaydipsinh K. Dodiya, ed. *Perspectives on Indian English Fiction* (New Delhi: Sarup & Sons, 2006), p. 1.
38. William Pfaff, "Nationalism and Identity." The Way: Contemporary Christian Spirituality, January (1994), pp. 12-13.
39. H.S. Komalesha, "History, Colony, Nation and Nationalism: Revisiting Raja Rao and His Kanthapura." Jaydeep Sarangi (ed.) *Raja Rao: The Master and His Moves* (New Delhi: Authors Press, 2007), p. 59.
40. Rabindranath Tagore, *Nationalism.* Ramachandra Guha (ed.) (New Delhi: Penguin Books, 2009), pp. 67-68.
41. Mithun Bhattacharya, "Spatial Fixity and Postcoloniality—the Issue of Language in Indian Writing in English." *Language in India* 12.4 (2012), p. 288.
42. C.D. Narasimhaiah, "National Identity in Literature and Language: Its Range and Depth in the Novels of Rajo Rao." K.L. Goodwin (ed.) *National identity.* (US: Heinemann, 1970), pp. 153-68, p. 54.
43. D. Maya, "Raja Rao's Fiction: Cultural Reassertions in the Context of Globalisation." Sarangi Jaydeep (ed.) *Raja Rao:*

The Master and His Moves (New Delhi: Authors Press, 2007), p. 22.

44. Haydn Moore Williams, *Studies in Modern Indian Fiction in English* (A Writers Workshop Publication, 1973), p. 95.
45. Rumina Sethi, "Contesting Identities: Involvement and Resistance of Women in the Indian National Movement." *Journal of Gender Studies* 5.3 (1996), p. 307.
46. Vinay Kumar Pandey, "The Effect of Myth in the Novel of Raja Rao's Kanthapura." Jaydeep Sarangi (ed.), *Raja Rao: The Master and His Moves* (New Delhi: Authors Press, 2007), p. 92.
47. M.K. Naik, *Raja Rao*. 1972 (Madras: Blackie & Son, First Published in Twayne's World Authors Series, 1982), p. 214.
48. H.S. Komalesha, "History, Colony, Nation and Nationalism: Revisiting Raja Rao and His Kanthapura." Jaydeep Sarangi (ed.), *Raja Rao: The Master and His Moves* (New Delhi: Authors Press, 2007), p. 68.
49. M.K. Naik, *Raja Rao*. (New York: Twayne Publishers, 1972), p. 26.
50. Himadri Roy, "Deconstructing Femininity: The Image of Indian Women During the Freedom Struggle in Kanthapura." Jaydeep Sarangi (ed.), *Raja Rao: The Master and His Moves* (New Delhi: Authors Press, 2007), p. 92.
51. K.S. Anish Kumar, "Deconstructing the Power Structure: A Contemporary Reader's Response to Raja Rao's *Kanthapura*." Jaydeep Sarangi (ed.), *Raja Rao: The Master and His Moves* (New Delhi: Authors Press, 2007), p. 209.

4

Literary Representation of the Indian Ethos in Post-independent Period

CHAPTER OUTLINE

4.1. Post-independent Period

A long cherished dream of Indians was fulfilled on 15 August 1947. However, the historical event led not to ease but to a responsibility—to create a developed India.[1] Along with the age-old noble values and national consciousness of freedom fighters, Indians had been begun a pilgrimage to a new destiny. They took up the challenge to shape their own destiny. Indians were confronted with many obstacles which needed immediate attention. The unity and development of the country has always been a matter of hot discussion within the nation as well as in international circles. Defeating the predictions of many like Winston Churchill about the disintegration of India, it has been surviving as a single entity due to its strong bound of ethos. However, it is true that India is a bundle of contradictions, which cannot fully adhere to any one or any particular theory. It has gone through many harsh challenges. As an infant nation she had to face one of the world's cruellest riots following the partition. This was followed by three major wars. The nation suffered set backs in the form of lack of proper leadership, undemocratic practices, economic crisis, fundamentalism, regionalism, and corruption.

The growth of a nation is a dynamic and continuous process through various troublesome situations. In such situations, the strong bond of relationship between the people of the nation based on a common unifying ethos, works as a catalyst to weaken the disintegrating elements. As for India, the unseen force of ethos was the saviour that kept the nation as an entity at the time of the pre-independent period. To form the national identity was a Herculean task in the midst of partition, poverty, and the various problems with caste, religion, and class. Under the leadership of Nehru, India began to walk at its own pace.

4.1.1. *Democratic Culture*

The democratic way of life is not entirely new to Indian culture since its rudimentary form existed in the Vajjian territory in the sixth century BC. Two millennia ago, in the present Bihar,

Lichhivis had a common meeting place where assemblies were held at regular intervals to decide matters falling in the public domain. Here, both men and women participated, although the seating arrangements were separate.[2] However, the modern political culture of India is formed through the freedom struggle. The mass participation under the leadership of Gandhiji was exceptionally great compared to any other movement in the world. It fostered to build a strong bond between the people and the nation. They began to pay keen attention to the political movements of the nation. Since the political culture was not born out of hatred or hostility to others but out of a purified heart, there was peace and order in the country to a certain extent and non-violent methods became the means of protest. "During the freedom struggle Mahatma Gandhi insisted that the independence movement was against the servitude and exploitative mechanism of the colonial order and not against the British."[3] This facilitated to keep India united apart from its diversities. The leaders of the post-independent India like Jawaharlal Nehru, Vallabhbhai Patel, Rajendra Prasad, Maulana Abul Kalam Azad, Jayaprakash Narayan, C. Rajagopalachari and so on also based their work on democratic culture. So the nation began to root itself in democracy.

On 26 January 1950 the Indian Constitution, the cornerstone of Indian democracy, officially came into effect and the post-independent India took steps to form in its spirit. It is one of the great achievements of India and benefited the establishment of the democratic culture among people. The basic values and objectives are sovereignty, unity and integrity of the republic, democracy, justice, liberty, equality, fraternity, dignity of the individual, socialism, secularism and international peace. The preamble expresses the basic philosophy of the constitution and a call to ensure justice, liberty, equality and fraternity. The true spirit of India is well defined in the constitution and it is the hallmark of the ethos of post-independent India. It has all aspirations of the Indian masses. As a multi-cultural nation, the rights of the minorities, both religious and linguistic are protected in the constitution. Democratic decentralization is the spirit of the constitution and only through it, the unity of

India can be maintained. The upliftment of various oppressed groups is also considered. The national flag and the national anthem have become the pride of India. The song, Jana-gana-mana, composed by Rabindranath Tagore was accepted as the National Anthem of India. The national flag consists of the colours—saffron which stands for courage and sacrifice; white which denotes purity and truth; and green which symbolizes faith and fertility. The wheel in the centre is the Wheel of Law.

4.1.2. *Secularism*

When religion became the major defining factor of identity during pre-independent period, *Bharat Mata* got an incurable scratch. The multi-religious land, for its peaceful existence, should accommodate various religious faiths without giving any special preference to any of them and should promote tolerance, which is an element in Indian ethos, among people. In post-independent period, there was a powerful ideological movement under the banner of secularism, against religious fundamentalism. Religion is a part and parcel of Indian culture, so to have a complete detachment from it is impossible for the people of India. Hence, the Indian constitution took a neutral stand towards religion; neither anti-religious nor pro-religious. The relationship between state and religion can be seen under three categories. First of all, the Articles which ensure that religion has nothing to do in imposing Constitution, for example all equally enjoy the fundamental rights. Secondly, the Articles which ensure that the state does not have any official religion, nor does it promote any religion. Thirdly, the Articles that guarantee religious freedom. By ensuring freedom of conscience, the constitution advocates a constructive approach to religion. The constitution made sure that religious fundamentalism and communalism have nothing to do with the democratic republic of India. "Today the antithesis of communalism is secularism, [...]. Before 1947 the term secularism was rarely used in this context; the antithesis of communalism was nationalism."[4] Secularism is one of the basic features of the Indian Constitution.

4.1.3. *Socialism*

The term socialism influenced most of the freedom fighters; so it reflected in the functioning of the government and in the Constitution. According to Gandhiji "In socialism all the members of society are equal—none low, none high. [...] Even as members of the individual body are equal, so are the members of society. This is Socialism."[5] Gandhi and Nehru agreed on socialism in spirit but they had two different approaches. Gandhi stood for small-scale production and self-sufficient villages where as Nehru wanted large-scale industrialization. For him "Indian socialism is the extension of democracy from the political into the social and economic realms."[6]

Even though socialism is reflected in the directive principles, the word was not added in the Constitution. Dr. B.R. Ambedkar was against it because the social and economic policies should be determined by the government according to the time and circumstances. Ambedkar says

> The Socialist wants two things. The first thing they want is that if they come in power, the Constitution must give them the freedom to nationalize or socialize all private property without payment of compensation. The second thing that the Socialists want is that the Fundamental Rights mentioned in the Constitution must be absolute and without any limitations so that if their Party [The Communist Party] fails to come into power, they would have the unfettered freedom not merely to criticize, but also to overthrow the state.[7]

He had the apprehension that it might destroy democracy altogether. Though the term socialism was not there in the initial constitution, India followed democratic socialism to achieve the welfare of all in the socio-economic field.

4.1.4. *Spirit of Nation Building*

Losing the father in the fifth month of one's birth is a great tragedy for any child. India lost Gandhiji, the Father of the Nation on the 169th day of independence. From then onwards the absence of Gandhiji was felt very much, especially at the time of deep crisis. Vinoba Bhave followed the footsteps of Gandhiji. "Saintly politics is important as a language of comment rather than of description or practical behaviour. The outstanding figure of nation-wide importance in this idiom is Vinoba Bhave, the 'Saint on the March' who tours India on foot preaching the path of self-sacrifice and love and polity without power."[8] He contributed to a great extent but not as much as Gandhiji.

In the post-independent period, India was led by the Nehruvian vision. According to it the nation should be based on four major pillars: democratic institution-building, staunch secularism, non-alignment, and socialist economics. The first two were indispensable for the country's survival; the third preserved its self-respect and enhanced its international relationships; the fourth was to build-up a welfare society.[9] He approached democracy from three perspectives: individual, social and international. For him, democracy should empower the self. "[Nehru's] concept of 'the fullest democracy' aimed at giving the individual an opportunity for the fullest development in material and mental spheres under a sense of participation that he or she was one with the others in running the State."[10] He tried to remove disparities between the rich and the poor as well as rural and urban. For international relationship, he adapted non-alignment principle to promote global relationship between all the countries and in 1961 the Non-Aligned Movement was formed. "To Nehru, nationalism was essentially a sense of belonging together and facing the rest of mankind for good. He coined a phrase to define that objective—the emotional integration of people."[11] He also visualized a democratic society where all citizens have active participation in the nation building.

Not only the leaders and intelligentsia, but the common people also actively participated in the process of nation building. So Jayaprakash Narayan was concerned about the decentralization of power. "The foundation [of our polity] must be self-governing, self-sufficient, agro-industrial, urbo-rural, local communities."[12] The village panchayats should be self-created, self-governing and self-reliant with responsibilities. In independent India Jayaprakash Narayan followed the Gandhian path and stood for decentralizing the economic institutions, transparency in government activities, and 'owner-worker' or cooperative industries. Nation building was a major concern of the time and the nationalist movement inspired the people to contribute to the progress of the nation.

4.1.5. *Developmental Crisis*

The Five Year Plans, the 1956 Industrial Policy Resolution, Green Revolution, and the vision of self-sustained growth facilitated the growth of Indian economy. On the other hand, the slow growth in agricultural sector from 1961 to 1964, the Indo-China war of 1962, two successive bad monsoons in 1965 and 1966, the Indo-Pakistani war of 1964, the industrial recession, the upcoming election of 1967, political uncertainty after the death of Nehru in 1964, etc., drastically affected the economic growth of the country. "The Indian authorities as well as the public retained a bitter memory of this [1966] period."[13] 1961 census shows that the population went up unexpectedly.

The distinction between the rich and the poor, disempowerment of the weaker sections of society, unemployment, and malnutrition increased. Chowdhary Charan Singh in his book *The Economic Nightmare of India* writes "India may at best be described as a qualified success in politics, but it is an unqualified economic failure."[14] From 1965 onwards, unemployment among the lower middle classes affected the society. The polices of the government did not benefit the common people as a result many blamed the leaders. In short even economic crisis continued in this period without a proper solution.

4.1.6. *Marginalized Voices*

The unity of India formed out of diversity was threatened by inequality and lack of mutual respect between different castes and ethnic groups. To avoid or neglect any of these groups would shake the core of the unity of the polity and lead to a fundamental crisis. Hence, it was essential to empower the downtrodden in a democratic India for its very existence. In the present Indian Constitution there are many provisions for the empowerment of the tribes and lower caste. Along with many other articles, Article 17 prohibits untouchability, and Article 15(2), gives freedom to all without any discrimination to use the public spaces such as shops, wells, bathing ghats, etc. It also accepts positive discrimination or affirmative action such as reservation for the holistic growth of the oppressed. In certain situations, political parties tried to get the confidence of the scheduled castes, scheduled tribes and other backward classes because of their voting power. On the one hand, it facilitated the political unification of lower castes and increased their political bargaining power, while on the other, it became an exploitation of caste consciousness to attain power. Caste influence is an unavoidable factor in Indian democracy.

In 1950, L.M. Shrikant was appointed the first Commissioner to study the caste system. His report stated that the caste system was strong in India and government had to take legal and economical means to empower the untouchables. According to the later reports, in 1953-54 government spent ₹ 2,686,000 and in 1959-60 government spent ₹ 1,43,84,000 for scholarships for students of Scheduled Castes and other backward classes for pursuing post-matriculation education.[15] Such aid promoted the growth of the lower caste. In its strict sense, caste system prohibits transgression of job, marriage, etc., but studies show that there is improvement in mobilization. The study of Andre Beteille in 1965 revealed that the caste of an individual in a Tamil village no longer influences the selection of jobs.[16] However, the growth was marginal in the post-independent period and social acceptance of the lower caste hard to improve.

4.1.7. *Status of Women*

The daughters of India actively participated in the nationalist movements and organized many programs to attain independence. However, in the post-independent period their role declined in the nation-building process. The interesting fact is that in a lot of cases women were promoted to political positions in the absence of a proper male candidate or out of legal obligation. The politics of inclusion and exclusion of Indian women to the public spaces even in the family, limits their involvement and participation. Priority always goes for the opposite gender, men. Women contribute to family, society, and to state, but in turn the beneficiaries fail to enrich women. Violence such as sexual abuse, harassment, trafficking, rape, battering, female child abuse, dowry, marital rape, and female genital mutilation endangers the peaceful existence of women in the society. "Women in India have to contend with oppressive traditions, exploitation and the lack of self-worth or identity that continues to disadvantage them."[17]

Providing a nurturing environment to women in the society is one of the primary duties of the state. The Indian Constitution prohibits any kind of discrimination on the basis of sex. More than that creative programmes should be planned by the state to empower women. However, post-independent India neglected them. "Significantly, issues identified by the National Planning Committee's Sub-Committee on Women were not considered by the official planners a decade later."[18] Their social, economic, and civil rights are not protected and rules are not implemented properly. The Hindu Succession Act and the dowry Prohibition Act came into force in 1956 and 1961 respectively. In 1953, the Central Welfare Board was formed for the welfare of women. The Community Development Programme (1952), the Drought Prone Area Programme (1959), etc., are various initiatives launched for the empowerment of women.

In the traditional Indian society, the male-ego is the major hindrance for the growth of women. Instead of interpreting women from the patriarchal point of view, men should put themselves in women's shoes. Only a sound male-ego can motivate women to the front. The empowerment of women includes: environment for holistic development, freedom for decision-making, participation in nation building, and job for economic independence. These parameters may facilitate women to contribute effectively to the nation-building process.

4.1.8. *Chauvinistic Movements*

The post-independent period was a decisive time for India. To a certain extent, India succeeded in building a unified nation with democratic principles under the leadership of Nehru, Vallabhbhai Patel and so on. Yet there were some undesirable sub-national identities which tried to overpower the unity of the nation such as regionalism, ethnocentrism, racism, and religious fundamentalism. Some were born out of the feeling of negation and fear of losing the identity.

India was born with the traumatic experience of partition which was born out of religious fundamentalism to a certain extend. Partition is considered as the fifth major factor (other factors: Aryan invasion, Muslim conquest, Western intrusion, and the freedom movement) in the formation of India.[19] The horrifying incident resulted in one of the biggest population transfers in human history. Around twenty thousand were ruthlessly massacred and 13,000 causalities were officially reported.[20] The unrest in Kashmir is a permanent mark caused by the partition of India. More than land division, it exerted influence on the ethos of Indians. The claim of religious identity became stronger. Sikhs, Hindus and Muslims began to focus on their community's benefits. Partition made a lasting impact on the chauvinistic thinking of various groups. N.V. Godse, a former member of RSS, assassinated Gandhiji because of Gandhiji's pro-Muslim attitude. The RSS was banned in 1948 and the ban was lifted in 1949. At that time, it was not a political movement but it stood for the reformation of Hinduism. However, Hindu fundamentalism began to take root in the country and they put forward religious nationalism which stands for an official religion for the state.

The rise of regional consciousness over nationalism was yet another alarming threat to the integrity of the nation. Some of the policies of the Central Government for the unification of the nation by rejecting the marginalized voices caused fear in the minorities. India is a multi-lingual nation and each language is an expression of a particular ethnic tradition. Instead of protecting all, without looking at the size of the population or place, some were stubborn and insisted on attaching Indianness to a particular ethnicity. In 1951, Hindi was declared as national language and it caused riots in Tamil Nadu. The linguistic minorities were wounded and different movements were started to protect regional ethnicities. The death of Potti Sreeramulu in 1952 compelled Nehru to take the decision on the division of states. On the basis of the report of State Reorganisation Commission, Andhra Pradesh, Kerala, Karnataka, were formed and in the following years, Gujarat and Maharashtra. "Until the 60s, more than a decade after independence, the greatest fear was that India would split up along linguistic lines."[21] Even the three-language formula remains a utopian idea.

Every ethnic group has a right to promote and keep their identity. This led to the formation of non-political organizations and regional parties. Regionalism and linguistic chauvinism are major threats to Indian unity after independence and with the rise and growth of regional parties, some of which hold the reins of power in their respective States, the idea of a separate nation for each language got more support. In addition to this, the local leaders politicized issues to attain power. Since the ideologies of the local political parties affected people more emotionally, they gradually united with them.

The strong willed ethnocentric leaders decided to protect the ethnic identity as a goal and it aroused protests against the Central Government. Ethnicity includes all the cultural uniqueness that descends from a common origin. It gave way to ethnocentrism and racism. Ethnicity gave a common identity and unity to a homogeneous geographical area. For instance, in 1949, Dravida Munnetra Kazhagam (DMK), the first regional political party, was formed. During the early period of independence, the extremists of Dravidian movements made claim for a sovereign nation namely the Dravida Nadu or Dravidistan. From 1967 onwards the Dravidian parties control the state governance.

Another example for regionalism was the pursuit for a Sikh nation namely Khalistan (the land of the pure) by the Khalistan Movement. As Tara Singh, the Akali Dal leader framed, "Muslims got Pakistan, Hindus, Hindustan, but what did the Sikhs get?"[22] The demand for a separate territory for Sikhs that started from 1950s onwards was fulfilled in 1966. Punjab was finally divided into three states—Himachal Pradesh, Haryana, and Punjab. Yet Sikh regionalism went on with Sikhetho-nationalism and resulted in many military operations, like Operation Blue Star from 3-8 June 1984 and the consequent assassination of the then Prime Minister Indira Gandhi on 31 October 1984.

4.1.9. *Cultural Decolonization and Search for Identity*

When different cultures encounter each other, do they enhance or endanger each other? The history of the world teaches that the powerful take the control. "Culture can be seen both as a historically constituted domain of significant concepts and practices and as a regime in which power achieves its ultimate apotheosis."[23] As a result, the voyages of Christopher Columbus and Vasco da Gama are symbols of Colonialism of cultures. The word 'native' itself is formed out of the Western superiority complex.

During the colonial period in India, the anti-colonial struggle was primarily focused on the political realm. The intelligentsia intentionally sidelined the problem of cultural regeneration and they focused on the political agitation out of the fear that the social reformation may deviate from the goal of political freedom.[24] Notwithstanding that the cultural decolonization was neglected, pre-independent period was the time to assert and establish Indianness. The period not only aimed at the political consolidation of the nation but also the assimilation of culture. This would not be a tie up of Indianness with a particular ethnic culture. Along with Hindi as the national language, all regional languages should be given an equal status. Indian ethos is the celebration of the 'multi', i.e. variety and plurality of the all indigenous traditions.

The regional cultures, which were marginalized, appropriated and displaced by the hegemonic power, would be refurbished. Politically, the colonial yoke was lifted but the mental mark had yet to be healed in order to assert the nation's identity. In the post-independent period, India had to resist the hegemonic influence of the west by building up the national identity. Decolonization is a process of self-discovery and a time to erase the painful memories of colonization, to become mentally sound to experience one's culture positively and to build-up universal brotherhood without losing one's national ethos. Decolonization is not the term for cultural isolation but establishment of self-identity. Thus, always constructive interactions of cultures are necessary. The independent India has attempted to form an underlying ethos out of the indigenous heterogenic ideologies and cultures. Developing a socio-cultural consciousness is vital.

4.1.10. *Fictional Representation*

In the post-independent period, the primary thrust was nation-building. The integrity of the nation, social reformation, economic development, and the upliftment of the weaker sections, were various challenges of the period. The post-independent Indic-ethos focused more on the individual and his/her rights. The individual, as a free agent, was ensured freedom for the self-fulfillment and was expected to meaningfully contribute to the nation. This was reflected in the Constitution and the activities of the great leaders. For instance, "To [Nehru], people were individuals rather than vague groups. To that individual he wanted to restore the bliss of freedom."[25] Modern rationalism and scientific temperament were the guiding spirit of the nation rather than intuition and tradition. Panikkar said, "Clearly, our new democratic, egalitarian and secular state is not built upon the foundations of ancient India, or of Hindu thought."[26] Indian secularism and socialism got due respect. The nation promoted multi-cultural ethos and democratic values. The creative writings reflected these aspirations and the period can be called, the nation-building phase of literature.

Even though the settings and stories of many novels of the post-independent period were based on the pre-independent period, they aimed at building up the nation, to bring social reformation, to promote democracy, etc. Some of the novels which narrate the pre-independent period are Mulk Raj Anand's *Seven Summers* (1951); Khushwant Singh's *I shall not Hear the Nightingale* (1959), Venu Chitale's *In Transit* (1950), etc. Mulk Raj Anand's *Death of a Hero* (1963) and Kamala Markandaya's *Some Inner Fury* (1955) are examples of violence that was rampant in India.

Attia Hosain's *Sunlight on a Broke Column* (1961) is the story of a Muslim family in Lucknow before and after independence. In the novel, Laila fought for personal freedom and aimed at reformation. Zeenuth Futehally's *Zohra* (1951) is about an upper-class Muslim woman who lived in the early twentieth century in Hyderabad. The novel combines the need for women empowerment and the growth of the Indian national consciousness. Some other Indian English fiction of the period are Menon Marath's *Wounds of Spring* (1961); Lambert Mascarenhas's *Sorrowing Lies my Land* (1955); Manohar Malgonkar's *The Princes* (1963), *Combat of Shadows* and *Distant Drum* (1960), Khwaja Ahmad's *Inquilab* (1955) and N. Kagarajan's *Chronicles of Kedaram* (1961), etc. Though the novel *A Suitable Boy* was published in 1993, it is about the struggle between political parties, communal riots, etc., during the period from 1950 to 1952.

The novels selected for the study of the ethos of post-independent period are R.K. Narayan's *Waiting for the Mahatma* (1955) and Khushwant Singh's *Train to Pakistan* (1956). *Waiting for the Mahatma* was written out of the post-independent outlook about Gandhiji, independence, freedom fighters, etc., which could guide the nation building and *Train to Pakistan,* was written against the background of the partition of India, an event which would always remain as a sear in the memory of the Indians. Hence, based on the theme and the author, these novels, are very apt for the research.

4.2. Analysis of *Waiting for the Mahatma* in the Light of the Post-independent Ethos

To give birth is difficult but to nurture is tougher. Indians attained freedom in 1947 but it was not mere delight but an unimaginable responsibility. It was a time to build-up the nation which had a bundle of problems such as poverty, regionalism, communalism, refugees of partition, underdevelopment, disunity, unstable governance, and lack of international relationships. All issues required immediate attention without delay. In the transition period, the passing away of the man who led the freedom movement with a strong ideology, created a strong absence in the leadership style. The paradox is that the apostle of non-violence ended as a victim of violence and it reveals the challenging situation the nation faced. At such a time literature had a great role to play, empowering the people to face the challenges with an optimistic outlook. R.K. Narayan's *Waiting for the Mahatma* published in 1955, is such a novel.

Since the novel was published after seven years of independence, the purpose may not be merely the narration of the freedom struggle. Moreover, it is a revisiting-novel, about the passionate exodus of freedom struggle with an eye on post-independent experience to revitalize the ethos of India. The political novels of the period have a teaching and motivating purpose to guide the nation to achieve the welfare of all. They reminded the people about the various theories, especially of Gandhism, or tried to give them confidence to march ahead without fear.

4.2.1. *Gandhism: Revisited*

Just after independence, people were highly idealistic. However, as they faced harsh realities, the joy of independence turned into despair. When the foreign imperialists had left, native imperialists took their place. "Fancy Nehru and Patel and the rest sitting there where there were haughty Viceroys before" (*WM* 177). The folly of independence celebration is very well narrated in the novel. "The sight of the Independence Day celebrations irritated him" (*WM* 179). At the time of suffering under the ruling class of India, along with Sriram and Bharati the common people longed for Gandhiji. Gandhiji who stood for the poor who in turn trusted him, was rejected by the ruling class. "The events of independence and partition brought a near-complete marginalization of Gandhi and Gandhism."[27] Yet Gandhism is significant and the novel revisits it in the language of common man.

Waiting for the Mahatma is not a novel which aims to teach Gandhism but a prophetic one which reminds us that an entire nation failed to comprehend Gandhism in its true sense. For example, the attitude of the people who surrounded Sriram, the protagonist of the novel, at the time of picketing a shop that sold English biscuits. The crowd felt that he was unreal and the act was linked with monkey-like acrobatics. Instead of taking the real spirit, the crowd suggests to the boy who came to buy snuff "Come and fetch your snuff after that fellow leaves." (*WM* 96). Still Gandhian ideas remain alien to the Indian, "He [Sriram] is not a man of this place" (*WM* 96). Narayan envisages a future India, which would move away from Gandhiji and misunderstand his activities. People might not accept little Gandhians. "The carter, while pulling the animals back to the road, swore at them and at the disturbance. 'These politicians, Gandhi folk, they won't leave anyone in peace. Why do you come and trouble us here?'" (*WM* 82). When Sriram wrote 'Quit India' a man commented: "Waste of time and paint" (*WM* 85). For the business class, Patriotism and Gandhism would become a non-profitable wastage.

Narayan who writes about the situations and persons which rejected Gandhism, did not aim at establishing relevance of Gandhism but only suggested it to be a solution to the problems which India had been facing after independence. The novel calls the nation to follow Gandhism. "India's political leaders paid much lip service to Gandhi and his ideals in the years after Indian independence [....]. Time and time again, however, the policies pursued in some of the most crucial areas of concern for modern India ignored all that Gandhi stood for."[28] To follow Gandhism is a challenge and needs a purified mind.

Gandhism is a decorative ornament for many. Mr. Natesh, gets *Chark* to please Gandhiji, not to practice it (*WM* 33). The timber-contractor gave five thousand rupees to the Harijan Fund as well as to the War Fund for the smooth functioning of his business (*WM* 84). Narayan has used such ironic and humorous incidents to facilitate the readers to reflect on their multidimensional consciousness. "In fact, the greater part of the novel stands on this dialogic relation between Gandhi's teachings and the people. Sriram joins Gandhi's volunteers in order to stay near Bharati. [...]"[29] The novel realistically narrates the influence and response of the multifarious facets of Gandhism on common people. It is a revisiting novel of Gandhism to regain its prominence among the Indian masses.

4.2.2. Construction of the Nation

The major linking chain of the novel is the national construction of India, which at that time was in its infancy. Just after independence, India struggled a lot to make itself a nation with peace and unity. The novelist emphasizes the pathetic situation of the country. "There is nothing very good now, sir, what with the present difficulty of getting rice and any pure food. Our government does not do anything about it yet" (*WM* 174). The leaders and the people experienced the hardships involved in building up a nation. "The trouble is that things are still disorganized" (*WM* 177). Many predicted that freedom, democracy, and secularism would not survive in India for long and sooner or later the Indian political system would collapse, and disintegrate into linguistic and ethnic fragments.[30] In spite of the challenges, *Waiting for the Mahatma* is a novel that inspires to continue to sail as a democratic nation. One of the key sentences of the novel is that: "Ours is an infant State, still a baby, many things have still to be done [...]. We must be happy that things are being done and not spend the time finding fault with anyone" (*WM* 177). It reminds each one of his duty to contribute to the nation and to be tolerant of the shortcomings for resolving the crisis period.

After independence, many became dissatisfied with the functioning style of the government and the selfish attitude of leaders in power. "After all, what do I get for all the trouble I took and the risks I ran? Are they going to make me the minister of this and that? Not a chance, sir," (*WM* 178). In the post-independence India, the lay people of the independence struggle were neglected and the privileges were shared by the politicians. At this situation, *Waiting for the Mahatma* which functions as a healing novel attempts to give a transcendental meaning to the common folk who took on themselves the pain for independence. "I'm not complaining or grumbling. What I have done, I have done with the utmost satisfaction. I am not worried about it at all" (*WM* 178). The faceless freedom fighters faded away in the history and "[...] there are others waiting for the privilege" (*WM* 178). To comfort Jagadish, the photographer and freedom fighter, Sriram repeats the words of Jagadish himself that "After all, as you said now, we are an infant nation." The word was very convincing, "it had a homely and agreeable sound, nobody need worry what it meant or why it was mentioned" (*WM* 178). They consoled and inspired each other with an optimistic outlook for building the nation.

Further, *Waiting for the Mahatma* is an instructional novel and it advices the leaders as well as bureaucrats to work selflessly for the nation. The novel presents the Municipal Chairman and the District Collector as their representatives. Mr. Natesh, the representative of political leaders of the nation, reveals the hypocritical nature of politicians and their value system that contradicts Gandhiji. Mr. Natesh did all the arrangements for Gandhiji not out of love and respect for him but to make use of his popularity and recognition among the people. The love of Gandhiji towards the untouchable and the aversion of Mr. Natesh towards them are emphasized in the novel. Gandhiji did not make any comment about the reception at 'Neel Bagh' because he was more concerned with the poor. "Mahatmaji had the young urchin hoisted beside him on the divan...He nestled close to the Mahatma, who was smoothing out his matted hair with his fingers, and was engaged in an earnest conversation with him" (*WM* 36). However the Chairman did not like it and he had 'a sinful emotion' (*WM* 36). His introspection goes: "Of course people must like poor people and so on, but why bring in such a dirty boy, an untouchable, up the steps and make him so important?" (*WM* 36). The spirit of nationalism of the great leaders of freedom struggle shifted to make way for the tenor of madness for power. In democracy, the bureaucrats have a good role to play for good administration. However, a lot of incidents reveal that Indian bureaucrats do not hold the attitude of service but the imperial aristocratic view. "The Collector had taken the trouble to go through the address [...] to make sure that it contained no insult to the British Empire" (*WM* 30). The author counsels the politicians and the bureaucrats to keep themselves away from luxuries, and be with the poor. "For me?

Don't trouble yourself. I can sleep in any hut. I can live where others are living. I don't think I shall demand many luxuries" (*WM* 69-70). Gandhian simplicity is highlighted as a model.

The novel begins with the scene of Granny preparing Sriram to take the responsibility. "He's old enough to take charge of his own affairs. How long should I look after him! I'm not immortal" (*WM* 7). As Granny explains the use of money 'in a mystifying manner' (*WM* 10), the Indian independence also should be seen as a responsibility which should be handed carefully. By potraying the young Sriram, who spends his early years without taking responsibility, the author warns the political leaders that they should be more accountable and should not move with the newness of 'power.' The time may pass soon and India may lose its opportunities for development. 'Another Dussehra!' or 'Another Deepavali! It looks as though I lighted crackers only yesterday!' he would cry, surprised at the passage of time' (*WM* 14). After meeting Bharati and Gandhiji, Sriram became more duty-bound. The author emphasizes that it is high time to make new resolutions. Sriram met Bharati on 'New Year's Day' (*WM* 14). The novel advises the Indians to internalize and follow Gandhism.

Ultimately the responsibility to build-up the nation falls on the people. 'We the people of India' are the custodians of the sovereignty of the nation. The novel envisages that all must take up the path of Gandhiji and the task of building the nation must not be limited to any political party. The novelist indirectly reminds the readers of the last desire of Gandhiji "to disband the existing congress organization and flower into a Lok Sevak Sangh" to keep out "unhealthy competitions with political parties and communal bodies."[31] In the novel, on the day of the assassination, Nehru and Patel meet Gandhiji (*WM* 194) but he does not give them any promise. On the contrary, he blesses and commands Sriram and Bharati. "I [Gandhi] want to be there very much, but I don't know. [...] Anyway you are not to put off your marriage for any reason, remember," he said, with a new command in his voice' (*WM* 199-200). Thus, Gandhiji entrusts the followers to carry on his work and it is a novel of commissioning. Burton says, "Gandhi had not wanted the Congress to become a conventional party, preferring instead that the politics of the new nation find expression in factions representing different interests and programmes, including a Gandhian one. In his view, the Congress would wither away or become a non-partisan arena for discussing the nation's problems."[32] Gandhiji does not wish that the Congress continue as a political party that opts for power. Hence, the novel limits the narration of the assassination of Gandhiji to a few lines and gives importance to the conversation with Sriram and Bharati. There Gandhiji reveals the last will and testament which advocates to continue his efforts to face the challenges of the nation.

The novelist stresses the word 'today' (*WM* 196) by repeating and italicizing because Gandhiji wants to anoint them on that day. The next day is in God's hand. "If God wills it I shall come" (*WM* 199). The final scan can be called as handover scan. Three things are emphasized: the means of non-violence (*WM* 198), purification act of fasting (*WM* 198), and love the needy as 'their father and mother!' (*WM* 199). Sriram accepts the mistake of following the path of violence and Bharati is ready to fast herself for purification. They are blessed for marriage to look after the needy who are always the manifestation of God. 'God reveals himself to us in the shape of children' (*WM* 197).

The novelist brings the schoolmaster, the guru of Sriram as a moral voice. The guru is considered as the last word for every decision in Indian culture. The master certifies the decision of Sriram as right. "The teacher said, 'I am proud to see you here, my boy. Join the Congress, work for the country, you will go far, God bless you [...]' Whatever happens, don't let down our country" (*WM* 26). When Granny expresses her dissatisfaction about the stay of Sriram with the Gandhian group, the guru said: "Our country needs more young men like him" (*WM* 48). Master, the school teacher of Sriram, may be a minor character but he is an authentic person who calls the youth to participate enthusiastically in promoting the glory of Bharat Mata. Thus, the novel can be considered as a prophecy exhorting Gandhism and strongly emphasising it to be the only way to build the nation. It tries to convey the need to build up the nation by being faithful to Gandhism. It looks for a brighter future of India and it can be seen as a novel of hope.

4.2.3. *Search for Indianness*

Colonialism has an enduring unconscious control over its subjects. "The postcolonial world is one in which we may live after colonialism but never without it."[33] *Waiting for the Mahatma* has a strong cultural and mental decolonization purpose. It rejects the culturally dominant 'other' and establishes the 'self' through rewriting the colonial 'hidden transcript'[34] with Gandhism which reflects the typical Indian ethos. It can be called an indigenous re-Indianization novel. "Narayan's intimacy, as a writer, is with ordinary persons, their personal predilections, oddities, hysterics, and illusions and through them, he generally gets concerned with the whole predicament of man's existence as such, his search for identity somewhere, for some standby in life, something that could carry him across."[35] Narayan writes the metamorphosis of Sriram into a true Indian in five stages.

In the first stage, Sriram has a fair complexion and acts as Lord Macaulay has envisaged "We must at present do our best to form a class of persons, Indian in blood and colour, but English in taste, in opinions, morals, and in intellect." He is chronically colonized and even he does not like his mother's Indian look. "[Sriram] didn't feel pleased with her [his mother's] appearance" (*WM* 1). On the other hand, he liked the unknown European queen. "...he wished she [his mother] looked like that portrait of a European queen with apple checks and wavy coiffure hanging in the little shop opposite his house..." (*WM* 1). At any cost, he wanted to possess the portrait of the European queen. Likewise, Kanni the shopkeeper shares the intellectual servitude. He considers the portrait of a European queen, as precious because it 'brought luck' (*WM* 2). The imperial rulers colonize even the aesthetic sense of Indians. The Indians have appreciation for the west and blindly follow Western culture.

In the second stage, Sriram is shaken when he encounters with alluring Indianness. "She [Bharati] looked so different from the beauty in Kanni's shop; his critical faculties were at once alert, and he realized how shallow was the other beauty, the European queen, and wondered that he had ever given her a thought" (*WM* 15). Bharati becomes an instrument that reveals the real Indianness to Sriram. She, the sincere follower of Gandhiji, is the daughter of Bharat. "Bharat is India, and Bharati is the daughter of India" (*WM* 45). Sriram gets attached to Bharati and he is ready to accept her advice. "Why don't you [Bharati] take me [Sriram] as your pupil?" (*WM* 45). Here, Sriram, also meets Gandhiji, who is the embodiment of the real ethos of India. Although he joined in the crowd with Gandhiji, he does not follow him as a disciple. Since Sriram was introduced to the Indianness he began to reflect on it. "This was the first time he was assailed by doubts of his own prowess and understanding" (*WM* 21). Sriram feels that he has to change his lifestyle. "Yes, Bapuji, I will be a different man." (*WM* 53). Gandhiji initiates him to discover himself. "Why do you say 'different'? You will be all right if you are fully yourself" (*WM* 53). This is an allegory to discover the Indian ethos and to live according to it.

In the third stage, Sriram adopts the Pseudo-Gandhian philosophy and actively participates in the freedom struggle. "Learning that she is a follower of Gandhiji, he decides to become his disciple to be able to be close to her—neither understanding nor having any interest in Gandhiji's philosophy."[36] He scolds Granny for speaking ill about Gandhiji. "I won't hear anyone speak lightly of him." ...'He [Gandhiji] is not a man; he is a Mahatma!' cried Sriram' (*WM* 64-65). In spite of the fact that, he tries to practice Gandhism without proper conviction. At this level the transformation process was progressing. "He felt he was becoming a citizen of an entirely new world" (*WM* 56). The author compares the departure of Sriram from Granny to that of Buddha who set out to attain enlightenment at night from his wife Yasodhara. Sriram participates in the 'Quit India' movement in his own way and experiments Gandhian way of *satyagraha*. He tries to imitate Gandhiji blindly like a child who fails to behave prudently according to the situation. The crowd is a projection of the inner world of Sriram who moves with a shallow Gandhian conviction. The crowd does not have a thorough understanding of Gandhiji but they just wish to get a glimpse of the 'great legend.' The crowd is a symbol of those who do not practice Gandhism. After independence the Indian leaders except very few failed to follow Gandhism.

In the fourth stage, Sriram moves to the extremist group when the Indian National Army goes ahead under the leadership of Subhas Chandra Bose. Jagadish praises him: "I'll have a lavani composed of Subhas Babu's life, his sacrifice, patriotism, courage, and make it compulsory to sing it every day in every school" (*WM* 118). In 1939, Indira Gandhi wrote: "[Subhas] had come to be regarded as the leader of the 'left.'"[37] Bose and collaborators dedicated their life 'to free our dear motherland' (*WM* 116). More than self they loved the nation. "Our lives are not very important. Our work is more important" (*WM* 121). At the end Sriram is arrested.

The fifth stage commences at jail. "My jail seems to be on my back, all the time," he reflected (*WM* 190). The jail life enlightens him like Buddha who attains enlightenment under the bodhi tree. At last, he makes the confession before Gandhiji (*WM* 198). Sriram and Bharati take the great mission entrusted by Gandhiji: "May you be their father and mother" (*WM* 199). Thus, Sriram dedicates his life for India.

Sriram and Bharati are the archetypes of the true sons and daughters of India. The word 'Sriram' has multiple dimensions which signifies Indian culture. Obviously, it stands for an average adolescent boy who represents the identity of the average Indian. It also denotes 'Ram' in the *Ramayana* who kills Ravana and it proclaims the glorious Indian ethos. Narayan uses popular gods and goddesses of India to convey Indian messages. The words Ramayana, Gita, Ram, Sita, are used three, five, twelve, and three times respectively in the novel. It, also, connotes the *manthra* of Gandhiji which Sriram repeats for his spiritual renewal: "Raghupati Raghava Raja Ram, Pathita Pavana Sita Ram" (*WM* 74).

The lives of Sriram and Bharati have similarities with that of Jayaprakash Narayan (JP) and his wife Prabhavati. Prabhavati lived with Gandhiji for seven years and Kasturba died in her arms in 1943.[38] JP joined the Gandhian movement in 1921 for the non-cooperation movement. Later, during his studies in America he moved to Marxism. "JP was as much if not more impatient than the group of younger leaders of the Congress, such as Subhas Chandra Bose [...] to begin the fight to capture power from the British."[39] Whereas, Prabhavati stood for non-violence without the influence of Marxism of her husband. Like Sriram, JP also was a part of an underground movement during the Quit India movement and was jailed.[40] Many senior leaders were released from jail after the war of 1945 in Europe but JP was released only in 1946. Later he accepted non-violence like Sriram. For the rest of his life, JP ardently followed Gandhism. Identifying with Bharati, Gandhiji considered Prabhavati as a true hero of non-violence.

4.2.4. *Pan-subaltern Spirit*

Waiting for the Mahatma is a humanistic novel that depicts Gandhiji as a person who understands the romance between Bharati and Sriram, lives with the untouchable, moves with the common folk, and sympathizes those who suffer. It projects the people outside the hegemonic power structure. In the novel, all the characters except Gandhiji are from common folk and the novel is designed for average people. It is a pan-subaltern novel which narrates the story of independence from the angle of the downtrodden. It focuses on little Gandhians, women, and untouchables. In order to inspire the post-independent Indians to participating in nation construction, the novel brings out the heroic sacrifice of the little Gandhians to attain independence. People are the strength of Indian democracy and they should be the custodians of it by drawing from the spirit of the freedom fighters.

The novel is the story of romance between Sriram and Bharati, two ordinary people set against the backdrop of Gandhian freedom struggle. The romance itself leads the protagonist to Gandhiji and he participates in both non-violent and violent means for the independence movement. Sriram, is an ordinary and lazy adolescent boy who meets visionary people like Gandhiji, the School Master, and Bharati on the one hand, and short-sighted people like, the collector, the municipal Chairman, the shopkeeper, and the timber-contractor on the other. The novel unfolds the change in the protagonist. At last, when transformed completely he dedicates his life for the nation. He practices the Gandhian principles such as non-violence, in such a manner so as to build the identity based on Indianness in common people. William Walsh writes "'a rare piece of triumph' in which the genius of Mahatma is exquisitely projected."[41] The novel is a redefinition and reinterpretation of Gandhism from the point of view of common people.

The novel is not a blind acceptance of Gandhism or its promotion. It is not the glorification of Gandhism and cannot be called a Gandhian novel. Even though the title of the novel has the great legend's name, the novel starts with an average adolescent boy's usual day. The story is told from the perspective of different sections of people. Not all the characters of the novel are rooted in Gandhian principles but are developed through their own life experiences. This gives the scope for a deep analysis of the novel and gives more understanding about the reality of the freedom movement. The novel is a new subaltern reading of the understanding of Indians about Gandhiji with the comic and ironic presentation of how the principles are implemented in the actual life of people. Though the Indian freedom struggle is a mass movement, the novel portrays a subaltern history of independence. The novel thoroughly exposes Gandhism for dialogue. Even though Gandhiji is a character in the novel, he has only a minor role. As a result, Narayan is able to narrate the freedom struggle from an average person's perspective and the protagonist shifts from non-violence to violence and again turns to non-violence. The leaders are always accepted with great awe and their contributions are written in golden letters. On the other hand, the common folk who suffer for the country are often ignored. The faceless Gandhians, who follow Gandhiji with *nishkama karma*, are also great people. They who really suffer are the real heroes. Sriram represents the common people who selflessly participated in the freedom struggle. "Throughout the novel Sriram is a voice-sometimes the inner voice and often the outer, the louder one. Thus, he is left to our imagination, never to be finalized."[42] Through Sriram, Narayan echoes the voice of Malgudi, which is the microcosm of India.

The first subaltern group in the novel is the little Gandhians of the country who carry Gandhiji as a living reality to the illiterate and rural villagers of India. Like Gandhiji who walked 1279527 feet for the Dandi March in 1930, Sriram "climbed 4,000 feet above sea level" (*WM* 86) to spread the message of 'Quit India.' The word 'quit' is used twenty-four times in the novel. Men of power attempt to resist the subaltern. "Wherever he went he wrote, 'Quit India'. And it was followed by loyalists amending it with: 'Don't' or an 'I' before 'Quit'" (*WM* 85). Bharati and Gorpad, the little Gandhians are the sincere followers of Gandhi. Bharati, whose "father died [...] when he was beaten by the police" (*WM* 58), is the role model for the Gandhian disciples. She guides Sriram to Gandhiji and inspires him to become his follower. It is true that at the initial stage Sriram moves with the crowd to meet Bharati and that love continues until the end. However, as the story develops the relationship which starts with lust become nobler based on Gandhism. Gorpad, with whom Sriram shares the room in Gandhi's camps, is also a true Gandhian at heart. He unveils his noble thoughts. "I will not rest till the British are sent out of India" (*WM* 48). After hearing the atrocities of the Britishers, Sriram said "All Englishmen deserve to be shot" (*WM* 59). Yet, Gorpad corrected him, "You should not even think on those lines, if you are going to be a true satyagrahi" (*WM* 59). The presence and sharing of the pathetic life experience of Gorpad helps Sriram to understand Gandhism in its true sense.

The novel is not a ruminative analysis of Gandhism but the view of ordinary people. It inspires the common folk to contribute to the nation with the vision of Gandhiji. The novel takes the message to the people. The voice in the novel is of one among the crowd, sharing the feelings of the subaltern. It is an attempt at demythologizing the homogeneous history of the national movement and brings out the real nameless and faceless heroes of the national movement who suffered in India. The process is essential to whittle away the so-called over projected heroes. This helps to motivate people for enthusiastically participating in the nation-building process. The novel is a motivational novel for the common people.

The second subaltern group that speaks through the novel is the woman. In 1936, Gandhiji states, "When woman whom we call *abala* becomes *sabala*, all those who are helpless will become powerful."[43] The novel narrates the contribution of women for the Indian freedom struggle. Bharati who is depicted as a 'daughter of India' (*WM* 45) stands for all women who sacrificed themselves for India. "The freedom movement also had the distinction of bringing, for the first time, millions of women into the political realm of civil disobedience and satyagraha campaigns."[44] Bharati is a true *satyagrahi* and temptations could not detach her from the noble principles of *satyagraha*. Even though Bharati is young, she is emotionally mature. Moreover, through the character Gandhiji, Narayan upholds the dignity of women. "All women are your sisters and mothers. Never look at them with thoughts of lust" (*WM* 23). Even though there are pitfalls, respect for woman is an Indian tradition. It is the responsibility of the society to ensure the woman's safety. "He said that if a country cannot give security to women and children, it's not worth living in" (*WM* 191). Gandhiji considers Bharati as the guru of Sriram (*WM* 72) and she is able to guide him. This shows that Gandhiji is open enough to accept the qualities of women. Gandhiji also reminds them about their duties to serve society. Narayan attempts to empower women and talks about their contribution in the freedom struggle.

The third major subaltern group in the novel is the untouchable. Narayan gives an account of the supportive behaviour of Gandhiji, so that the Indian society becomes more aware of their pathetic condition. In addition, it can be seen as a defensive Gandhian novel. Because there may be a few who began to consider Gandhiji as against the untouchable. For instance, Ambedkar says "The only reaction and a very natural reaction of the Untouchable would be to run away from Gandhism."[45] On the contrary, the novel highlights the empathetic approach of Gandhiji and his contribution for the uplift of the untouchable. Even though many rich want him to be in their luxurious villas (*WM* 28), Gandhiji stays with the untouchable to express his solidarity with them. His mind is always with the downtrodden and he has friendly talks with the untouchable boy. He wants to be with the untouchable and shares their suffering. "Mahatmaji gave his forefinger to the young boy to clutch and allowed himself to be led down the veranda steps" (*WM* 38). In 1946, Gandhiji stayed in the slum-quarters of Bhangi untouchables to express solidarity with them in Delhi.

For the high caste Gandhiji is a rebel. "For her (Granny) the Mahatma was one who preached dangerously, who tried to bring untouchables into the temples..." (*WM* 48). The Chairman is annoyed by the behaviour of Gandhiji who expresses love towards the boy. Social exploitation is well narrated in the novel. The underdogs are living in the dirtiest area of the city. The arrival of Gandhiji compels the government and people to clean the whole area. After the cleaning Gandhiji commented: "Now one can believe that the true cleansers of the city live here" (*WM* 39). He makes a lot of efforts to eradicate untouchability. One of the reasons for the success of Gandhiji is his mobilization of subaltern group. "[Gandhiji] tried to incorporate subaltern politics into his alternative by purging it of its violent aspects, so as to give it a strong moral superiority as against the coercive and violent politics of both the colonial state and the indigenous elites."[46] The average Indians move with Gandhiji and he envisages a means to empower all.

4.2.5. *Indian Secularism*

Religion is both a blessing and a curse to humanity. To keep it always as a grace, persistent openness and dialogue are essential. If not, it can turn into a closed fundamental group. Therefore, Narayan makes every effort to bridge between extreme secularism which keeps hostility with religion and theocracy which is fully controlled by religion. It upholds the secularism of India, which keeps a respectable distance with religions on the one hand, and has a healthy relationship with them on the other. Secularism is a major feature of the ethos of independent India. *Waiting for the Mahatma* emphasises the secularism of India in the midst of fundamentalism. "Don't ask whether they are Muslim children or Hindu children or who they are. It is no use asking that; we don't know. We have given them only the names of flowers and birds. [...] You see one child was called Malkaus, that's a melody: a girl is known as Gulab, that is a rose. These children must grow up only as human beings" (*WM* 193). Religious harmony is the beauty of Indian ethos.

Narayan laughs at the superstitions in religions by the narration of the recovery of Granny at the cremation ground. "People seemed to have suddenly lost all common sense" (*WM* 142). Since people are too orthodox, they do not allow her to come back to her house. They believe "it was inauspicious and might blight the city" (*WM* 160). The misuse of religion and rituals without humanism and spirit are also mirrored in the novel. Religious fanaticism makes society equivalent to hell. Even if Granny gets her life back, she goes back to the similar style of life. Granny, the pious orthodox woman follows all the meaningless rituals in her life. On the contrary, Sriram has a continuous transformation in his life and each moment in his life is a time of rebirth towards a better life. "At one level, therefore, *Waiting for the Mahatma* is a story of progress of young, irresponsible, carefree Sriram into a passionate lover, a responsible citizen of the country with a record of considerable sacrifice and a term in jail to make him a complete patriot."[47] The novel is an example for how a person can change his life for a better cause.

Gandhiji stands for the change of heart and a meaningful life through religion. He not only works for independence but also for the character formation of people which is underlined by humanism and moral righteousness. "I want you to clear your hearts and minds and make certain that only love resides there, and there is no residue of bitterness for past history. Only then can you say to the British, 'Please leave this country' (*WM* 24). The independence movement led by Gandhiji is more of a self-realisation march because its end is not to attain independence but a life in the soul. Gandhiji incorporates spirituality with day-to-day life: *karma marga*. Gandhiji goes beyond ritualism. "God is everywhere, and if you want to feel his presence you will see him in a place like this with a beautiful river flowing, the sunrise with all its colours, and the air so fresh. Feeling a beautiful hour or a beautiful scene or a beautiful object is itself a form of prayer" (*WM* 52). Mutual understanding is more important in life than religion and caste.

Narayan emphasises the tolerance and inclusiveness of religions because fundamentalism is growing in India. The partition of the country and the assassination of Gandhiji, the two greatest sorrows of modern India, happened because of an extreme form of fundamentalism. Consequently, Narayan emphasises the 'truth' for inculcating tolerance and inclusiveness. The constitution of life should be the inner voice. "Your work should be a matter of inner faith. It cannot depend upon what you see or understand. Your conscience should be your guide in every action. Consult it and you won't go wrong" (*WM* 100). Gandhiji always listens to the inner voice. "During the last fifteen minutes of this walk the Mahatma said nothing; he walked in silence, looking at the ground before him [...]. The Mahatma's silence was heavy and pervasive..." (*WM* 53). Gandhiji also emphasises renunciation, and simplicity instead of religious rituals: the *bhakthi marga*. "There was a class of society where luxuries gave one a status, and now here was the opposite. The more one asserted one cared for no luxury, the more one showed an inclination for hardship and discomfort, the greater was one's chance of being admitted into the fold. [...] Here the currency was suffering and self-mortification" (*WM* 56). Abstention and detachment facilitate focus on the core of life and help to lead a meaningful life.

4.2.6. *Swaraj: Self Reliant Villages*

When one says India is the land of villages, people may imagine a romanticized greenish place. The concept of village in Sriram which is formed out of Tamil films (*WM* 67) is beautiful. Nevertheless, the reality is horrific. "Hungry, parched men and women with skin stretched over their bones, bare earth, dry ponds, and [...]. Sriram could hardly believe he was within twenty miles of Malgudi and civilization" (*WM* 69). Narayan presents the 'other India': the non-shining India. Gandhiji always has an empathetic heart towards the poor. Lohia says

"No matter to what part of the world one might go, one would find numberless people who look upon Gandhiji as the world's greatest symbol for resistance to oppression and injustice and solace in suffering, suffering that may have nothing to do with government and laws, suffering that may result out of the very fact of living."[48] Only a purified heart can love the poor who have nothing to return. "Mahatmaji had set out to study the famine conditions at first hand, and to put courage and hope into the sufferers. It was a grim, melancholy undertaking" (*WM* 68). Gandhiji lives as one among them. Indirectly the novel criticises the leaders of post-independent India who fail to provide hope to the poor. Gandhiji's life is always with the poor. "Bapu said his place was where people were suffering and not where they were celebrating" (*WM* 191). To serve them is a spiritual act.

Gandhiji envisages a self-sufficient village and it is called as trusteeship. "[...] village Swaraj is when it is a complete republic, independent of its neighbours for its vital wants [...]"[49] He recommends small scale industry because mechanization leads to the rule of a few. "Gandhiji had presented him with a spinning wheel in one of the villages with the explanation: 'This is the key to your future'" (*WM* 74). Charka is a symbol of hope and self-sufficiency. "We will spin the charka, wear khadi; live without luxury, and we shall have India ruled by Indians" (*WM* 88). India is blessed with natural resources but not to fulfil the greed of human beings. Spinning is not only an economic activity, but a self-actualization endeavour too. "[...] Khadi is or should be the symbol of its freedom, both economic and political. If it cannot be that, it is meaningless."[50] Work and worship are complimentary. Gandhiji places the spinning wheel next to the sacred books. He spiritualizes the outlook of life and charka.

In spite of this, India moves to industrialization and promotes exploitation. Narayan presents it humorously. The arrival of Gandhiji to Malgudi is celebrated as a commercial festival. Soda-water, cucumber, crescent lime dipped in salt, etc., become commodities for sale. The attitude of the timber-contractor is to make money at any cost and he is not at all interested in patriotism or independence. He does not want to cooperate with the *swadeshi* movement. Selfishness and greed lead to poverty and exploitation. Indians should be proud of their Indianness. Khadi and the spinning wheel become a matter of identity. Indians should take the pain to ensure the welfare of all. "I [Sriram] will never again wear clothes spun by machinery. The dhoti and jibba were heavy, it was as if a piece of lead were interwoven with the texture. But he felt it was something to be proud of. He felt he had seen and reached a new plane of existence" (*WM* 77). Narayan uses the term 'spin/ning/ner' for twenty-nine and 'spun' for six times respectively. The novel emphasises the concept of a self-sufficient village which is a part of Indian culture.

4.2.7. *Non-violence*

A country which attained independence through *ahimsa* ended up in violence. Religious fanaticism, regionalism, and political agitations caused a number of brutalities in post-independent period. In such a situation, *Waiting for the Mahatma* was written as a novel to promote non-violence. The story is the victory of non-violence over violence. Sriram joins Gandhian movements but later moves to violence. At last he comes back to Gandhism. Sriram is convinced by the Gandhian *marga* of truth. "It is our duty to propagate truth wherever it may be" (*WM* 120). Even though Gandhiji practised non-violence, along with independence incidents of violence and bloodshed are reported. "On the fifteenth of August when the whole country was jubilant, [...] do you know where Bapu was? In Calcutta where fresh riots had started" (*WM* 191). Gandhiji consoled the victims and remained with them with an empathetic heart. The power of the *satyagrahi* is proved at its toughest time. "We followed the Master through burning villages. [...] There were a few places where they showed their anger even against Mahatmaji [...]. But in such places he stayed longer than in other places. And ultimately he held his ground" (*WM* 192). A lot of children become refugees and the disciples of Gandhiji take care of them.

Gandhiji teaches the *mantra* of love which is his ultimate goal. "Before you aspire to drive the British from this country, you must drive every vestige of violence from your system. Remember that it is not going to be a fight with sticks and knives or guns but only with love. [...] You must gradually forget the term 'enemy'" (*WM* 60). Gandhiji wants Indians to move against the imperial rulers in peace. Since narrow chauvinism endangers the unity, Gandhiji taught to forgive the enemy. Narayan uses the word 'truth/ful' seventeen times in the novel to emphasize it. *Ahimsa* is the real ethos of India.

Even though the Indian democracy faced a lot of challenges and crises, the Gandhian discipline helped the country to settle down after independence. Mahatma Gandhi said: "I see before me a vast army. Every one of you has certain good points and certain defects, and you must all strive to discipline yourselves before we can hope to attain freedom for our country" (*WM* 19). To build-up a nation, everyone should be disciplined.

4.2.8. *Indianized Usages*

Narayan uses a wide-range of Indian vocabulary to feel the Malgudi-ness. Some of them are given in the Table 4.1. He gives importance to native language. "At the outset Mahatma Gandhi explained that he'd speak only in Hindi as a matter of principle. 'I will not address you in English. It's the language of our rulers. It has enslaved us'" (*WM* 19). The novel takes a radical view against English: "get the English out of India, as that venerable saint Mahatmaji explained untiringly" (*WM* 24). In his personal life, Narayan recommends three-language formula. The novel is written at a time when linguistic-based state are in debate and Telugu based state was formed in 1953. So the 'Sons of the soil' mentality is reflected through the influence of regional language.

In short, constant search for truth is a part of the Indian ethos. The whole life of Gandhiji is an experiment with truth that is constantly evolving with the experience. Accordingly, he is open to dialogue. *Waiting for the Mahatma* also adopts the style of dialogue. "Here, unlike Anand's Gandhi who appears as a legend, an oracle, the Mahatma stands in a dialogic relation with the people of Malgudi. [...] Narayan brings the image of Gandhi among diverse and contradictory elements, the image thus entering into various relationships with other life-positions, and the result is there for us to consider."[51] By the presentation of the ironic image of Gandhiji, the author portrays the Indian ethos like religious harmony, secularism, empowering the needy, *ahimsa*, and patriotism in the actual life of the common people. The author gives a vivid account of the impact of Gandhiji on the Indian masses both urban and rural. Sriram meets heterogeneous persons with varied outlooks. In the end, he is rooted in Gandhism. The novel envisages that Gandhism will become a style of thinking and living of Indians. It ensures that "there was no sense of fear where Mahatmaji was" (*WM* 192) and call all to 'be natural and truthful' (*WM* 196). Besides, it conveys confidence in nation building.

Table 4.1: Indian Vocabularies in *Waiting for the Mahatma*

Regional Words	No. of Times Used	Regional Words	No. of Times Used	Regional Words	No. of Times Used
ahimsa	2	Guru	4	puja	1
Anna/s	19	Halwa	2	Pulav	2
Ao	2	Idli/s	3	Pyol/s	5
badam	2	Ingeva (Tamil)	1	sadhaya	1
badmash	1	ji		sambar	1
beedis	2	jibba	6	Saree/s	11
Bhai	1	jutka	3	Satyagrahi/s	2
bhajan	3	karma	1	Shastras	4
Bonda	1	khaddar	15	sircar	3
Chappati/s	3	khadi	13	Sri	
Charka	5	Lathi	2	subedar	1
cholam	1	Lavani	1	Taluk	5
deepavali	2	Mahatma		Thali	2
dhoti	13	Mantra/s	2	Vadai	2
Dosai	1	Nai Dheheli	1	Vilas	2
Goondas	1	namaste	3	Zamindar	1
		nam	1		

4.3. Analysis of *Train to Pakistan* in the Light of the Post-independent Ethos

Pluralism is a lunar phase and partition is the dark phase of India. These two sides continuously influence the destiny of

India. So a constant analysis of both is needed. "Partition was the defining event of modern, independent India and Pakistan, and it is hardly an exaggeration to assert that partition continues to be the defining event of modern India and Pakistan even now after fifty years of independence."[52] Hence, it influences the ethos of independent India. On the one hand, the negative factors have been waning India and so many try to wax it on the other. Khushwant Singh is one among many who eulogizes the Indian ethos.

Train to Pakistan (1956), Singh's first novel, is an artistic narration of a village named Mano Majra which was ruined by the tempest of partition. Mano Majra is a small peaceful village on the border of Punjab in India through which a rail track goes to Lahore. The total equation of the village changes with the announcement of partition and Singh narrates the communal flare-up which can be considered as the microcosmic account of the brutal and violent incidents that happened at that time. All the chaos that happens in the novel is between late August and early September (*TP* 111) of 1947. The novel narrates one of the brutal episodes in the human history, in which around 12.5 million are displaced, and between 200,000 and 1000,000 die. The novel attempts to alleviate the sorrow of the Indian minds without blaming any community. It acclaims the Indian ethos of harmony and non-violence. N.D. Tank says that Mano Majra which is the primary symbol in the novel represents of the spirit of India herself—India, the land of *ahimsa*. Here the picture of unity in diversity is very well portrayed as the Hindus, Sikhs and Muslims live together peacefully since time immemorial.[53] Thus, the primary aim of the novel is not the narration of the tragic tale of the partition but to repaint the social harmony in the midst of cultural and ethnic mosaics. Indian sages continuously prayed for 'Santhi' (peace) in hymns and it is a goal of life in Indian ethos.

4.3.1. *Social Harmony*

Train to Pakistan projects social and religious harmony, which is the symphony of Indian culture. It conveys the ethos of deep relationship between Indians and promotes interethnic unity.

For this purpose, Singh selects a remote village, Mano Majra, a place of 'oasis of peace' (*TP* 10). It is a small village and the people lead a harmonious life irrespective of their belief and faith. Seventy families including the Sikhs, Muslims and Hindus live together and they are not aware of the consequence of the political partition of the country into two, based on religion. "The riots were confined mostly to the urban areas. The rural population, which comprises nearly 90 per cent of the total population of India, has always remained peaceful."[54] Coexistence of different ethnic and religious groups is the ethos of India. "Robbing a fellow villager is like stealing from one's mother" (*TP* 53).

Cultural pluralism is the identity of India and any attempt of homogenization will kill the unity of the nation. "A policy of integration, which discounts cultural pluralism and the composite character of Indian society and seeks to impose uniformity, homogenization and regimentation on the country's heterogeneous population, will ultimately prove to be self-defeating."[55] Multiculturalism is one of the prominent features of the Indian ethos which is formed out of multiethnic, multilingual, multi-religious, and multi-cultural ethos. The people have unity in diversity of race, caste, creed, and religion. Multiculturalistic Indian ethos inspires people to be open-minded and to respect the socio-cultural diversity.

The number of members in the family is also a sign of the relationship between people. In a big sized family, the members are collective rather than individualistic. "Iqbal thought of his first reaction on reaching Bombay. Milling crowds-millions of them—on the quayside, in the streets, on railway platforms; even at night the pavements were full of people. The whole country was like an overcrowded room" (*TP* 58). In the Indian culture, home is not only just the space under the roof but the whole village itself is a part of it. Home has an extended meaning in Indian culture which includes the local society and the geographical area. There are similarities in the outlook of the people. "The youth of the Punjab were as alike as the news. The qualities they required in a wife were identical" (*TP* 88). They share the same ethos and the spirit of oneness. "For them truth, honour, financial integrity were 'all right', but these were placed lower down the scale of values than being true to one's salt, to one's friends and fellow villagers" (*TP* 54). The mental agony of leaving the place without a word to the neighbours is heartbreaking for the Indian villagers who are bonded to the home, place, and people beyond religions.

One's native village is also an extension of the home. The place links horizontally with peer group and vertically with generations. Being uprooted from one's native village is extremely painful. "What have we to do with Pakistan? We were born here. So were our ancestors. We have lived amongst you as brothers. Imam Baksh broke down" (*TP* 147). The sense of family history and the attachment to the land are very powerful in Indian culture. Family and kinship are closely related with the place too. Singh paints the pain of the villagers who undergo the trauma and massacres that accompany the partition of the country. "Could they ask their Muslims to go? Quite emphatically not. Loyalty to a fellow villager was above all other considerations. Despite the words they had used, no one had the nerve to suggest throwing them out, even in a purely Sikh gathering" (*TP* 145). Attachment to the native village is part and parcel of one's existence. Moving away from the native village arouses such sentiments and emotions as that of the departure of one's parents.

The politics of the elite class is similar to imperialism but for the villagers rootlessness to one's land is the great loss. Nooran says: "Who will throw us out? This is our village" (*TP* 150). The poor girl does not understand or cannot accept the tragic event of going away from the village. "One should also not forget the emotional suffering of the refugees, forced to quit all of a sudden and forever the familiar scenes of childhood and youth or, maybe, of a lifetime."[56] Sentimentality of uprootedness may not be understood by those who dwell in flats that can be changed according to convenience.

The conversation between the Sikh and the Mussulman of Mano Majra on the previous night when the latter ones are going to a refugee camp is heart breaking. From all the nearby villages, all the Muslims are evacuated except Mano Majra.

However, the Sikhs do not want to leave their fellow Muslims and in turn, Muslims did not like to depart from Mano Majra. It was unimaginable for the Sikhs to ask the Muslims to vacate the village. The Sikhs love Muslims and are ready to die for their wives and children. "If anyone speaks rudely to you, your wives or your children, it will be us first and our wives and children before a single hair of your heads is touched" (*TP* 147). Since the villagers have been living harmoniously, they do not find any need for the partition. "It is a fact that millions of people on both sides of the new border refused to accept the finality of partition long after it was announced, and that is one major reason why the transfer of population became such a frenzied, last minute affair."[57] For the people, root breaking is heart breaking since all are attached to the home place.

The adieu scene at Mano Majra is filled with lachrymosity. "Imam Baksh [...] started to cry loudly. Sikh and Muslim villagers fell into each other's arms and wept like children" (*TP* 149). For the villagers', religious identity is never a hindrance to social harmony. At Mano Majra, the Muslims and the Sikhs live together for generations. Many believed that "they would only go to the refugee camp for a few days and then return" (*TP* 156). After the departure of the Muslims, even the deserted houses of Muslims arouse sadness in the Sikhs. In this regard, Anup Beniwal remarks: "The author in a nutshell seems to advocate the existence of a composite Punjabi identity which is more powerful than and subsumes within it the Sikhs and Muslim dichotomy. He however does not present it as a romantic idyll, sans problems and conflicts."[58] *Train to Pakistan* is primarily a story of harmonious life in a pluralistic society.

Above religious identity, people share Punjabiness. "Singers are neither Hindu nor Muslim in that way. All communities come to hear me" (*TP* 122). It is not the worship that creates the identity but the regional elements form the identity. "A person who has ethnic conscious does not believe in social discrimination on the basis of caste, race, religion, language and so on. Ethnic consciousness expects people of various faiths and religions to co-exist and live in peace and harmony."[59] Culture, values, relationships, etc., are shared and nourished for generations and help to form unity. "The large peepul tree in the middle" (*TP* 10) of the *gurdwara*, the mosque, and the house of Lala Ram Lal who is a Hindu is a symbol of the unity between religions and their cooperation. Another image used to express the unity of people in spirit is "the local deity, the *deo* to which all the villagers—Hindu, Sikh, Muslim or pseudo-Christian—repair secretly whenever they are in special need of blessing" (*TP* 10-11).

4.3.2. *The Root of Evil: Imperialism*

Singh never takes the side of the Hindu, the Muslim, or the Sikh but he indirectly blames imperial rule for the mass madness and fratricidal conflict. The five dacoits who come to Mano Majra crossing the river are a symbol of the whites who came to India through water. They are the 'professional robbers' (*TP* 14). The anonymous dacoits who are not from Mano Majra and who spark violence in the peaceful village, represent the colonizers who encourage enmity between different sectors of the country. "The colonial government's conciliatory policy towards the Muslim League bore fruit during the Second World War, and stiffened Mohammad Ali Jinnah's resolve to achieve his Muslim homeland."[60] The invisible evil sowed by the colonizers was greater than the visible atrocities.

On charge of the murder of Ram Lal, the Police arrest Iqbal who is in the field at the time of the crime. However, the accused is immature and acts imprudently in various situations like the Indian leaders who acted according to the capriciousness of the colonizers. The innocent represents the local leaders and people who are blamed for the partition and the acts of barbarity. The leaders act imprudently without vision, for power and that results in atrocities. Partition is not the result of a day but has a long history where colonizers give a religious identity to the parties. The basis of imperialism is 'othering' and the partition of India is the climax of the same. The communal-national binary at the cost of nationalism is the result of the policies of imperialists. "Unity was only a preference for the British, not a conviction for which they were willing to sacrifice anything, let alone their lives. They sat back and let civil war unfold, as it did not affect them directly."[61] The attitude of Hukum Chand, who is called as 'Government' represents the corrupt and indifferent bureaucracy of the imperial rule, reveals the attitude of the British before they leave India. 'Well, Inspector Sahib, let them kill,' said Hukum Chand wearily. 'Let everyone kill' (*TP* 177). The colonizers encourage the evil of chauvinism to such an extent that they themselves cannot control it.

On 20th February 1947, the British Prime Minister Attlee declared that the British Government would transfer power to Indians by June 1948 at the latest. However, it was Mountbatten who decided the date seeing the critical situations in India. The British wanted to wash their hands off the atrocities that were going to happen. "The British could escape responsibility for the rapidly deteriorating communal situation. [...] a hasty retreat was perhaps the most suitable action."[62] Everybody knows that the division can be avoided and the violence related to it. It is very clear from the date of announcing the boundaries between India and Pakistan, i.e. the next day of the independence on 16th August 1947. Lack of proper communication arouses unnecessary anxiety and the misleading orientation of the fundamentalists lead to massive violence and slaughter. "Incredible confusion, mayhem, and violence followed, because many people did not know whether their villages were now in Pakistan or India, and did not know in which direction they were to migrate."[63]

The police, who collectively represent the colonial rulers even though colonizers hand over the power, make radical mistakes. The oppressive attitude of the colonizers can be seen in the police. "They knew that they had made a mistake, or rather, two mistakes. Arresting the social worker was a blunder and a likely source of trouble. His belligerent attitude confirmed his innocence. Some sort of case would have to be made up against him" (*TP* 74). The police behave inhumanly to people even before they know who the real culprits are. Through the inhuman behaviour of the police, the brutality of the empirical force is exposed. In the colonial rule, "the police are the kings of the country" (*TP* 126). The religious fundamentalists are aware of the attitude of the police. Iqbal foresees the democratic rule in the country. "You made up the warrant in front of me.

This is not going to end here. The days of police rule are over. If you dare put your hands on me, the world will hear about it. I will see that the papers tell the people how you chaps do your duty" (*TP* 66). Iqbal speaks about the need to shift the colonial attitude to a democratic way of life.

4.3.3. *The Non-elite Class*

On 15th August 1947, colonialism politically marked its end but the undertone continues. Apart from the cultural colonization, the Indian elite class took the colonizers' place externally to a certain extent. "Yes, the Englishmen have gone but the rich Indians have taken their place" (*TP* 76). The 'mental make-up' (*TP* 87) of Indians has been framed by colonialism. Instead of democratic equality, colonial hierarchy is still followed in India. "If caste was abolished by legislation, it came up in other forms of class distinction" (*TP* 87). The poor remains poor and suffering is their fate. They are ignorant about the wider world. At the time of independence, there were Indians who were ignorant about the drastic political changes. Mano Majra is a typical village of India and the people have little knowledge "I am sure no one in Mano Majra even knows that the British have left and the country is divided into Pakistan and Hindustan. Some of them know about Gandhi but I doubt if anyone has ever heard of Jinnah" (*TP* 33). There was nothing new in their lives after independence. "Freedom is for the educated people who fought for it. We were slaves of the English, now we will be slaves of the educated Indians—or the Pakistanis" (*TP* 62). For the poor, satisfying the basic needs is more important than anything else.

The most tragic fact is that the villagers are not even aware of the partition which will affect them radically. The partition of India based on religion was unofficially accepted much before August in 1947. "Congress officially referred to partition in early March 1947 when a resolution was passed in the Congress Working Committee that Punjab (and by implication Bengal) must be partitioned if the country was divided."[64] The government failed to make the people conscious about it. That led to a great bafflement and the unscheduled stop of an east-bound train symbolizes this unawareness. No one in the village was aware of the 'ghost-train.' The elite took the decision of division, but the poor suffered. In a democracy, the leaders should feel with the suffered. Just after independence, India began to move away from the Gandhian principles. If Indian democracy neglects the poor and misuses freedom, the poor might state, "We were better off under the British" (*TP* 64). The gap between the rich and poor should be reduced. The novel stands for the equality of all and declares that the binary attitude of the imperial rulers should be annihilated.

4.3.4. *Socialism*

Socialism moved many great leaders of India and was deeply rooted in its ethos. "Democracy, in the Indian context, had to be associated with socialism."[65] The current trend is reflected in the novel too. Iqbal is a 'social worker' (*TP* 48) and belongs to the People's Party of India (*TP* 80). His proclaimed aim is to make the people ready to face the consequence of partition. Iqbal expresses his wish to organize the villagers. "We have to get together and rise. We have nothing to lose but these chains" (*TP* 76). However, he does not like to be called a villager. "I am not a villager. I come from Delhi" (*TP* 75). It throws light into his inner mind. His attitude is ironic even though Iqbal is presented as an active and dynamic person who dedicates his life for the poor and the unorganized, he is a failure in the end. The socialist's words are less supported by his actions. More than the upliftment of the poor, his basic motive is to become a leader. Hence, he attempts various means for the same. He is not ready to take pains for the people and 'dreaming of peaceful life in jail' (*TP* 65). He wishes to "start his political career by finding an excuse to court imprisonment" (*TP* 65). Regardless of his wish to be a political prisoner, he is arrested along with Jugga for the murder.

While bloodshed is going on and all the villages are suffering, Iqbal is waiting for a class revolution to help the people. "The stage had not arrived. The proletariat was indifferent to political freedom for Hindustan or Pakistan, except when it could be given an economic significance like grabbing land by killing an owner who was of a different religious denomination" (*TP* 65). The socialite speaks a lot about class and revolution without any action. Iqbal also looks for communal means to become famous. "All that could be done was to divert the kill-and-grab instinct from communal channels and turn it against the propertied class. That was the proletarian revolution, the easy way" (*TP* 65). In the end, the insincere nature of Iqbal becomes very explicit. When many are worried about the massacre that would happen at that night, he is worried about the publicity of his arrest. The socialist hypocrisy is revealed when Jugga comes to call Iqbal to help him to save the Muslim who is in the train.

Meet Singh whispers to Juggut, "Do not disturb him [...] He has been taking medicine to sleep" (*TP* 200). The medicine which Iqbal has taken is whisky and it is a short cut to get away from reality. "He [Hukum Chand] took another whisky and dismissed his conscience. Life was too short for people to have conscience" (*TP* 39). It shows that Iqbal likes to live in sleep and dreams (*TP* 65, 197). The sub-inspector's comment suits Iqbal: "It did seem unlikely that an educated man would risk his neck for any cause" (*TP* 183). Singh ironically presents Iqbal as a man of high ideologies but fails pathetically in its implementation.

4.3.5. *Regional Influence*

Khushwant Singh adapts the behavioural pattern social relationship, and vernacular linguistic usage to create Indianness in the novel. He makes use of a lot of regional usages to give a native taste to the novel. The style of English usage with a cultural flavour gives the reader the feeling of the Indian culture. Influence of Punjabi, Hindi, Arabic, and Urdu also can be seen in the novel. Some of them are highlighted in the Tables 4.2 and 4.3. Along with these linguistic features, the style of the conversation of the local people is reflected in the novel. The typical Indian style of conversation and intrusion in the individuality and activities of others can be seen in the dialogue between Iqbal and a passenger in a train (*TP* 52).

The conversation starts as if the passenger knows Iqbal for a long time. There is no self-introduction or greetings as per the English style, such as 'Good Morning' or 'Good After Noon.' For a foreigner, it may seem impolite or uncourteous. However, for an Indian, formality is a hindrance for an intimate relationship. Indian ethos gives much importance to relationship; so the interactions are more personal and intimate. It is because of the collective nature of the society. People take more freedom in others' matters. A lot of kinship words are used in the novel; for example, bhai/ji, sister/s, brother/s, father-in-law, father/s, grandmother, mother, and uncle are used 44, 10, 26, 37, 1, 54, 10 times respectively. The style of behaviour may be negatively viewed as the curiosity to know about others or unnecessary interference in others matters. Formalities are formed from the protocol or binary attitude of the west. A person with western education like Iqbal may be irritated by such interactions. For example, when the passenger asks 'what are you reading?' Iqbal gives a shallow and insignificant answer as he does not want to continue the conversation. But the passenger moves forward from that hollow reply. It reveals the collective ethos of the culture.

The novel acknowledges the deep-rooted influence of English on Indian culture. The language of the colonizer performs 'vital function' (*TP* 129) in the society. The villagers interpret even the freedom on the basis of knowledge about 'English'. "Freedom must be a good thing. [...] Educated people like you, Babu Sahib, will get the jobs the English had" (*TP* 62). The dialogue exposes two categories of Indians: the English-learned and the English-non-learned. The first group is considered as upper class because the colonized mind evaluates the colonizer's culture as great. Due to inferiority complex, the colonized considers English as a powerful language to convey a message. People use English words in between their vernacular language as a mark of gentle nature. "The girl started to sing a song which had several English words in it" (*TP* 40). They also consider 'English' as the sign of education. When Meet Singh sees that Iqbal is reading an English book, he concludes: "You must be educated" (*TP* 51).

To know even a little of the English language is considered a mark of social status. To learn one's 'own language' is not a 'pleasing suggestion' to the natives (*TP* 128). But at the end people are saved not by Iqbal, the English-learned, but by Jugga, the English-non-learned. Hence the novel has undone the civilization mission. "The use of nonstandard language in creoles and worldwide Englishes becomes a politico-ideological issue, connected with minority identities and cultural deprivation."[66] Singh also satirically presents the way Indians imitate the colonizer. Hukum Chand, The magistrate-cum-deputy commissioner, is from a middle-class family yet he blindly follows the Western styles. "The sub-inspector lit the magistrate's cigarette and then his own. Hukum Chand's style of smoking betrayed his lower-middle-class origin" (*TP* 29). The novel is a fight against the cultural deprivation and participates in the process of identity creation.

Table 4.2: Regional Usages from *Train to Pakistan*

Regional Words	No. of times used	Regional Words	No. of times used	Regional Words	No. of times used
Achha	2	'git mit'	1	naradmi	3
ajingle	1	golmohur	1	peepul	9
Anna/s	4	Haseen/a	14	punkah	7
Babu sahib	21	Hijra/s	6	Pye	1
Babu/ji	62	Huzoor	2	Pyjamas	7
Bairah	2	inspector sahib	25	rahu	1
Bhai/ji	44	Kalyug	3	Sahib	94
Budmash/a/i	27	Keekar/s	10	Salaam (peace be upon you; Arabic usage)	6
Chacha	4	khas	1	Sardar/a/s/ji	15
Charpoy/s	39	kirpans	1	Sat Sri Akal (God is truth)	37
		kraak	2	Shabash	2
Dakoo	3	lambardar	87		
deo	1	mausem	1	tamasha	1
dhak	2	Wah	15	Toba	9
		zulum	2	tonga	16

Table 4.3: The Native Influence in the Language

Usages with Regional Influence
you son of fornication (*TP* 16)
That incestuous lover of his sister (*TP* 25)
his hands were soiled with the blood of a fellow villager (*TP* 54)
you became a *naradmi*-a he-man who had defied authority (*TP* 54)
being true to one's salt (*TP* 54)
a snake can cast its slough but not its poison (*TP* 55)
This saying is worth a hundred thousand rupees. (*TP* 55)
how long can a snake keep straight? (*TP* 55)
The winds of destruction are blowing across the land (*TP* 64)
What seducer of his mother can throw bangles at me? (*TP* 72)
bad acts yield a bitter harvest? (*TP* 85; 143)
And didn't you see how that pig's penis spoke to Chacha? (*TP* 99)
but it is only the nimbus south-west winds of summer that make a mausem (*TP* 108)
The dose of salts gurgled down pleasantly (*TP* 113)
who kills a hen which lays eggs? (*TP* 125)
you son of pig (*TP* 136)
They have been eating our salt for generations (*TP* 144)
What honourable noun does your honour bear? (*TP* 52) (means: 'what is your name)
Where does your wealth reside, Babu Sahib? (*TP* 53) (means: where is your home)
Cherisher of the poor (*TP* 37, 77, 79-80, 181)
King of Pearls (*TP* 90, 92)
May your fame and honour increase. May your pen write figures of thousands and hundreds of thousands (*TP* 37)
May you ever rule. May your pen write hundreds of thousands. May... (*TP* 38)
Pigeon-kabootur, oodan-fly (*TP* 129)
Look-dekho, usmatl-sky (TP 129)
Chakravartyrajagopalachari (TP 109).
'Teet-tittee-tittee-whoot, tee-tee-whoot, tee-tee-whoot, tit-tittee-whoot' (*TP* 25) (the sound of lapwing)
sala, wife's brother. ("I would like to sleep with your sister") (*TP* 127)
susra, father-in-law ("I would like to sleep with your daughter") (*TP* 127)

4.3.6. *Humanistic Religion*

In the midst of religious fundamentalism, *Train to Pakistan* presents a humanistic religion. The novel begins with the narration of the brotherly coexistence of the "three brick buildings enclose a triangular common with a large peepal tree in the middle" (*TP* 10). The three buildings represent three religions, namely Hindu, Muslim and Sikh. Even though each religion has its own identity, there is a common uniting divine spirit above the individualistic religiosities. Religion and faith are part of their ethos. "Their [Hindus and Musalmans] past is imbedded in their religion, and for each to give up its past is to give up its religion. To hope for this is to hope in vain."[67] Respecting others' religion is a part of the culture of Mano Majra. The addresser uses the greeting verses of the person whom s/he addresses as a part of high regard to the addressed. Sikhs salute Muslims with 'Salamm' and Muslims greet Sikhs with 'Sat Sri Akal' (*TP* 146, 152-53). The novel gives due importance to the real spirit of religion. It uses the phrase 'Sat Sri Akal' (God is truth) 37 times. Gandhiji is considered as a model of being receptive to other religions. The novel describes a community with high-level purified religious consciousness and the villagers have a common identity, which is above religion. The partition which is caused by religious fundamentalism is the clear profanation of the sacred. "An unbiased study of contemporary history will show that it was not religious feeling itself but extraneous elements which had become associated with religion, and the vested interests which used the name of religion for their own purpose, that started the separatist movement culminating in the partition of the country."[68] Religious harmony is a sign of the true spirit of religion.

In the first part of the story, Jugga is not a religious person. But at the end Jugga takes inspiration from the Guru. It shows that the true religion can inspire people for self-sacrifice for the good of others. Thus apart from communalism, the novel portrays the true meaning of religion. The novel is a true search to find the inner meaning of religion. "If religion gets dissociated from culture, imbalances in society would take place. At the same time, if culture is dissociated from religious fundamentalism, culture would become more secular."[69] The Indian secularism facilitates the spiritual journey and at the same time it keeps itself from the danger of religious fundamentalism. "The Indian democratic system too has succeeded admirably in not being guided by organized religions or listening to the voices of temples or mosques in polity management. It is equally significant that spirituality has sustained India's culture and helped ensure its continuity."[70] True religion can provide substantial contribution and the novel calls for religious reconstruction.

4.3.7. *Lamentable Discord*

'Until yesterday' (*TP* 148) everything was entirely different. But 'today' "the head constable's visit had divided Mano Majra into two halves as neatly as a knife cuts through a pat of butter" (*TP* 141). The cacophony of the catastrophe is heard from all around. People begin to flee and there is a lot of confusion. "The same thing was repeated again and again, till the compartment meant for fifty had almost two hundred people in it, sitting on the floor, on seats, on luggage racks, on trunks, on bedrolls, and on each other, or standing in the corners. There were dozens outside perched precariously on footboards, holding on to the door handles. There were several people on the roof" (*TP* 51-52). Famine has reached its peak. The most inhuman atrocities take place. One among the suffered states that "During about half this period there were on an average six deaths daily-mostly old people and infants."[71] Those who are friendly neighbours and lived peacefully become enemies and a deep chasm is created in their relationship. Everyone 'felt wretched' (*TP* 204) about the Partition of India. "The dawn of Indian independence was marred by massacres and migrations in the Punjab on a scale unparalleled in world history in time of peace."[72] The minds of people are filled with vengeance and all act in retaliation.

The entire law and order collapses and the officials have no means to solve it. The riots and killings go out of our control. "There is darkness over the land" (*TP* 115). The number of murders in one incident of massacre itself is reported: "fifteen hundred innocent people" (*TP* 115). It is impossible to count the number of the dead. People behave like animals and they kill each other. Many innocent people are victimized and brutally torn apart, bodies of the dead are simply burned, and the saddest situation is narrated in the novel. "A soft breeze began to blow towards the village. It brought the smell of burning kerosene, then of wood. And then—a faint acrid smell of searing flesh. The village was stilled in a deathly silence" (*TP* 100). Melancholy fills in the air. In other words, it can be described as 'Kalyug' and the word is used three times in the novel (*TP* 53, 96, 115).

Since the mob turns against women, their condition became worse. Violence and abuse cause terrible physical and emotional torture. Nooran the heroine represents the suffering of all the women who suffer due to partition. The pain of partition still continues. Ambedkar points out "I am sure burying Pakistan is not the same thing as burying the ghost of Pakistan. So long as the hostility to one Central Government for India, which is the ideology underlying Pakistan, persists, the ghost of Pakistan will be there, casting its ominous shadow upon the political future of India."[73] Though Pakistan is separated, the ghost still remains.

4.3.8. *Hope: Beyond Partition*

Train to Pakistan is not a partition novel but a reconciliation novel. The partition remains in the background to open the eyes of chauvinistic personalities. "Behind every holocaust there lies the birth of a new generation. Khushwant Singh has the affirmative assumption of a birth of a harmonious human society of India overriding religious, linguistic and caste divisions."[74] The novel is a fight between hope and hopelessness; ghost-train and hope-train. It brings out the ironic reversal of an anti-hero, Jugga, who becomes a noble-hero. It is a transformation story. Jugga who is considered as budmash by the society, is turned into a martyr of love. Singh projects that often the noblest acts of generosity and self-sacrifice are from the persons who are looked down by the people as immoral deviants[75] and illiterate. Jugga is a criminal. "[Juggut Singh's] name was entered in register number ten and he was officially declared a man of bad character" (*TP* 75). However, when religion, law, and ideologies fail, the romantic love between Jugga and Nooran succeed in saving the lives of many innocents. "The engine was almost on [Jugga]. There was a volley of shots. The man shivered and collapsed. The rope snapped in the centre as he fell. The train went over him, and went on to Pakistan" (*TP* 207).

The train, which regulates the time and life of Mano Majra 'until the summer of 1947' (*TP* 14), is a powerful symbol in the novel. As the novel develops, the nature of the train also changes. The train that seems to be very neutral in the beginning, shifted to ghost-train as the flames of communal violence increase. "Ghost trains went past at odd hours between midnight and dawn, disturbing the dreams of Mano Majra" (*TP* 93). The irregularity of trains in the second phase represents the disorder and mess. "There are no lights on the train. The engine did not whistle. It is like a ghost" (*TP* 163). However, at the end it turns into hope-train that moves to new horizons carrying the beloved to nurture new life.

The horrific violence in the aftermath of the partition is another challenging face of the independence struggle. It has been continuing as a process of re-ordering of national identities of the newly erected nations: India and Pakistan. In spite of that, the novel narrates the harmonious pro-existence which is a part of Indian ethos. Here Pakistan is seen as the life partner or a child, which is the most intimate relationship in human society.

The ultimate call of the novel after seven years of victimization of partition is that the uprooted people of India could go back to a state of peaceful village life as before the incident. In other words, Nooran may be able to return to Mano Majra to cherish the romance and nurture the spirit of sacrifice in the unborn child of Jugga. Yet even today, Indians do not come out of the high politics of communalism and colonization which lead to the enmity of brothers and sisters. It has been continuing as a process of nationalizing the nations. In order to build-up a new hegemonic national identity the Indians have projected Pakistanis as the Other, the extreme antagonist, and vice versa. "For each trainload of dead they send over, send two across. For each road convoy that is attacked, attack two. That will stop the killing on the other side. It will teach them that we can also play this game of killing and looting" (*TP* 171). The binary attitude of the old colonizers still rules the minds of the colonized. Instead of sending bogies loaded with mutilated bodies, Singh sends bogies of sacrifice and love. "His [Jugga] soul, like that of the phoenix, rises from its ashes only to proclaim that at least this 'Train to Pakistan' is a symbol of hope and light amidst the cruel world of darkness and despair."[76] The altruistic act may restart the flow of warmth of harmony beyond any political boundary. Generations may praise the greatest self-sacrifice of Jugga who becomes the embodiment of love. The chance for repentance is always open to all. 'To err is human, to forgive divine' (*TP* 185). The novelist also endorses the goodness in every human being. "The novelist succeeds in showing the supremacy of love and finer human qualities over communalism and brutality."[77] The novel foresees a bright future when the hegemonic powers and fundamentalists in India and Pakistan would repeat the words of the sub-inspector: 'I admit my mistake' (*TP* 185). The novel provides hope for unity beyond partition.

In short, *Train to Pakistan* which was set in 1947 in the backdrop of Indian partition holocaust is a classic saga of pro-existence. The novelist depicts the positive and negative forces of Indian ethos of the particular horrific situation not to blame any one of the community but to highlight the cordial relationship and interaction, which they have. "We will defend you with our lives" (*TP* 148). Hence, the novel is a dialogical novel that inspires the Hindu and the Muslim communities to enter into dialogue. Even though India and Pakistan are politically separated, culturally they are still united. The novel establishes that Indians and Pakistanis are brothers and sisters. The novel proclaims the Indian ethos of unity in diversity.

More than land, the partition cripples the ethos of inter-ethnic unity of India. Even the remote harmonious village, which is initially not disturbed by violence, at last immerses in the religious hyper consciousness. "Partition was a major political as well as a civilizational failure."[78] The pain of the victims should be healed for peaceful existence of humanity and cosmos, with the positive energy of love. The proverb, 'No fool like an old fool' (*TP* 200), is applicable to nations too. As India and Pakistan pass through the ages, they should realize that without solving the issue there cannot be a peaceful existence for both. "What is important is not the winning of independence but having the sure means of maintaining it."[79] The novel highlights the Indian ethos of harmonious pro-existence of different religious ethnic groups.

Notes

1. A.P.J. Abdul Kalam, *India 2020: A Vision for the New Millennium.* Y.S. Rajan (ed.) (New Delhi: Penguin Books, 1998), p. 22.
2. Balmiki Prasad Singh, *India's Culture: The State, the Arts, and Beyond* (India: Oxford University Press, 2011), p. 232.
3. *Ibid.*, p. xxv.
4. Donald Eugene Smith, *India as a Secular State* (1963) (New Jersey: Princeton Press, 1967), p. 140.
5. M.K. Gandhi, *Socialism of My Conception.* Anand T. Hingorani (ed.) (Bombay: Bharatiya Vidya Bhavan, 1957), p. 1.
6. Ludden David, "India's Development Regim." Nicholas B. Dirksed (ed.) *Colonialism and Culture* (USA: The University of Michigan, 1992), p. 277.
7. B.R. Ambedkar, "The Indian Constitution Defended and Interpreted." Ramachandra Guha (ed.) *Makers of Modern India* (New Delhi: Penguin Books, 2010), p. 321.
8. W.H. Morris Jones, "India's Political Idioms." Thomas R. Metcalf (ed). *Modern India: An Interpretive Anthology* (America: The MacMillan Company, 1971), p. 279.
9. Shashi Tharoor, *India: From Midnight to the Millennium* (India: Penguin Books, 1997), p. 29.
10. M.N. Das, "Political Thought of Jawaharlal Nehru." Indira Gandhi Abinandan Samiti. *The Spirit of India.* Vol: II (New York: Asia Publishing House, 1976), p. 366.
11. *Ibid.*, p. 365.
12. Jayaprakash Narayan, "A Plea for Political Decentralization" (1959). Ramachandra Guha (ed.) *Makers of Modern India.* 2010. (New Delhi: Penguin Books, 2012), p. 408.
13. Isabelle Milbert, "Building the Economy: 1947-1980" Christophe Jaffreloted. *India Since 1950: Society, Politics, Economy and Culture.* (New Delhi: Yatra Books, 2012), p. 90.

14. J.K. Bajaj, "Chowdhary Charan Singh and the Politics of Independent India." Anand Amaladass (ed.) *Political Thinkers of India* (Chennai: Satya Nilayam Publications, 1998), p. 114.
15. Raj Kumar, *Encyclopaedia of Untouchables Ancient, Medieval and Modern* (Delhi: Kalpaz Publications, 2008), p. 392.
16. Gurcharan Das, *India Unbound: From Independence to the Global Information Age.* 2000 (New Delhi: Penguin Books, 2002), p. 142.
17. Vani Xaxa, "Globalization, Culturalism and Mass Media." *Women's Link* 15.2 April-June 2009.
18. Vina Mazumader, "Women: From Equality to Empowerment." Hiranmay Karlekar (ed.) *Independent India: The First Fifty Years* (Delhi: Oxford University Press, 1998), p. 260.
19. T.K. Oommen, "Citizenship and National Identity in India: Towards a Feasible Linkage" T.K. Oommen (ed.) *Citizenship and National Identity: From Colonialism to Globalism* (New Delhi: Sage Publications, 1997), p. 147.
20. Koenraad Elst, *Decolonizing the Hindu Mind* (New Delhi: Rupa & Co., 2001), p. 508.
21. Deccan Herald, "Defining Indianness: Multiple Voices." Assessed: 4th September 2013. <http://www.deccanherald.com/content/171602/defining-indianness.html>
22. Vaugier-Chatterjee Anne, "Sikhs: Between Integration and Separatism." Christophe Jaffreloted (ed.) *India Since 1950: Society, Politics, Economy and Culture* (New Delhi: Yatra Books, 2012), p. 291.
23. Nicholas B. Dirks, "Introduction: Colonialism and Culture." Nicholas B. Dirks (ed.) *Colonialism and Culture* (USA: The University of Michigan, 1992), p. 5.
24. K.N. Panikkar, *Colonialism, Culture and Resistance.* 2007 (New Delhi: Oxford: Oxford University Press, 2009), p. 52.
25. M.N. Das, "Political Thought of Jawaharlal Nehru." Indira Gandhi Abinandan Samiti. *The Spirit of India.* Vol. II (New York: Asia Publishing House, 1976), pp. 365-66.
26. K.M. Panikkar, *The State and the Citizen* (Bombay: Asia Publishing House, 1956), p. 28.
27. Omvedt Gail, *Dalits and the Democratic Revolution: Dr. Ambedkar and the Dalit Movement in Colonial India* (New Delhi: Sage Publications, 1994), p. 226.

28. Hardiman Davi, *Gandhi in his Time and Ours* (Columbia: Columbia University Press, 2003), p. 198.
29. Sravani Biswas, "The Dialogic Imagination in R.K. Narayan's *Waiting for the Mahatma*: A Bakhtinian Analysis" M.K. Bhatnagar, *New Insights into The novel of R K Narayan* (New Delhi: Atlantic Publishers and Distributors (P) Ltd., 2008) p. 125.
30. Chandra Bipan, *India Since Independence* (New Delhi: Penguin Group, 2008), p. 4.
31. "Draft Constitution of the Congress," 29 January 1948, *The Collected Works of Mahatma Gandhi.* Vol. 90, p. 527 (hereafter CWMG).
32. Stein Burton, *The History of India* (Oxford: Oxford University Press, 1998), p. 369.
33. Nicholas B. Dirks, "Introduction." Nicholas B. Dirks (ed.) *Colonialism and Culture* (United States of America: The University of Michigan Press, 1992), p. 23.
34. James C. Scott, *Domination and the Arts of Resistance: Hidden Transcripts* (New Haven: Yale University Press, 1990), p. xii.
35. Rameshwar Gupta, "The Gandhi in Narayan." Ram Atma (ed.) *Perspectives on R.K. Narayan* (Ghaziabad: Vimal Prakashan, 1981), p. 51.
36. P.S. Ramana, *Message in Design: A Study of R.K. Narayan's Fiction* (New Delhi: Harman Publishing House, 1993), p. 46.
37. Indira Gandhi, *Two alone, Two together: Letters between Indira Gandhi and Jawaharlal Nehru 1922-1964.* Sonia Gandhi (ed.) (New Delhi: Penguin Books, 2005), p. 217.
38. Ajit Bhattacharjea, *Jayaprakash Narayan: A Plitical Biography* (Delhi: Vikas Publishing House, 1975), pp. 46-47.
39. *Ibid.*, p. 45.
40. David Hardiman, *Gandhi in his Time and Ours* (Columbia: Columbia University Press, 2003), p. 198.
41. Walsh William, *R.K. Narayan: A Critical Appreciation* (Great Britain: University of Chicago Press, 1982), pp. 86-94.
42. Sravani Biswas, *A Study of R K Narayan's Novels: A Celebration of the Carnival* (New Delhi: Atlantic Publishers and Distributors (P) Ltd., 2010), p. 87.
43. CWMG: LXIV, "*Message to the All-India Women's Conference.*" Sent before 23 December, 1936, p. 165.

44. Balmiki Prasad Singh, *India's Culture: The State, the Arts, and Beyond* (India: Oxford University Press, 2011), p. xlvi.
45. B.R. Ambedkar, "Gandhism: The Doom of the Untouchable." Valerian Rodrigues (ed.) *The Essential Writings of B.R. Ambedkar* (New Delhi: Oxford University Press, 2002), p. 171.
46. David Hardiman, *Gandhi in his Time and Ours* (Columbia: Columbia University Press, 2003), p. 295.
47. Tripti Tiwary, "R.K. Narayan's Waiting for the Mahatma: A Reappraisal." *Indian Scholar* 3.2 (1981): 79-87, p. 86.
48. Rammanohar Lohia, *Marx, Gandhi and Socialism* (Hyderabad: Navahind, 1963), p. 121.
49. CWMG: LXXVI, "Village Swaraj." *Harijan* 26th July 1942, p. 308.
50. CWMG: XXVII, "Harijan," 21st July 1946. p. 308.
51. Sravani Biswas, *A Study of R.K. Narayan's Novels: A Celebration of the Carnival.* (New Delhi: Atlantic Publishers and Distributors (P) Ltd., 2010), p. 87.
52. Gerald James Larson, *India's Agony over Religion* (Delhi: Oxford University Press, 1997), p. 182.
53. N.D. Tank, "The Trauma of Partition in *Train to Pakistan* by Khushwant Singh and the Foreign Aggression and Its Impact on Indian Politics in *Shadow from Ladakh* By Bhabani Bhattacharya." Web page: 2011. Accessed: 1st June 2013 <www.shodhganga.inflibnet.ac.in/bitstream/10603/2301/.../07_chapter%202.pdf>
54. Gopal Das Khosla, "Stern Reckoning: A Survey of the Events Leading up to and Following the Partition of India." *The Partition Omnibus* (New Delhi: Oxford University Press, 2002), p. 5.
55. A.R. Momin, "Interface of Cultural Identity Development: Cultural Pluralism, National Identity and Development, The Indian Case." Web page. Accessed: 4th September 2013. (New Delhi: Indira Gandhi National Centre for the Arts, 1996), <http://ignca.nic.in/ls_03016.htm>
56. Penderel Moon, "Divide and Quit: An Eyewitness Account of the Partition of India." *The Partition Omnibus* (New Delhi: Oxford University Press, 2002), p. 259.
57. Bipan Chandra & et al., *India's Struggle for Independence* (New Delhi: Penguin Books, 1989), p. 502.

58. Anup Beniwal, *Representing Partition, History, Violence and Narration* (Delhi: Shakti, 2005), p. 33.
59. Grishma Manikrao Khobragade, "Reflection of Multiculturalism in Khushwant Singh's *Train to Pakistan*." *Galaxy: International Multidisciplinary Research Journal* 2.2. Accessed: March 2013.
60. Mushirul Hasan, "Partition Narratives: Introduction." *The Partition Omnibus* (New Delhi: Oxford University Press, 2002), p. xi.
61. Sucheta Mahajan, *Independence and Partition: The Erosion of Colonial Power in India* (New Delhi: Sage Publications, 2000), p. 386.
62. *Ibid.*, p. 386.
63. "Train to Pakistan 2007: Decolonization, Partition, and Identity in the Transnational Public Sphere." Accessed: 1st June 2013. <www.temple.edu/tempress/chapters_1800/1958_ch1>
64. Bipan Chandra & et al., *India's Struggle for Independence* (New Delhi: Penguin Books, 1989), p. 501.
65. M.N. Das, "Political Thought of Jawaharlal Nehru." *The Spirit of India.* Vol. II. Indira Gandhi Abinandan Samiti (New York: Asia Publishing House, 1976), p. 366.
66. Taavitsainen Irma and Gunnel Melchers, "Writing in nonstandard English: Introduction." Irma Taavitsainen and et al. (ed.) *Writing in nonstandard English* (USA: John Benjamins Publishing Company, 1999), p. 21.
67. B.R. Ambedkar, *Pakistan or The Partition of India* (Bombay: Thacker & Communication. Ltd., 1946), p. 19.
68. S. Abid Husai, *The National Culture of India* (India: Asia Publishing House, 1961), p. 9.
69. Balmiki Prasad Singh, *India's Culture: The State, the Arts, and Beyond* (India: Oxford University Press, 2011), p. xxvi.
70. *Ibid.*, p. xxxiv.
71. Penderel Moon, "Divide and Quit: An Eyewitness Account of the Partition of India." *The Partition Omnibus* (New Delhi: Oxford University Press, 2002), p. 258.
72. *Ibid.*, p. 7.
73. B.R. Ambedkar, *Pakistan or The Partition of India* (Bombay: Thacker & Communication Ltd., 1946), p. xix.
74. Moirangthem Linthoingambi Devi, "Multiculturalism and Conflict in Khushwant Singh's *Train to Pakistan*." *Journal of*

Literature, Culture and Media Studies. III. 5-6 (2011). Accessed 31st May 2013.

75. Harish Raizada, ""*Train to Pakistan*": A Study in Crisis of Values", R.K. Dhavan (ed.) *Commonwealth Fiction,* Vol. 1 (New Delhi: Classical Publishing Company, 1988), p. 167.
76. Vasant A. Shahare, "Theme, Title and Structure in Khushwant Singh's *Train to Pakistan* and Chaman Nahal's *Azadi.*" *The Literacy Criterion* 25.2 (1990), pp. 58-66.
77. N.D. Tank, "The Trauma of Partition in *Train to Pakistan* by Khushwant Singh and *The Foreign Aggression and Its Impact on Indian Politics in Shadow from Ladakh* by Bhabani Bhattacharya." Web: 2011. Accessed on: 1st June 2013. <www.shodhganga.inflibnet.ac.in/bitstream/10603/2301/.../07_chapter%202.pdf>
78. Balmiki Prasad Singh, *India's Culture: The State, the Arts, and Beyond* (India: Oxford University Press, 2011), p. lxiv.
79. B.R. Ambedkar, *Pakistan or The Partition of India* (Bombay: Thacker & Communication Ltd., 1946), p. xix.

5

Literary Representation of the Indian Ethos during De/re-democratization Phase

CHAPTER OUTLINE

5.1. De/re-democratization Phase

Ups and downs, crossroads and challenges are natural on the way to progression of any nation. Independent India is not an exception to this general phenomenon. Even though India could be proud about many remarkable achievements, the downturns in various areas hit the development. The frustration of deterioration was gradually over reflected in the public. The phase can be called de-democratization because though democracy commenced with great zeal various hazards weakened the democracy and the unity of the nation. Its climax was the declaration of the State of Emergency on 26th June 1975, a period of political depression. Many regretted "that a great experiment had come to an end—the experiment of India's development within a pluralist democratic framework."[1] There were personal, political, social and economic reasons for the declaration of the national emergency. However, it was not an end forever. In 1977, as democracy got the upper hand the period can be called a time of re-establishment of democracy. The phase can be called de/re-democratization and the period extended from 1975 to 1990.

During the period, India faced a lot of crises and spent enormous amount of energy to solve the conflicts. First of all, there was an economic crisis. It began to form in the 1960s and continued in 70s and 80s. Instead of a liberation policy, the government adopted the policy of mixed economy. With the socialistic influence, the public sector got prominence and took many strategies to overcome the crisis. On 19th July 1969, the government issued the Banking Companies' Acquisition and Transfer of Undertaking Ordinance. Even though along with many other programmes, fourteen largest banks that had 85 per cent of the bank deposits of the nation were nationalized, the country could not overcome the financial crisis. The low development, lack of employment opportunities, and difference between the rich and the poor affected the peace and unity of the country. Chowdhary Charan Singh, one of the Prime Ministers of the period commented of the early 1980s, "we have failed most conspicuously in the matter of food. Today, towards the end of 1990s, the failure looks even graver, because during the last twenty years many of the so-called developing countries of the world have advanced much farther, both in agriculture as well as industry."[2]

The second major challenge was the political instability of the period. After the death of Nehru, there was a lack of leadership in the country. Later Indira Gandhi was selected by the Congress Party to lead the country. "In her, the party chose a leader who had shared the vision and ideology of Jawaharlal Nehru, and who would carry forward his mission of building a modern, progressive, and prosperous India, which would be a force for world peace."[3] In 1977, Mrs. Gandhi was out through the election and a coalition government came into power but the Janata Government of 1977 could not make a stable government. It failed to have well-defined economic priorities and there was not much deviation from the Mrs. Gandhian policies. They could not come up as an alternative to the Congress.

The third obstacle faced by India was religious fundamentalism and regionalism. By the rise of various extremists like Muslim and Hindu fundamentalists, the Nehruvian secular consensus began to breakdown. Communal riots took place in different parts of the country like, Aligarh (1978), Jamshedpur (1979) and many other places. Later, Hindu fundamentalists came up with the Ayodhya issue and the general election of 1989 was explicitly coloured with communalism. The Sikhs extremists also stood for a separate sovereign nation with the unifying identity of religion. Both religious fundamentalism and regionalism were involved in it. It had predominantly grown from the partition of 1947. In the 1980s, it reached its aggressive form and culminated in the assassination of Mrs. Gandhi. As a response to it, 800 Sikhs were killed in anti-Sikh riots in 1984. Another regional issue raised was in North-East India and it claimed for a Greater Assam. The seven states found themselves in great difficulty in being loyal to the Indian Nation which has formed out of Aryan-Dravidian culture. Guerrilla attacks and mass agitations became very common in the region. The United Liberation Front of Assam (ULFA) which was formed on 7th April 1979 claimed for a separate nation and in 1990 the Government of India banned it on the basis of its terrorist nature. Another regional organization was the Nationalist Socialist Council of Nagaland (NSCN) which stood for a separate Naga nation. Moreover, regional parties also emotionally participated in these movements to secure votes. "Yet, defining Indianness has become more important than ever, as India experiences separatist movements all throughout its territories."[4] It was at the brink of a breakdown.

The fourth major threat of India was the corruption and criminalization of politics. Widespread corruption in all realms of Indian democracy had been one of the major negative forces which vexed the development and functioning of the Government of India. In certain situations the so-called public servants became public promoters of corruption. In 1985, Rajiv Gandhi remarked, "corruption is not only tolerated but even regarded as the hallmark of leadership."[5] The elected representatives should be ideal but many who are elected are from criminal background. This situation adversely affected the just functioning of the Legislature, the Executive, and judiciary.

The fifth major problem was the oppression of the downtrodden people including the lower caste as well as the women. The evils related to the caste system continued, not only the suffering of the lower caste but also the rise of casteism. "The study also reveals the strange paradox that the caste is getting stronger and weaker at the same time. Caste at the level of endogamy is generally not breaking down. Members feel a strong sense of solidarity when it is a question of mutual benefit."[6] The caste consciousness and activities to attain a political goal led to the formation of casteism. Caste has begun to function as a political pressure group with narrow vision only for the benefits of a particular community instead of a wider perspective of nationalism. Another category, which was the most neglected group in India was women. In the patriarchal society, women were subjugated both in and out of the house. Modern India viewed women not with the vision of her integral development but as a means to reduce population. Commenting on the report of the Committee on the Status of Women in India

(1974-77) Vina wrote, "The growing emphasis on population control highlighted women's reproductive rather than their productive roles, influencing a 'populationist' approach to women's development needs."[7] The women policies should be framed with pro-woman attitude.

Without being disintegrated, India continued its journey in the midst of these challenges. India experimented many solutions to overcome various crises. First of all the nation was to attain the whole hearted participation of all the citizens in the process of nation building. Just after independence, a mass of people who suffered under colonial rule, remembered only their rights. Hence, they failed to remind the citizens about their duties. Through the Forty Second Amendment (The Constitution Act, 1976), the Fundamental Duties were incorporated in the Constitution for orienting the citizens to contribute to the development of the country. Secondly, to promote equality among the citizens, the nation promoted socialism and the word was included in the Constitution. It emphasized the need to be committed more in justice in socio-economic and political fields. The Representation of the People Act of 1989 compelled all the political parties to include 'socialism' as one of the objectives. When Swatantrata Party failed to align socialism with their principles, the Election Commission rejected the party. It highlights, that the state should stand for the welfare of all the citizens.

Thirdly, to overcome the religious fundamentalism and regionalism, the government emphasized the ethos of secularism and national integrity. The word 'secular' was also incorporated in the constitution to resist the growth of religious fundamentalism. Since, India was threatened by regionalism, the phrase 'unity of the nation' was modified to 'unity and integrity of the nation.' Thus, according to the signs of time India gives more emphasize to certain elements of ethos. Fourthly, to overcome the economic crisis, India began to move to liberalization policy. In the economic and technical field, the first step for radical change was initiated by Rajiv Gandhi. In his time, India was searching for a solution in the total darkness of political and economic crises. His period was a bridge between nationalization and liberalization, in other words the threshold of neo-liberal period. "[Narasimha Rao] watched Rajiv Gandhi's modest attempts at reform in the 1980s. Even these small efforts had yielded significant benefits."[8]

The de/re-democratization phase was a period of transition from degeneration to re-generation of Indian democracy. It was a period of tribulation for the nation and its democratic existence was questioned due to economic crisis, communalism, regionalism, political instability, and corruption. The undemocratic events of the phase paved the way for a deep evolution in the functioning of the democracy in India. "The period of the National Emergency can be defined as a crucial historical watershed that marked the beginning of Indian intellectuals' reassessment of the meaning of Indian democracy and its achievements, of the postcolonial stage."[9] At the time, Indian democracy was pictured as a failure and may be the darkest period in the history of independent India. Proper democracy is needed for the self-fulfilment of each individual and discipline without free thinking is like a house without love. Amongst all these challenges, India was unified in spirit. Mrs. Gandhi herself said, "Despite many difficulties and contrary to certain predictions, the country has not broken into warring states. We have not succumbed to civil anarchy. [...] This does not justify complacency but it does give us confidence that the Indian people can rise to whatever challenge the future may hold."[10] Even in the midst of all the troublesome catastrophes, India was united by its strong ethos which is the underlined linking principle. India continues to dance to the tune of democracy and even a minute disturbance will disturb its rhythm.

Indian English writers also responded to the situation and oriented the people about the need to respond creatively to build the nation. They used satire and allegory to criticize the personalities who misused power. They presented social evils and sufferings of the people for upholding the democracy. Some of the novels which were written during this period that highlight the political scenario of India are, Salman Rushdie's *Midnight's Children* (1981) and *The Satanic Verses* (1988);

Amitav Ghosh's *The Shadow Lines* (1988); Shashi Tharoor's *The Great Indian Novel* (1989). Though Rohinton Mistry's *A Fine Balance* was published in 1996, it also deals with the suffering of people from 1975 to 1984 and the story is set in Bombay. The novels selected for the analysis are *Midnight's Children* and *The Great Indian Novel.* Both novels depict the decadence of Indian democracy and debasement of the leaders. At the same time, they are powerful as stars which guide the fisherman to the shore. They can empower Indians to embrace Indianness in all their endeavours. The novels enkindle the Indian hearts to be faithful to Indian ethos and the development of the nation.

5.2. Analysis of *The Great Indian Novel* in the Light of the De/re-democratization Ethos

5.2.1. *Re-reading of India*

Since India is a complex reality the multiplicity of its nature cannot be easily comprehended. Varieties of interpretations and analysis can be drawn from its history. In addition to plurality of religions, languages, and cultures Indian democracy is also complicated. "Understanding Indian politics is an endless intellectual challenge."[11] How did Indian democracy solve its challenges and survive? The question gives rise to multiple sets of responses. Here, a satirical novel which has the liberty to highlight infirmities along with proficiency of personalities can do much better than a historical book. *The Great Indian Novel* (1989) written by Shashi Tharoor is such a satirical novel on Indian political history from 1930 to 1980. It handles the causes and effects from a personal point of view. The novel takes its name from the literal translation of the *Mahabharata*. In Sanskrit, 'Maha' means great and 'Bharat' stands for India. The novel makes it clear that "[Ganapathi's] task would be no less than transcribing the Song of Modern India in my prose" (*GIN* 18). The novel uses the words 'Indians' and 'we Indians' for eighty and nine times respectively. Thus, the novel ensures that it comprehends the antique and modern ethos of India with new dimensions.

The novel sketches out achievements and drawbacks of India as well as strengths and weaknesses of the great leaders. In narration, the outlook of optimism and pessimism are incorporated. The novel says "today's India is a land of adulteration, black-marketing, corruption, communal strife, dowry killings, you know the rest" (*GIN* 412). At the same time, it states 'India is eternal' (*GIN* 418). By connecting an ancient text with the modern history of India, Tharoor attempts to comprehend the whole Indian ethos. In other words, it re-vitalizes of the spirit of India and re-reads the past and present with a future vision. Analyzing the religious text and modern political scenario simultaneously the novel follows the traditional Indian approach of holistic understanding of person and society without the separation of the sacred and the secular.

5.2.2. *The Great Itihasa*

The *Mahabharata*, one of the epics of India, is not merely a part of literature but it was formed out of Indian ethos and in turn, it influenced the later evolution of the ethos of India. "The *Mahabharata* has not only influenced the literature, art, sculpture and painting of India but it has moulded the very character of the Indian people."[12] Hence, the selection of the epic to narrate the story of modern India has a wider vision of making Indianness relevant and great; antique and contemporary. The novel has a futuristic vision too. "The story [The *Mahabharata*] becomes a 'prophetic vision' because it so manifestly exceeds the linear narrative of history, and the story of India is known in a way which cannot be confined by History."[13] The retelling of the story of the *Mahabharata* is a symbol of the rebirth of India. Hence, it never dies away. India is not young; so a great and noble ethos has been formed from its own rich heritage. "In terms of India's post-independence history there is also no real beginning. India's history is not some appendix to the story of an empire."[14]

The *Mahabharata* is an *itihasa* which is the result of public imagination. By re-writing the story of the *Mahabharata*, the novel reappraises the Indian modern itihasa. Itihasa which includes oral as well as written traditions, official history as well as subaltern history, is an Indian way of approach to the history. It incorporates stories, events, narrations, moral teachings, comments, imaginations, etc., and it reveals the internal spirit of inside of India. "The Indian idea of history/*itihas* being cyclical, Tharoor suggests that history repeats itself offering new interpretations and new lesions."[15] With this intention, the major events, places and personalities of the *Mahabharata* and of modern Indian history are allegorically linked together. Table 5.1 shows the allegorical reading of some names, places and events of the novel. The events and personalities are decisive factors which determine the destiny of India. "Thematically, Tharoor's novel deals with divisions and conflicts that constitute the history of India from its remote past to the present."[16]

Table 5.1: Allegorical Representations of the Names

Names/events in the novel	Representations for the *Mahabharata*	Allegories from the modern Indian
Chakra invasion		Indo China War
Gelaby Desh War		Bangladesh War
Big-Mac Line		L.O.C.
Siege		Emergency
Ballot game		Dice game
Dice		Election
Draupadi	Draupadi	Democracy
Karnistan		Pakistan
The Bibighar Garden Massacre		The Jallianwallah Bagh Massacre
Laslut		Lahore
Tibia		Tibet
Ved Vyas (V.V.-ji)	Vyasa,	Acharya Kriplani, or C. Rajagopalachari, or Sanjeeva Reddy
Ganga Datta (Gangaji or the Mahaguru)	Bhishma (Devavrata)	Mahatma Gandhi
Vidur	Vidura	Sardar Vallabhbhai Patel
Pandu	Pandu	Shubhash Chandra Bose
Jayaprakash Drona	Drona	Jayaprakash Narayan
Dhritarashtra	Dhritarashtra	Jawaharlal Nehru
Gandhari	Gandhari	Kamala Nehru

Names/events in the novel	Representations for the *Mahabharata*	Allegories from the modern Indian
Shishu Pal	Shalya	Lal Bahadur Shastri
the Kaurava Party	the Kauravas	the Congress party
Kaurava Party (Real)		the Congress (I) party
Kaurava Party (Old Guard)		the Indian National Congress
the People's Front	The Pandavas	the Janata Party
Mohammad Ali Karna	Karna	Muhammad Ali Jinnah
Priya Duryodhani	Duryodhana	Indira Gandhi
Yudhishtir	Yudhishtira	Morarji Desai
Bhim	Bhima	The Indian Army
Arjun	Arjuna	the Indian news media
Ekalavya	Ekalavya	Fakhruddin Ali Ahmed, or V.V. Giri

5.2.3. *Personalities*

One of the major thrusts of the novel is an in-depth reading of the personae and the *Mahabharata* which presents so many characters from day to day life of the society, makes it possible to accommodate a lot of personalities from the present Indian scenario. Following the epic, the novel gives an eagle-eyed biography of national leaders with their strengths and weaknesses. More than events, it makes a microscopic analysis of the characters with the background of characters in the epics. "Tharoor is far more politically engaged than most other Indo-English novelists. His fictionalization is transparent, and the figures onstage are easily identifiable political giants of the last fifty years."[17] Allegory facilitates to reveal the hidden aspects of history. A few personalities are also analyzed here.

The greatest personality of pre-independent India is Gandhiji and he is symbolized by Gangaji in the novel. The novel presents Gangaji as a man with virtues and vices. The greatness of Gandhiji is summarized by saying, "While he was alive, he was impossible to ignore; once he had gone, he was impossible to imitate" (*GIN* 47). He takes decisions according to his inner voice even if many find disagreement. His way of behaviour is so unique and it moves even the enemies. "Yet I have asked you to be strong, for he who gives in now not only admits his weakness but weakens the strength of the others" (*GIN* 101). He gives a new turn to the freedom struggle as it becomes a mass movement. However, he is satirized in relation to his *brahmacharia* and his relationship with Nehru.

The post-independent India is equated with Nehruvianism. "In death, as in life, Jawaharlal would become India."[18] The novel takes the character Dhritarashtra to represent Nehru and presents him as an idealist. "Dhritarashtra toured the lecture-halls and the meeting-rooms of urban India" (*GIN* 111-12). The novel also appreciates 'non-alignment' (*GIN* 295) and other unique contributions of Nehru. Yet, Nehru fails to fulfil his *gribastha dharma*. "Dhritarashtra is not loyal to his wife. He is a true politician with selfish motives. He guides his daughter not as a father but as a political trainer into a political manipulation."[19] Another prominent leader of pre-independence, who still lives in the hearts of many Indians, is Subhash Chandra Bose. He is represented by Pandu in the novel. He is pragmatic and 'his slogan was a can do!' (*GIN* 176). Pandu tries to combine idealism and realism. "He balanced an hour of meditation with an hour of martial arts" (*GIN* 85). He selflessly moved to the villages of India. "It was Pandu who took the party banners into the most remote villages" (*GIN* 111). More than non-violence, he attempts violence as a means to attain freedom. Even though he toiled for independence, he could not see the free India. 'Pandu himself was gone' (*GIN* 210) but people of India are waiting so that he might 're-emerge at the right time' (*GIN* 210).

Priya Duryodhani is the most criticized character in the novel and she stands for Indira Gandhi. She is a "self-made woman, with firm conviction."[20] She takes firm decisions and "acted only according to the dictates of her own conscienceless mind" (*GIN* 155). Even in times of trials and tribulations, she dares to declare emergency. "Determination had always been Priya Duryodhani's greatest asset" (*GIN* 342). She is 'equal to a thousand sons' (*GIN* 74). Tharoor makes a better psychological understanding about Priya who faced loneliness in childhood and shared the pains of her mother. "After what she saw in her childhood Priya Duryodhani would never be able to trust another human being, no, not even—especially not—her own father" (*GIN* 152). The unique formation given by Nehru who called his daughter 'Indu-boy'[21] also makes her different. "Even at the age of twelve, overkill was already her problem. Perhaps things might have been different had Dhritarashtra taken her in hand, rather than his pen" (*GIN* 155). If a person is not emotionally mature, s/he cannot make a balanced judgment. "The *Mahabharata* shows that it is not until one's relationship with one's self is right that one's relationship with the other can be right and the two being inseparable, it is by achieving a right relationship with the other that one comes to one's self, fulfilled."[22] The novel cannot have an easy rejection or acceptance of Priya. "To some, Duryodhani is a revered figure, a saviour of India, a Joan of Arc burned at the democratic stake by the ignorant and the prejudiced" (*GIN* 416).

Jayaprakash, the Gandhian of pre-independent period is illustrated by Drona. "Throughout his life, during his days of violence and of peace, his years of teaching and of withdrawal, Drona had been one of India's simplest men" (*GIN* 403). He keeps himself away from power but fought for the people. "[Drona] believed, in-the tradition of our great sages, that my material needs were irrelevant, for a Brahmin's upkeep is the responsibility of society" (*GIN* 158). Yet he lacks originality (*GIN* 403).

5.2.4. *Spirit of Nationalism*

The Great Indian Novel is a nationalist novel that proclaims the pre-eminence of Indian ethos and promulgates 'India as eternal' (*GIN* 418). To substantiate that India is a developed country, the author gives a wider perspective to the term development, which encompasses many other factors along with economic elements. If development stands for holistic growth, then India is a developed country. The very act of colonization proves that India is a developed country. "Do you think the merchants and adventurers and traders of the East India Company would have first sailed to a land of poverty and misery? [...] they came to an India that was fabulously rich and prosperous, they came in search of wealth and profit" (*GIN* 95). The novel highlights the great contributions of Indians to humanity. The holistic view of life is emphasized in the novel. For Indians, science and philosophy are not two separate entities but they go hand in hand. Here, the zero is not something limited Mathematics but extended to internal reality. "The Indian zero is no empty shell. It reflects the perpetual intangibility of the eternal, it embodies the calm centre of the whirling tornado of life, it stands for the point where our verified values die transcended by the enigma of the void" (*GIN* 158). The sacred and secular outlooks of the same entity enhance human life. The victory of India is continuous and independence is considered as one of as one of its greatest triumphs.

At the same time, the glorification of the golden age of India is not to keep away from the present reality. "I was born with the century, a bastard, but a bastard in a fine tradition" (*GIN* 19). Even though he is proud of the past, the author is very critical about the present situation of India. The usage of 'overdeveloped' (*GIN* 17) is ironic. After stating that 'everything in India is over-developed,' the author points out certain areas where misconduct dominates, "particularly the social structure, the bureaucracy, the political process, the financial system, the university network and, for that matter, the women" (*GIN* 17). Furthermore it adds, "a man who lives in the past, a dog who has had his day" (*GIN* 17). The phrasing can be either laughing at Indians who are blindly proud about 'Great India' or defending India against those who claim "India is an underdeveloped country" (*GIN* 17; 419).

5.2.5. *Great Principles of Indian Ethos*

Values play a prominent role in the nation-building process. From time immemorial Indian ethos has been giving due significance to noble values and it is reflected in the social scenario through various customs, teachings, and religious practices. About the modern values of a nation, Sachchidananda says, "building different communities into a nation does not necessarily involve the removal of cultural differences between them. But there are certain basic values, such as democracy, secularism, equality of opportunity and freedom of thought and speech, which have got to be accepted by all irrespective of caste, creed or religion."[23] Every stable and celebrated culture is rooted in moral values. *Dharma* is one of the major ethical concepts which controls the personal and social life of Indians. "If there is one great Indian principle that has been handed down through the ages, it is that of the paramount importance of practicing *dharma* at any price" (*GIN* 417). Not only in the structure but also in spirit, the novel follows the *Mahabharata*. The primary preoccupation of the epic may be the concern over the nature and execution of *dharma*. Similarly, the novel assesses characters on the basis of the fulfillment of their *dharma*. For instance, Priya fulfils her *grihasthashra dharma* by looking after her mother in her illness but Dhritarashtra fails in the same. *Dharma* should be the guiding principle of behaviour. "Between obedience to the law and obedience to my conscience I can only choose the latter" (*GIN* 53).

Dharma also, places a vital role in nation building. Indian nationalist spirit is a fight between *adharma* and *dharma* and India exists because it upholds *dharma*. Indian ethos teaches that "Life itself is worthless without *dharma*" (*GIN* 417). The war of Kurukshetra, the independence struggle and the vote against emergency, which were not against the Kaurava, the British or Priya Duryodhani but against *adharma*, were to show the ultimate victory of *dharma* over *adharma* and of India. 'Only dharma is eternal' (*GIN* 417). *Dharma* is paramount than victory and it is the primary principle of life. Hence, pre-independent India adopted the vision '*Satyamevajayate*, Truth will Prevail' (*GIN* 410). *Satyam* should follow non-violence as a means to attain the goal. *Dharma* should be attained by the means of non-violence, which is a prominent element in Indian ethos. In the 20th century, Gandhiji became the icon of non-violence. He practiced love and argued "We cannot point to the injustice of British rule if our opposition to it takes equally unjust forms" (*GIN* 127). He fired true nationalism in the hearts of millions (*GIN* 111) and for him "Non-violence, non-cooperation, non-alignment, all mean more, much more, than the concepts they negate" (*GIN* 48). He brilliantly used non-violence as an effective weapon where colonizers surrendered completely. Tharoor narrates the victory of non-violence over colonization and democracy over emergency.

5.2.6. *Indian Democracy*

The credit of being the largest democratic country with a stable democratic rule are the paramount achievements of India. However, Indian democracy is quite confusing. "The Indian paradox is not the familiar apparent contradiction between India's poverty and India's democracy, but the far more puzzling contradiction between India's high level of political violence and its success to sustain a democratic political system."[24] It began with the great exception to Nehruvianism. In spite of that, the image of Dhritarashtra shattered gradually. "Criticism in the party was vociferous and unrestrained: many of our MPs howled with the jackals of the Opposition for sacrificial blood" (*GIN* 304). After the reign of Dhritarashtra, Priya Duryodhani becomes the Prime Minister and the novel criticizes the family for controlling the political scenario. "A political party is like a family, Yudhishtir. A family does not decide in the street who will cook its dinner tonight" (*GIN* 340). Thus each election leads closer to a political crisis. Election is the major tool of democracy but the voting system is corrupt. Indian elections are criticized as 'a great Indian *tamasha*' (*GIN* 390). All kinds of manipulations are seen in elections. Political parties and the corrupt leaders can control the democracy. Even Priya is selected not with right motive because the Kaurava Party needs someone to 'decorate the office' (*GIN* 318) of Prime Minister.

Indian democracy is represented by Draupadi, the illegitimate daughter of Dhritarashtra and Lady Drewpad. The narrator describes Draupadi, in relation to the change in Indian democracy. The real complexity of India is well portrayed through Draupadi. "She stood erect and calm amidst the confusion" (*GIN* 315). Priya becomes more autocratic and the rule becomes unpopular. "While striking trade unionists were beaten [...], all this while more and more laws went into the statute books empowering Priya Duryodhani to prohibit, proscribe, profane, prolate, prosecute or prostitute all the freedoms" (*GIN* 357). Gradually Draupadi falls into a coma in 1975. The democratic ethos of India is arrested.

Emergency is a dark chapter in the history of Indian democracy. The Fundamental Rights were suspended. "Duryodhani censored the press, [...] she was bulldozing through Parliament like the steel-rimmed chakras of an invincible juggernaut" (*GIN* 372). Priya misinterprets that Parliament is controlling everything. To the essence, parliament has only delegated power of the people to govern the nation in the democracy. "It is not Parliament that is supreme, but the people" (*GIN* 384). The act of Priya is described in two phrases: *vinasha kale, viparitabuddhi* and "whom the gods wish to destroy, they first make mad" (*GIN* 369). The election after emergency was the selection of the people either for 'dictatorship' or for 'democracy.' The people of India uphold the ethos of democracy in the general election of 1977. Authoritarian rule is controlled by the principle of *adharma* since the ruled one has no freedom. More than material development individual realization is important.

5.2.7. *Multi-culturalism*

The complex nature of India is a blessing and a curse. It is a gift because it gives beauty to India and a harm because differences lead to conflicts. In the novel, Draupadi symbolizes the 'unity in diversity' of India. Draupadi has to accommodate, Yudhishtira, Bheema, Arjuna, Nakul and Sahadev. Indian identity is formed out of multiculturalism. "The evolution of national identity in India is a result of a long process of inclusion of cultural practices, either internally generated or originating from outside."[25] Because of its pluralistic nature, it can never tie to a particular ethnic group. One of the reasons to select the *Mahabharata* as the background to analyse the modern India may be its acceptance throughout the country. It is a story of 363 communities with high regard to all ethnic groups. At the same time, it proclaims the unity with vast number of genes in common. Communities share a very high percentage of traits and their perceived diversity is often deceptive. For instance, although Indians speak hundreds of dialects, and have as many as seventeen recognized languages, their entire vocabulary has its source in four major language families.[26]

The novelist blames the colonizers for the outgrowth of communalism in India. "It was the British Civil serpent who made our people collectively bite the apple of discord. *Divide etimpera,* they called it in the language of their own Roman conquerors—divide and rule" (*GIN* 134). The British gave special preference to Muslims not to empower them but to extend the colonial rule. 'Karna was creating his constituency' (*GIN* 147). He openly goes against the Hindu leadership. "Independence without Hindu domination was Karna's new slogan" (*GIN* 148). The religious fundamentalism ends in partition. In *India: From Midnight to the Millennium*, Tharoor himself says, "The major challenge for Indian democracy is therefore to absorb and resolve the clashes that may arise between contending interests, while ensuring the freedom, safety, security, and prosperity of all Indians."[27] To keep the unity within the real and vested interests of various regional groups is an arduous effort. The novel warns against the growth of religious fundamentalism and rejects all kinds of chauvinist thinking. For the unified existence of India, the ethos of multi-culturalism should be promoted. "So we Indians are open about our differences; we do not attempt to subsume ourselves in a homogenous mass, we do not resort to the identity-disguising trick of standardized names or uniform costumes or even of a common national language" (*GIN* 134). The novel suggests a mantra for the unity of India: "Uphold decency, worship humanity, affirm the basic values of our people —those which do not change—and leave the rest alone. Admit that there is more than one Truth, more than one Right, more than one dharma..." (*GIN* 418). Tolerance towards even the opposite point of view is a value in Indian ethos.

5.2.8. *The Subjugation of Women*

The patriarchal society makes very deceptive comments on women. On the one hand, the writings seem to be enhancing the power of women but on the other, the same words endangered their empowerment. Manu says, "women must be honoured and adorned by their fathers, brothers, husbands, and brothers-in-law, who desire (their own) welfare."[28] The commandment is meant for the protection of women but it takes away the decision-making power. Over protection and lack of freedom lead to the inferior status of Indian women. The novel mentions the freedom of women. "Indian women were free to make love with, whomever they wished, without being considered immoral. There were even rules about it: the sages decreed that a married woman must sleep with her husband during her fertile period, but was free to take her pleasure elsewhere the rest of the time" (*GIN* 71). However, the underlined intention of the freedom favours the high caste men to have sex with any woman and not to empower women. "The lower caste man who approaches a girl of the highest caste, whether she be willing or unwilling, must be put to death."[29] If a woman enjoys sex with the highest caste, it is not punishable. In other words, high caste men can have sex with any woman according to his wish. Gangaji says "Don't forget that we have a long tradition of Brahmins coming to the rescue of barren Kshatriyas" (*GIN* 31). Satirically, the unjust sexual caste system is described in the novel. "In Kerala the men of the Nair community only learn that their wives are free to receive them by seeing if another man's slippers aren't outside her door" (*GIN* 71). The statement created controversy as Tharoor accused the Nair women by characterizing them as immoral and justifying polygamy by distorted facts.[30]

The novel ironically presents the practice of *brahmacharya*. Gangaji is over-anxious about his celibacy. "Ever since his vow Ganga had developed something of an obsession with his celibacy, even if he was the only one who feared it to be constantly under threat" (*GIN* 28). The celibate Ganga thinks that it is woman who seduces man. If celibacy fails to respect the womanhood, it becomes worse than the married life. Tharoor ridicules the oppressive patriarchal system. The consumeristic patriarchal view is made clear in the words of Dhritarashtra about wife. 'How often must I tell you that you would be more useful to me the way you are?' On the contrary, the female perspective is revealed when Gandhari says, "Useful? It is not a wife's role to be useful" (*GIN* 64). As per Indian ethos women are equal to men in every sense. Gandhari thinks that, "Her duty is to share the life of her husband" (*GIN* 64).

The real ethos of India about women is to respect them. Against this spirit, in course of time various practices are introduced by the patriarchal society to put women down, for example, both the empowering and oppressive customs can be seen in the wedding system. The uprising of the weaker sections such as women and the lower caste of the society is symbolically represented by Ekalavya and Kunti. In the epic, Ekalavya gave the thumb of his right hand to the guru but the modern Indian Ekalavya refuses to do so: "I... I'm sorry, sir, but, I cannot destroy my life and my mother's to pay your fee" (*GIN* 199). Against the grievous system, Kunti is presented as a modern and liberated woman. She is free from society's stereotype concepts. Everyone has become aware of their rights.

5.2.9. *Indianization*

The novel is a part of the post-colonial way of viewing and of being viewed. It gives a re-interpretation to the civilizing mission from the perspective of the colonized. "[...] the simple logic of colonialism, under which the rules of humanity applied only to the rulers, for the rulers were people and the people were objects. Objects to be controlled, disciplined, kept in their place and taught lessons like so many animals" (*GIN* 80). Not only political freedom, but also cultural and social liberation are needed for the fullness of liberation of a nation. The adapted form of the *Mahabharata* in the novel functions as a re-inventing of the cultural perception. It is an outcome of the self-confidence of a colonized, to work with one's own great culture and introduce its immense wealth to the colonizer. "Perhaps Tharoor's lasting accomplishment is that he has reminded Indians (unobtrusively) of the continuing significance of their ancient scripture and has persuasively drawn many Westerners into it for the first time."[31]

The hybridity of post-colonialism is expressed through the character, Draupadi, who is born from Dhritarashtra (Indian) and the Vicerine (British), represents the post-colonial India.

"The baby was called Draupadi, a subtle Indianization of her mother's family name, and she took the uncouth patronymic of her adoptive father, Mokrasi" (*GIN* 245). The oriental perspective influences Indians who get Western education. For example, Dhritarashtra who symbolizes Nehru has a Western outlook that influences the formation of the post-independent India. "[Nehru's] books reveal a Western intellect articulating an Indian heritage in the voice of the Enlightenment."[32] In spite of that, Gangaji champions for Indianization. "Mine is a dress. [...] is best suited to the Indian climate and which, for its simplicity, art and cheapness, is not to be beaten on the face of the earth" (*GIN* 61). Panikker also remarks that more than any other leader in the modern times, Gandhiji has a comprehensive view of the anti-colonial struggle.[33] Drona also tries to establish the Indianness. "[Drona] now made a special effort to Indianize his diction with the colonials: they had to realize he had both an axe and an accent to grind" (*GIN* 240).

By adapting the great epic, the novel makes a great contribution in introducing the Indian vocabulary in English and some of these words are given in Table 5.2. The mythical names and stories are made known to the global population. The Indian mythical characters such as Ashwathama, Bheema, Chitragada, Dhritarashtra, Ekalavya, Ganapathi, Hidimba, Jatila, Karna, Kunti, Madri, Nakul, Pandu, Sahadev, Shakuni, Shantiparvan, Subhadra, Tilottama, Ulupi, Vahana, and Yudhishtir become part of world literature. Other than names, a lot of Indian concepts and ideas are also placed in the global market such as Yama, Vedas, Swayamvara, Puranas, Kundalini, Yoga, Kama Sutra, and Arthashstra. Indian literary usages are also given in the novel. For example, 'vinasha kale, viparitabuddhi' (*GIN* 81, 369). The usage of 'ji' as suffix to show the respect to great people, is used more than three hundred times in the novel.

Not only language, but other cultural elements such as places, monuments, and rivers are also used for Indianization. For instance, the word 'Ganga' (including Ganga Datta, Gangaism, Gangaji) is used 447 times in the novel. "[The Ganga] has been a symbol of India's age-long culture and civilization, ever-changing, ever-flowing, and yet ever the same Ganga."[34] Ganga comprehends the secular and sacred ethos of India. Another symbol used in the novel is The Taj Mahal, which is used six times. "There was, Ganapathi, one brief shining moment of hope, when the Front's leaders, [...] gathered together before that symbol of the nation's enduring greatness, the Taj Mahal, and swore a collective oath to uphold India's glory and its traditional values [...]" (*GIN* 403).

In *India: From Midnight to the Millennium,* Tharoor criticises the aggressive native rulers who change the names of cities such as Mumbai, Chennai, Kanpur, and Pune. Even though Tharoor uses a lot of Indian words in the novel, he gives their meaning at the end of the novel. Hence, the novel is not an aggressive 'writing back,' but follows moderate re-colonization. Instead of violent resistance, the novel adopts creative-installation process for cultural coexistence, i.e. cordially presents the native culture with its pre-eminence before the colonized for accepting without any prejudice. The novel presents Indian culture into the world intelligentsia. It is a non-violent way of establishing one's identity. It instils confidence in the native people and forms the world population to use the native's cultural usages without any hesitation.

Table 5.2: The Indian Vocabularies Used in the Novel

Indian Vocabularies			
aarti	dal bhaat	kurta	sadhu
adharma	darshan	madallam	sahib
angrez	davanis	mahaguru	sainiks
apsara	dhamas	mahawaja	sannayasi
asana	dharna	marumakattayam	sardar
ashram	dharti	mofussil	satyagraha/i
ayah	dhoti	moksha	—
azhichapadippu	dhoti-wallahs	mullah	shama
babu	doodhwala	mundu	shamiana
baniya	durwan	mundus	shastras
barfis	durwan	naga	shunyabindu
bhai	guernica	namaskar	sloka
bharatiya	hitopadeshi	namaste	subedars

bharatmata	holi	namaz	sudra
bhisti	huzoor	nautch	swadeshi
chakra	—	nawabs	swaraj
chakravarti	janmabhoomi	neta	swatantra
chappals	jawans	ottamthullal	tabla
chaprassi	karanavar	padayatra	zenana
chaya-kadakaran	kaalam	Panchatantra	taluk
chela	karma	panchayat	tamasha
dal	karman	Pandal	thana
puja	khadi	patideva	thozhilalis
razai	khidmalgar	patwari	yuddha
rishis	kukri	payals	zamindars

5.2.10. *Call for Change*

The Great Indian Novel is not just a story, that links the ancient and modern India but it tries to set a vision for the future. "In my epic I shall tell of past, present and future, of existence and passing, of efflorescence and decay, of death and rebirth" (*GIN* 18). There are failures but it is not an end. India will continue its journey but only with the changes most necessary. The pre-independent India moved away from the path of *dharma*. The lack of visionary leaders and corruption are highlighted in the novel. The narrator says that 'our country is a story of betrayed expectations' (*GIN* 411). The novel strongly and directly uses the weapon of satire against great leaders. For example, after the death of Gandhiji, many hypocritical leaders misused fasting, the great means that was used for independence. The novel criticises the act. "What could be more absurd than the widely practised 'relay fast' of today's politicians, where different people take it in turns to miss their meals in public?" (*GIN* 106). The charm of 'fasting' faded away by its 'over-use' (*GIN* 100). The novel is not pessimistic but optimistic. "We Indians have a great talent for deriving positives from negatives" (*GIN* 48).

The novel suggests the way out of this crisis. "It is essential to recognize virtue and righteousness, and to praise him who, like yourself, has consistently upheld dharma" (*GIN* 413). It is a call for being firmly rooted in Indian ethos to go ahead. The novel itself is an allegory of *Geethopadesam* given by Lord Krishna. It can guide India to its right destiny and can correct the leaders as well as the citizens to become effective contributors to the society. To bring change he ridicules all the irrational practices in politics, religion, and society. The novel is a parody of the sacred book the *Mahabharata* which gives a satirical glimpse of Indian history. "The novel may provoke an Indian reader who holds the epic in high reverence and has high regards for the characters in it."[35] The provocation and response are needed to build-up an active Indian democracy. A dynamic public is essential for responsible governance.

In short, the novel effectively narrates the realistic situation of de/re-democratic phase of India. On the one hand, the novel glorifies the greatness of India and on the other, it is anxious about corrupt democracy. "History is Kurukshetra. The struggle between *dharma* and *adharma* is a struggle our nation, and each of us in it, engages in on every single day of our existence" (*GIN* 391). It was a great period of struggle. Although, once India worshipped 'truth and honour and valour and dharma' 'as the cardinal principles of existence' (*GIN* 411) presently it has moved away from those values. However, India has the inner oil to keep its lamp enlightened. The mystical nature of India is narrated, "Draupadi was like the flame of a brass lamp in a sacred temple of the people" (*GIN* 309). The narrator is quite sure about the future existence of India with unity and integrity. 'India had all the answers' (*GIN* 418) so the novel hopes for a new India. "India has been born and reborn score of times, and it will be reborn again" (*GIN* 245). For that people should take up the challenge. In the midst of these deformities, India will exist in its glory forever. 'India is forever being made' (*GIN* 245).

5.3. Analysis of *Midnight's Children* in the Light of the De/re-democratization Ethos

Historical events and ethos are reciprocal. Ethos influences events of future and past incidents to shape the ethos of the present. "I am the sum total of everything that went before me, of all I have been seen done, of everything done-to-me. [...] each 'I', every one of the now-six-hundred-million-plus of us, contains a similar multitude" (*MC* 535). The twentieth century ethos of India was constantly revised with a lot of historical milestones. To comprehend these historical events with their influence on Indians is a strenuous effort and such work cannot be simple but serpentine. *Midnight's Children* of Salman Rushdie is a similar attempt to fathom the historical events with the views of the narrator. The novel, a blockbuster, deals with the power centres of 32 years of the colonial rule and of 31 years of post-colonial democracy. It is an attempt to narrate the hidden aspects of the representation of power by the colonizer and the native rulers.

In the novel, the personal life of Saleem and the history of India are presented in an Indianized manner. "Memory's truth, [...]. It selects, eliminates, alters, exaggerates, minimizes, glorifies, and vilifies also; but in the end it creates its own reality, its heterogeneous but usually coherent version of events; and no sane human being ever trusts someone else's version more than his own" (*MC* 211). The tragic life story of Saleem who was born at the very stroke of midnight when India was born into freedom, is intricately intertwined with India. The novel, which narrates the story from personal, ancestral, and national perspectives, is highly complex. It is a search for Indian identity and expresses Indian sensibility in English. "Fantasy in Rushdie's novel fulfils a similar purpose as it does in Bollywood movies: it functions as a narrative component that helps to convey metatextual truths and as a strategy through which an 'Indian' identity can be expressed."[36] Its publication marked a cockcrow in Indian English novel writing and it won 'booker of bookers'.

5.3.1. *National Allegory*

Midnight's Children, where the characters, events, and places symbolize Indian culture, is an Indian national allegory. The novel is an interweaving of Indian history, saga of Saleem's family and the ethos of India. "From the moment of my conception, it seems, I have been public property" (*MC* 77). The personal history unfolds along with the national events with Indian sensibility. Here, the physical body of the narrator fuses with land of the nation; the personal biography fuses with the history of the nation; the individual spirit fuses with the ethos of the nation. The magic realism used in the novel facilitates for the synthesis in its best manner. Saleem could comprehend the history of India with the authoritarian and subaltern perspectives because of "the greatest talent of all—the ability to look into the hearts and minds of men" (*MC* 277). The person who knows a little about Indian history can identify the historical facts behind the novel. "In the West people tended to read Midnight's Children as a fantasy, while in India people thought of it as pretty realistic, almost a history book."[37]

Midnight's Children is the story of twins, Saleem Sinai and India who are born at the stroke of midnight, on 15 August 1947. "Time matters, [...] On the stroke of midnight, as a matter of fact. [...] spell it out: at the precise instant of India's arrival at independence, I tumbled forth into the world" (*MC* 3). Not only the time, but they are physically identical too. The geography teacher literally considers Saleem's body as the map of the undivided India. "'In the face of these ugly ape you don't see the whole map of India?' [...] 'See here-the Deccan peninsula hanging down!' [...] birthmark on the right ear is the East Wing; and thus horrible stained left cheek, the West!" (*MC* 321). In the decolonization period, stories about a person can be seen as an allegory about the destiny of a nation. The warm greeting given by the clock with 'hands joined palms' (*MC* 3) itself symbolizes a chained person without resistance but surrenders himself either to a so-called god or to a godman. This was again emphasized by the usage of 'indissolubly chained' (*MC* 3) and the case of the nation is also not something different. Saleem and the nation, which are in the hands of people who tear the dreams of freedom fighters, have no 'say in the matter' (*MC* 3).

Saleem Sinai, himself, is an allegory of India: his birth, life, failures, incidents, and body. "I am not speaking metaphorically; [...] I have begun to crack all over like an old jug-that my poor body, [...] I shall eventually crumble into (approximately) six hundred and thirty million particles of anonymous" (*MC* 31). Six hundred and thirty million particles refer to the population of India. The unity of Saleem with the nation is not incidental and peripheral but deep rooted and substantial. It is mentioned repeatedly in first person and third person pronouns. "He was mysteriously handcuffed to history, his destinies indissolubly chained to those of his country" (*MC* 586). The personal history of Saleem is fully subjected with the national history like a prisoner. At last, the personal and national spirit emerges into one. Saleem transcends the physical existence for identifying with India. "Since he literally becomes the semi-transcendental mirror image of the nation; yet, with the very same gesture, he is also emptied of subjectivity, deprived of the basic sense of seeing the boundaries of his very own self."[38] Even the failures of Saleem as a hero, lover, leader, narrator, and visionary resemble the political failures of India. In the words of Rushdie, "I even made the boy and the country identical twins."[39]

The saga of Saleem's family and the historical events of India were manifested with a fusion of private and public lives to have an in-depth analysis. Some of the major events referred in the novel are the massacre at Jallianwalla Bagh in Amritsar, the Cripps Mission, the announcement of the partition of India, the independence of India at the stroke of midnight, assassination of Gandhiji, Five Year Plans of India, the elected communist government of Kerala, liberation of Goa, Sino-India war, Indo-Pakistan war, liberation of Bangaladesh, the first nuclear explosion of India, the verdict of the Allahabad High Court against Indira Gandhi, declaration of state of emergency, end of the emergency, and the General Election of 1977. The novel emphasizes not only the historical incidents but also the motives of various people behind them and how they affected the Indian ethos. Hence, the novel that describes the violence of colonizers and of the native rulers is a rereading of the history of India with the background of personal experience. 'Nose' functions as a meeting place of personal experience, which happens inside and national history which takes place outside. "The three drops of blood plopped out of his [Aadam Aziz] left nostril" (*MC* 4) foreshadows the massacre at Jallianwalla Bagh in 1919. Tai told Aadam 'follow your nose' (*MC* 15) and Aadam could experience tragedies which would happen. Hence, on the day of the massacre he had an unpleasant experience. "He is

[...] feeling very scared, because his nose is itching worse than it ever has" (*MC* 40). The ups and downs of the family depend on the progress of the nation.

The novel is a nationalist novel since it elevates the ethos of India to the top. The nationalists of pre-independent period had been presented to India like a paradise and emotionally glorified it to its highest level. Rushdie also develops a utopian idea of India through the romantic relationship between Saleem's body and India; and through the romantic life of three generations, namely Aziz to Naseem, Amina to Ahmed and Saleem to Jamila. The novelist tries to echo the rich heritage of India. "You [Saleem] are the newest bearer of that ancient face of India which is also eternally young" (*MC* 167). India is ancient as well as eternally young. For India, this was the need of the hour since during the 1970s and 1980s Indian democracy faced various unity-shattering challenges and many prophesized its disintegration. To overcome these tribulations, the writers like Rushdie attempted to revitalize the national spirit. To establish *Midnight's Children* as a national allegory, Patrick Colm Hogan identifies four techniques which are used in the novel: literalized idioms referring to events or persons (in the latter case, personification) for example, 'birth of the nation'; isolation of relevant historical details, for example, self-conscious use of errors; the contrasting of facts with aspirations, ideals, even simple alternatives, for example more than 1001 possibilities Midnight's Children narrates the possibilities which were cut short; and mythologizing i.e. to give resonance to images, places, and persons.[40]

Rushdie reminds the readers of the unity of the freedom fighters under the leadership of Gandhiji to have a united and free nation. At the time of independence, United India was still a concept in the minds and not a reality. India was the sum total of several princely states. "It is a sort of national longing for form-or perhaps simply an expression of our deep belief that forms lie hidden within reality; that meaning reveals itself only in flashes" (*MC* 417). This ardent national longing helped the people to transcend the sectarian and regional thinking. Instead of quarrelling because of diversities they began to take pride in difference and build-up a new aesthetical concept opposite to uniformity: unity in diversity. A unified nation was the ethos which guided people to sacrifice themselves for independence. Beyond differences, people were bound together in spirit. Through these descriptions, the novel rejuvenates the nationalistic spirit in 1980s to save India from disintegration.

5.3.2. *Search for Identity: Indianness*

The midnight of 15th August 1947 is a pivotal point in the Indian history. The paradigm shift in the power centre created the radiance of change in all realms of the nation. Along with other challenges, independence led to new aspirations to decolonize and resuscitate the socio-cultural ethos of India. On the same line, *The Midnight's Children* contributed to strive for a positive and distinctive national concept based on Indianness. The novel is an attempt to identify the true ethos of India and narrates the urge of Indians to be rooted in Indianness. The novel is a museum of national history, cultural archive and age old tradition. The notion of the identity between Saleem and India made clear through the then Prime Minister Jawaharlal Nehru's letter to the infant Saleem: "...it will be, in a sense, the mirror of our own" (*MC* 167). The identity crisis of the post-colonial subjects is also reflected in the novel. The mental agony of different persons and the true Indian spirit are the underlined thread of the whole story. The West could not satisfy Aadam but only created a negative force, so he returned to paradise. The identity crisis was symbolically portrayed by the fisherman's finger (*MC* 166) and the lions of Sarnath stood above the *dharma chakra* on the Prime Minister's missive (*MC* 167). Indians cannot escape from the Victorian painting 'in which my inescapable destiny hung' (*MC* 167). The midnight's child in Elizabethan costume and picture of the fisherman in Buckingham Villa (*MC* 166) represents the socio-cultural colonization of Indians. Rushdie satirizes the colonial mimicry but at the same time it is 'impossible to ignore' (*MC* 167) the colonial influence on the subjects of the post-colonial period.

The dilemma of the colonized cannot be solved easily because their basic mental frame work of perception itself is manipulated. It may be blocked or mediated by the experience of colonization. 'The beadsheet' and 'the lady wrestlers' (*MC* 22) indicate the barriers of perception. "The multilated square linen" (*MC* 4) "with a roughly circular hole some seven inches in diameter" (*MC* 4) is a block and an opening for the colonized. The Western education might diminish the brightness required to enjoy the beauty of India. The 'beauty' is transformed to 'narrowness.' The childhood aesthetic consciousness of the Indian might be adulterated by the proximity of the colonizer, so a conscious effort is needed to revive it. The colonizer's influence has not only a conscious realm but also an unconscious level which is deep rooted and tough to remove. 'Out to another sea which was not the sea in the picture' represents the hidden sea 'which obliged us to look at the city's dispossessed' (*MC* 168). 'Another sea' may be Atlantic which represents the colonizer and 'out to another sea' stands for the Arabian sea of the colonized. The displaced Kolis, who were the native ethnic group which represents the all indigenous people of India, could not see in the bright sun light but "a sea on which the sails of Koli dhows glowed scarlet in the setting sun..." (*MC* 168).

The inferiority complex of the colonized, promoted to mimic the colonizer but the nationalist rejected it to a certain extent. Aadam became aware of his uprootedness. However, the grandson became a symbol of neo-colonialism.

> Thus, Saleem begins his tale of the birth of the nation at the moment when the 'modern' Aadam becomes conscious that he is 'Indian,' a moment that is awakened by the brutality of imperialism. However, this 'beginning' is complicated by Saleem's discovery that both his own and the nation's origins also lead him back to Britain.[41]

Saleem is a product of the politically independent India. But as the nation is not yet culturally liberated, he is not a free man. The Methwold Estate symbolizes neo-colonialism which witnessed 'the unproductive labour' (*MC* 149) pain of Vanita. "Saleem's experience of India is coloured by his exposure to British representation and narrative, but Saleem's perception of the British painting is shaped by his experience of Bombay."[42]

Saleem represents the continued cultural control of the colonizer and hybrid identity of the post-colonial subjects.

The novel brings out the various responses to the colonial culture. Aadam and Tai are portrayed as two opposite poles of change. "Tai-for-changelessness opposed to Aadam-for-progress" (*MC* 143). Tai is conservative and traditional without change. "Nobody could remember when Tai had been young" (*MC* 10). He is a symbol of the orthodox Indian who hesitates to change the practices. It may be perceived that the traditionalists are the true custodians of the culture with its purity. Aadam stands for modernization. He had western education and assimilated the Western culture. However, he turned to Indianness, the root. More than god or man Aadam loved 'women and history' (*MC* 4) which symbolically stands for the ardent love towards India. Naseem who represents 'Mother India, Bharat-Mata' (*MC* 565) was married to Aadam. "To say that Aadam has a weakness for women is to say that he has a weakness for the imagined nation."[43] Tai and Aadam are two ways of responding to colonialism. Tai stands for the total rejection and Aadam represents assimilation of colonizers culture.

Another response to colonialism is reactionary traditionalism which means total rejection of westernization through asserting the native culture and is represented by Naseem. She did comprehend good or bad from the culture of the colonizer but adopted a negative approach towards it. The reaction was formed as a defence mechanism to protect the identity of oneself. She represents the nationalist who negatively responded to the culture of the colonizer. Naseem, who rejected modernization, was wedded to Aadam who looked forward to progression. Aadam says "Forget about being a good Kashmiri girl. Start thinking about being a modern Indian woman" (*MC* 39).

> The difference is clear: a 'good Kashmiri girl' is someone who follows communal traditions and a 'modern Indian woman' is someone who breaks with local traditions to assert a counter traditional nationalized identity. It is in response to this incursion of modernity and nationalism that Naseem turns tradition into a categorical identity, one to be asserted rigidity.[44]

All the responses to colonization show the mental agony of subjects of colonized and the novel makes clear that it cannot be treated by Western standards but with Indian ethos. "Just as the realist novel is ill-suited to represent the subaltern experience because of the genre's roots in the project of Western nation-building, clinical medicine is blind to the ex-colonial pains because it relies on an alien standard of interpretation."[45] Aadam who has an urge for modernity is also under stress. "He was caught in a strange middle ground, trapped between belief and disbelief, and this was only a charade after all" (*MC* 7). The forgotten 'Indianness' of Aadam was enkindled by the experience of 'three drops of blood plopped out of his left nostril' (*MC* 4) which symbolizes the imperialism. In addition to the expression of the crisis of colonial subjects, through the portals of the fisherman and the lions of Sarnath that authenticate the Indianness. Buckingham Villa which symbolizes Buckingham Palace, the icon of the English, was built in 1705 A.D. Whereas the lions of Sarnath is taken from the Pillars of Ashoka which was built by the great Emperor Ashok in 250 B.C. The comparison reestablishes the superiority of Indian ethos over the colonial powers. "National history transforms time into space: the heroes of the past join each other in the common space of the national portrait gallery where they become models to be invoked by the would-be heroes of the future."[46] Thus, the novel is a journey towards Indianness.

5.3.3. *Betrayal of Democracy*

Midnight's Children re-visits the 31 years of independent India, which is "the privilege and the curse of midnight's children to be both masters and victims of their time" (*MC* 647). The chains of the colonizer were thrown away in 1947 and a goal was set to attain the democratic values. "In fact, all over the new India, the dream we all shared" (*MC* 159). Nehru expressed the common feeling in the Assembly, "This is no time for petty or destructive criticism, [...] No time for ill-will. We have to build the noble mansion of free India" (*MC* 158). The nation, which 'is itself a sort of dream' (*MC* 159) set out to fulfil the vision. However, the very first step itself started with tribulations, which divided the nation into two. Rushdie narrates the partition of India from the perspective of time. "It was only a matter of time, [...]. It could even be partitioned: the clocks in Pakistan would run half an hour ahead of their Indian counterparts..." (*MC* 102). The announcement of partition led to Hindu-Muslim riots. "Proving once again that there was no escape from recurrence" (*MC* 396). The crumbling (*MC* 3) body of Saleem represents the disunited India which took birth along with the nation and screaming stands for the violence which India faces.

The shattering of the national dream continued mercilessly and it reached its climax with the assassination of Gandhiji in post-independent India. "Re-reading my work, I have discovered an error in chronology. [...] But I cannot say, now, what the actual sequence of events might have been; in my India, Gandhi will continue to die at the wrong time" (*MC* 164). The assassination of Gandhiji continues through corruption, regionalism, and fundamentalism. There are people like Aadam who "resolved never again to kiss earth for any god or man" (*MC* 4) yet many others instigated fundamentalism and destroyed the collective imagination.

The economic progress was also not up to the mark. "During those five years [end in 1961], the number of landless and unemployed masses actually increased, so that it was greater than it had ever been under the British Raj, [...] illiteracy survived unscathed; the population continued to mushroom" (*MC* 285). Lack of economic development affected Indian democracy too. The gap between the rich and the poor increased. A new elite class formed in India in the place of foreign colonizers. The new business class of 'India were turning white' (*MC* 177). They took the control not only over the economy but also over the politics. The disunity began to take an upper hand in pre-independent India. Indian democracy seemed to be an unrealised dream.

The catastrophe of the democratic values in India reached its climax when Indira Gandhi declared a state of emergency. "Saleem's nose (you can't have forgotten) could smell stranger things than horse-dung. [...]. When the Constitution was altered to give the Prime Minister well-nigh-absolute powers, I smelted the ghosts of ancient empires in the air" (*MC* 592).

The constitutional freedom was dismissed during the emergency which 'reducing member to specks of voiceless dust' (*MC* 459). The democratic hegemony took over the midnight's children. The impotency of Saleem symbolically stands for the suffering of the people during emergency. Saleem is a victim of the Widow's tyranny and the narrator railed at Indira's autocratic centralization of power. People would rise against the autocratic government. "Rushdie's 'Super-Sexy-High-Masala-Art' is an expression of the rebelliousness of the democratic forces rising up against the authoritarianism of the Emergency."[47] *Midnight's Children* is a political resistance novel. Since *Midnight's Children* highlights the failures of the nation, Timothy Brennan commented that, it is an 'aesthetics of resistance.'[48] The novel is a venture to create a political history against the hegemonic history of the authorities. It is the story of the defenders of Indian democracy at the time of its failures. The novel reveals the untold dark side of Indian democracy. 'How terrible, truly' (*MC* 105). The beautiful front side of Red Fort became an allegory of the glorious democracy of India. On the contrary, the awful incidents behind the Red Fort represent the dark realities of Indian democracy. Saleem's mother experiences the untold realities. 'She enters these causeways where poverty eats away at the tarmac like a drought, [...] something new begins to assail her" (*MC* 105). The visible allusions of the beautified cities are different from the invisible darkness of the slums and villages.

The trials and tribulations of Indian democracy did not disappear after emergency. Even though people voted against Indira in the general election of 1977, the post-emergency government was a failure. Therefore, they again went with Indira Gandhi. Rushdie could not find any alternative for the tyranny of Indira who moved to the extreme form to equate herself with the nation: 'India is Indira and Indira is India' (*MC* 597). Above all these criticisms, Rushdie wrote at the time of the assassination of Indira, "All of us who love India are in mourning today."[49] The failure of Indira did not compel Rushdie to accept any other political ideologies of the time. For instance, he does not show a favourable stand for the leftist ideology. "This utopianism seems to reject the political left because it implies that no legitimate political alternative to the Congress Party exists; Picture Singh as a representative of the left offers a glorious but failed promise to the nation."[50] Instead of moving to any ideologies, the novel gives an account of the political failures of India as if they themselves can generate solutions.

5.3.4. *Multiplicity of Voice*

Midnight's Children is an apologetic novel for the pluralism and the multi-voice of India. The very title of the novel 'children' indicates the pluralistic reality and Midnight's Children National Conference reflects these diversities. "The hundred squalling rows which are unavoidable in a parliament composed entirely of half-grown brats" (*MC* 354). The midnight children represent hundreds of ethnic diversities of India. The Conference celebrated the diversity of the nation and Saleem wanted to make it as a symbol of democratic equality. However, Shiva, the symbol of the distractive principle of democracy, turned against it.

The plurality is also highlighted in the very origin of Saleem. He who is the biological son of William Methold and Vanita, brought up by Ahmed and Amina, is a joint product of Hindu, Muslim and English like 'India'. "Saleem represents, within his often-unwieldy first-person narrative many voices, many languages, many characters, and he struggles to contain them all until the end of the story, where he foresees his imminent disintegration into 600 million separate identities."[51] Even the fragmentation is a time of joy since it is an expression of pluralism.

Furthermore, the plurality is accentuated through the hermeneutics of the body of Saleem. The body functions as an allegory for the historiography of the nation. According to the *ayurvedic* philosophy the body is the microcosm of the whole nature. "Because a human being, inside himself, is anything but a whole, anything but homogeneous; all kinds of every which thing are jumbled up inside him, and he is one person one minute and another the next" (*MC* 328). The metaphor of the body to explain state or society is an age-old literary device in India. In the *Purusasukta* hymn of Rig-Veda states.

> A THOUSAND heads hath Puruṣa, a thousand eyes, a thousand feet.
>
> On every side pervading earth he fills a space ten fingers wide.
>
> This Puruṣa is all that yet hath been and all that is to be;
>
> The Lord of Immortality which waxes greater still by food.[52]

The approach of the Indian Ayurvedic system is holistic to human health so any malfunction in the body is treated with an over whole understanding of the body. Similarly, the novel perceives the cracks of Saleem as not merely physical. The cracks of Saleem and of India can be identified only through deep meditation and other spiritual practices. According to Ayurveda, Human beings are related to the society and nature. Hence, any imbalance in the relationship can be considered as illness. The disease is caused not only through various external infections but also through the state of mind. It does not consider human body as a separate entity like in the Western concept. Along with all other things in the universe, human body is also made up of *panchabhuta* or five elements: *prithvi*, *jal*, *agni*, *vayu* and *akasha*. "Indivisible, a one-piece suit, a sacred temple, if you will. It is important to preserve this wholeness" (*MC* 328). Holistic understanding about life is needed to accept the diversities. More than compartmentalization holistic comprehension is the ethos of India. "Who what am I? My answer: I am the sum total of everything that went before me, of all I have been seen done, of everything done-to-me. I am everyone everything whose being-in-the-world affected was affected by mine" (*MC* 380). Holistic understanding includes not only in a research but also to accept the diversities in the nation.

The novel is a fight between the imagination of pluralism and the imagination of centralization. The unjust power centre tore down the democracy. The authoritative centralization is represented by Shiva and the Widow. They foresaw a single national party, single ethnicity, etc., and tried to make a homogeneous culture through emergency. The novel criticizes "the dictatorial discourse of Indira Gandhi's regime."[53] The individualistic perspective of Shiva crushed enemies. The mighty kneels represent the oppression of pluralism. "He can kill six persons at one time, break necks khrikk-khrikk between his knees" (*MC* 519). The novel tries to uphold the pluralistic democratic view through the harsh criticism against centralism. 'Chutnification' (*MC* 642-43) is the method used in the novel to accommodate the diversities of the nation. "Symbolic value of the pickling process: all the six hundred million eggs which gave birth to the population of India could fit inside a single, standard-sized pickle-jar; six hundred million spermatozoa could be lifted on a single spoon" (*MC* 642). Each element is important in a pickle for a better taste. In the same manner, plurality makes India more enchanting.

5.3.5. *Preservation of Indian Ethos*

The golden past is a precious pearl. For a nation, it is an epoch-making element to attribute eternity to the imagination. The plethora of the glorification of the past of India in *Midnight's Children*, gives an impression that even in the midst of pitfalls of Indian democracy, its ethos is renowned and should be preserved for generations. The novel is 'eternally researching into and immortalizing' (*MC* 547) the Indianness. Rushdie preserves the ethos of India through different ways such as mythologizing, utopianization, and chutnification. The narration is not limited with the despair of failures but also promise of the success. He tries to mythologize the chronicle of the nation.

Creation and celebration of myths are prominent means to hand over the ethos of a nation to the coming generation. One of the means used by Rushdie in the novel to eternalize Indianness and to establish its identity is mythologizing its history instead of a rational and chronological way of narration. "A new myth to celebrate, because a nation which had never previously existed was about to win its freedom" (*MC* 150). A new myth is needed to construct continuously the rationale for being united. "A country which would never exist except by the efforts of a phenomenal collective will-except in a dream we all agreed to dream; it was a mass fantasy shared in varying degrees by Bengali and Punjabi, Madrasi and Jat," (*MC* 150). The novel follows the oral tradition of India that includes folklore, and myths. "What is being narrated in the text is an oral picture in Saleem's mind that is being written by him."[54] Saleem learns the story through superpower. Instead of rationalizing, Rushdie mythologises the history. He does not make an attempt to perfect the story in a Western manner. Only an imperfect history can exhibit the emotion of the subaltern.

Moreover the places and persons are mythologized in the novel. Rushdie attributed greatness to Indian place. "[...] in the oldest living city in the world, the city which was already old when the Buddha was young, Kasi Benares Varanasi, City of Divine Light" (*MC* 604). 'Tai,' who 'had no idea of his age' (*MC* 10) symbolizes the ancient culture of India which has 'five thousand years of history' (*MC* 150). "He is the 'tie' that binds the present to the past, the people to their customs and to one another; and he is the boatman who, like Charon, ferries to and from the land of the ancestral dead."[55] Tai is not limited to time and place but represents the whole India and its eternal history. "Tradition feels eternal, though of course it is not. That is how Tai can be said to precede religion and empire."[56] 'Tai's gift' (*MC* 8), to see the hidden yet real notions of history. "Tai taught [Aadam] years ago: The ice is always waiting [...] just under the water's skin" (*MC* 8). He represents Indianness so 'Aadam Aziz had loved him' (*MC* 11).

Another allegory used to preserve the history of India is pickle. Out of the fear of forgetfulness, Saleem makes chutney and keeps it in jars. 'To pickle is to give immortality' (*MC* 644). Metaphorically, the novel is a pickle jar to preserve 'the remaining shards of the past' (*MC* 596) of Indian ethos. The Indian identity is based on its plurality and each element has its vital role to play. Therefore a homogenization is not possible but a chutnification is the only means for the democratic existence of India. "[...] the feasibility of the chutnification of history; the grand hope of the pickling of time!" (*MC* 642). Preservation of the plurality is the aim of the novel. India cannot exist on monism and every attempt to make it homogeneous is a step towards its death. A further allegory used to preserve the Indian ethos is 'Saleem' himself. He is 'a swallower of lives' (*MC* 4).

"Just as Saleem is India, he is the chutney jar, the text, and the family, a chain of identifications that aligns each term with all the others."[57] Preservation is an act of hope because it is for the future generation. Since *Midnight's Children* is the history of chutnification, it is a novel of hope too. 'One jar stands empty' (*MC* 643) is a hope. The emptiness can be filled with a better tasty pickle. Subalterns carry more empty spaces which were forced on them by the democratic hegemony. "Testicles were removed from sacs, and wombs vanished forever [...] and they drained us of more than that: hope, too, was excised" (*MC* 613).

The emptiness is to be filled not only with resistance against foreign colonizers but also a strong defense against the native democratic hegemony. The narrator, has a hope in the second generation of midnight children and Aadam Sinai, 'Emergency-born' who 'is stronger, harder, more resolute than I', 'does not (as far as I can tell) surrender to dreams' (*MC* 421). Even though Saleem crumbles to dust, the 'son' may interact with the written book and build-up a new life. The novel has an optimistic view for a new horizon. "There is the future to think of" (*MC* 620). Hope and despair are always mixed with the personal life and national existence. "For every ladder you climb, a snake is waiting just around the corner; and for every snake, a ladder will compensate" (*MC* 194).

In short, the novel can be described as 'a permanent alternation: a hole' (*MC* 7) through which one can have 'the authentic taste of truth' (*MC* 644) about India. It is an attempt to preserve and to establish Indianness for eternity. "I spend my time at the great work of preserving. Memory, as well as fruit, is being saved from the corruption of the clocks" (*MC* 31). It celebrates the pluralistic imagination which is the essence of democratic ethos of India and rejects every attempt to form a homogeneous India. It is a political critical epic and calls for a change. "The nearly-thirty-one-year-old myth of freedom is no longer what it was. New myths are needed;" (*MC* 454). The pitfalls loaded in the novel spouts optimism 'to live or die in peace' (*MC* 647) than pessimism about Indian democracy. The post-independent history of India seems to be the betrayal of democracy but a promise yet to fulfill. The search for Indian ethos is not a completed task and the empty space is a hope to toil. "Five empty jars tinkle urgently, reminding me of my uncompleted task" (*MC* 381). The 'discovery' (*MC* 22) for identity based on Indian ethos still continues.

Notes

1. Shashi Tharoor, *India: From Midnight to the Millennium* (India: Penguin Books, 1997), p. 201.
2. J.K. Bajaj, "Chowdhary Charan Singh and the Politics of Independent India." Anand Amaladass (ed.) *Political Thinkers of India* (Chennai: Satya Nilayam Publications, 1998), p. 114.
3. Shankar Dayal Sharma, "Indira Gandhi and the Congress." Indira Gandhi Abinandan Samiti. *The Spirit of India.* Vol. II (New York: Asia Publishing House, 1976), p. 381.
4. Sam Chacko, "Defining Indianness." Web: 14th September 2010. Accessed: 4th September 2013. <http://geography.about.com/od/indiamaps/a/Defining-Indianness.htm>.
5. Peter Lyon, "The First Great Post-Colonial Stage: India's Tryst with Destiny." James Mayall and Anthony Payne (eds.) *The Fallacies of Hope: The Post-Colonial Record of the Commonwealth Third World* (UK: Manchester University Press, 1991), p. 26.
6. Jagjivan Ram, "Casteism: Impediment to Democratic Socialism". Indira Gandhi Abinandan Samiti. *The Spirit of India.* Vol. II (New York: Asia Publishing House, 1976), p. 432.
7. Vina Mazumader, "Women: From Equality to Empowerment." Hiranmay Karlekar (ed.) *Independent India: The First Fifty Years* (Delhi: Oxford University Press, 1998), p. 261.
8. Gurcharan Das, *India Unbound: From Independence to the Global Information Age.* 2000 (New Delhi: Penguin Books, 2002), p. 217.
9. Neelam Srivastava, *Secularism in the Postcolonial Indian Novel: National and Cosmopolitan Narratives in English.* 2007 (New York: Routledge, 2008), p. 4.
10. Shankar Dayal Sharma, "Indira Gandhi and the Congress." Indira Gandhi Abinandan Samiti. *The Spirit of India.* Vol. II (New York: Asia Publishing House, 1976), p. 382.

11. Ashutosh Varshney, "Editor's Preface." Ashutosh Varshney (ed.) *In The Indian Paradox: Essays in Indian Politics* (New Delhi: Sage Publications, 1989), p. 15.
12. C.R. Deshpande, *Transmission of The Mahabharat Tradition* (Simla: Indian Institute of Advanced Study, 1978), p. 1.
13. Bill Ashcroft, *Post-Colonial Transformation* (London: Routledge, 2001), p. 109.
14. *Ibid.*, p. 110.
15. Preeti S. Pathak, "Itihas, History and Novel in *The Great Indian Novel*." Jaydipsinh K. Dodiya (ed.) *Perspectives on Indian English Fiction* (New Delhi: Sarup & Sons, 2006), p. 245.
16. *Ibid.*, p. 243.
17. Uma Parameswaran, "Shashi Tharoor." Emmanuel S. Nelson (ed.) *Writers of the Indian Diaspora: A Bibliographical Critical Source Book* (New Delhi: Rawat Publications, 2010), p. 434.
18. Shashi Tharoor, *Nehru: The Invention of India*. 2003 (New Delhi: Penguin Books, 2007), p. 218.
19. D. Samrajya Lakshmi, "Subtlety, Mockery and Dharma in Shashi Tharoor's *The Great Indian Novel*." *Language in India*. Web: 2nd February 2009. Accessed: 2nd April 2014. p. 22 <www.languageinindia.com>.
20. *Ibid.*
21. Shashi Tharoor, *Nehru: The Invention of India*. 2003 (New Delhi: Penguin Books, 2007), p. 228.
22. Chaturvedi Badrinath, *The Mahabharata: An Inquiry in the Human Condition* (New Delhi: Orient Longman, 2006), p. 12.
23. Sachchidananda, "Integration of Tribes in Indian Society." Indira Gandhi Abinandan Samiti. *The Spirit of India*. Vol: II (New York: Asia Publishing House, 1976), p. 495.
24. Myron Weiner, "Preface." Ashutosh Varshney (ed.) *The Indian Paradox: Essays in Indian Politics* (New Delhi: Sage Publications, 1989), p. 9.
25. K.N. Panikkar, *Colonialism, Culture and Resistance*. 2007 (New Delhi: Oxford University Press, 2009), p. 102.
26. Pavan K. Varma, *Being India: The Truth about Why the Twenty-First Century will be India's* (New Delhi: Penguin Group, 2005), p. 148.

27. Shashi Tharoor, *India: From Midnight to the Millennium* (India: Penguin Books, 1997), p. 335.
28. *Manusmrti* Book:III/55. J. Duncan M. Derrett (Tran & Notes) *Bharcui's Commentary on the Manusmrti* Vol. II (Wiesbaden: Franz Steiner Verlag Gmbh, 1975), p. 6.
29. *Ibid.*, p. 200.
30. "Now Tharoor's book under fire," *The Times of India*. 31, March, 2014. Kerala ed.
31. Uma Parameswaran, *Writing the Diaspora: Essays on Culture and Identity* (New Delhi: Rawat Publications, 2007), p. 121.
32. Shashi Tharoor, *Nehru: The Invention of India*. 2003 (New Delhi: Penguin Books, 2007), p. 227.
33. K.N. Panikkar, *Colonialism, Culture and Resistance*. 2007 (New Delhi: Oxford: Oxford University Press, 2009), p. 52.
34. Jawaharlal Nehru, "Will and Testament." S. Gopal and Uma Iyengar N.D. (eds) *The Essential Writings of Jawaharlal Nehru* (New Delhi: Oxford University Press, 2003), p. 741.
35. Preeti S. Pathak, "Itihas, History and Novel in *The Great Indian Novel*." Jaydipsinh K. Dodiya (ed.) *Perspectives on Indian English Fiction* (New Delhi: Sarup & Sons, 2006), p. 244.
36. Deepa P. Chordiya, "Taking on the tone of a Bombay talkie: the function of Bombay cinema in Salman Rushdie's Midnight's Children" *ARIEL*. 38.4 (2007), p. 97. Academic OneFile. Accessed: 27th June 2013 <http://go.galegroup.com>
37. Salman Rushdie, "Introduction." *Midnight's Children*. 1981 (London: Vintage Books, 2013), p. xv.
38. Ágnes Györke, "Rushdie's Postmodern Nations." *The Ana ChronisT* 15 (2010), p. 135. Ebscohost. Accessed: 5th July 2013 <http://ehis.ebscohost.com.ulm.idm.oclc.org>
39. Salman Rushdie, "Introduction." *In Midnight's Children*. 1981 (London: Vintage Books, 2013), p. x.
40. Patrick Colm Hogan, "Midnights Children: Kashmir and the Politics of Identity." *Twentieth Century Literature*. 47.4 (2001), p. 510. Academic OneFile. Accessed: 22nd June 2013 <http://www.http://go.galegroup.com/>
41. Teresa Heffernan, "The Nation in Salman Rushdie's Midnight's Children." *Twentieth Century Literature* 46.4 (2000), p. 470.

Academic OneFile. Accessed: 1st July 2013 <http://www. http://go.galegroup.com/>.

42. Neil ten Kortenaar, "Postcolonial ekphrasis: Salman Rushdie Gives the Finger Back to the Empire." *Contemporary Literature* 38.2 (1997), p. 232. Academic OneFile. Accessed: 25th June 2013 <http://go.galegroup.com>
43. Mark Mossman, "Salman Rushdie's Midnight's Children: National Narrative as a Liminal Voice." *The Midwest Quarterly* 41.1 (1999), p. 66. Academic OneFile. Accessed: 22nd June 2013 <http://www.http://go.galegroup.com/>
44. *Ibid.*
45. Jean M. Kane, "The Migrant Intellectual and the Body of History: Salman Rushdie's 'Midnight's Children." *Contemporary Literature* 37.1 (1996), p. 94. Academic OneFile Accessed: 27th June 2013 <http://go.galegroup.com>
46. Neil ten Kortenaar, "Postcolonial ekphrasis: Salman Rushdie Gives the Finger Back to the Empire." *Contemporary Literature* 38.2 (1997) p. 232. Academic OneFile. Accessed: 25th June 2013 <http://go.galegroup.com>
47. Neelam Srivastava, "Languages of the Nation in Salman Rushdie's *Midnight's Children* and Vikram Seth's *A Suitable Boy*." ARIEL. 36.1-2 (2005), p. 207. Academic OneFile. Accessed: 22nd June 2013. <http://www.http://go.galegroup.com/>
48. John J. Su, "Epic of Failure: Disappointment as Utopian Fantasy in *Midnight's Children*." *Twentieth Century Literature* 47.4 (2001), p. 545. Academic OneFile. Accessed: 29th June 2013 <http://go.galegroup.com>
49. Salman Rushdie, "Introduction." *In Midnight's Children*. 1981 (London: Vintage Books, 2013), p. xvi.
50. John J. Su, "Epic of Failure: Disappointment as Utopian Fantasy in *Midnight's Children*." *Twentieth Century Literature* 47.4 (2001) p. 545. Academic OneFile. Accessed: 29th June 2013 <http://go.galegroup.com>
51. Neelam Srivastava, "Languages of the Nation in Salman Rushdie's *Midnight's Children* and Vikram Seth's *A Suitable Boy*." *ARIEL* 36.1-2 (2005) p. 207. Academic OneFile. Accessed: 22nd June 2013. <http://www.http://go.galegroup.com/>

52. *Rig Veda*, HYMN XC. *Puruṣa*. Ralph T.H. Griffith (trans.). 1896. Accessed: 5th May 2014. <http://www.sacred-texts.com/hin/rigveda/rv10090.htm>
53. Neelam Srivastava, "Languages of the Nation in Salman Rushdie's *Midnight's Children* and Vikram Seth's *A Suitable Boy*." *ARIEL* 36.1-2 (2005), p.207. Academic OneFile. Accessed: 22nd June 2013 <http://www.http://go.galegroup.com/>
54. Himanshu Parmar, "The Indian Counter Narrative in Midnight's Children." *Language In India*. 11.11 (2011), p. 424. Academic OneFile. Accessed: 27th June 2013 <http://go.galegroup.com>
55. Mossman Mark, "Salman Rushdie's Midnight's Children: National Narrative as a Liminal Voice." *The Midwest Quarterly* 41.1 (1999), p. 66. Academic OneFile. Accessed: 22nd June 2013 <http://www.http://go.galegroup.com/>
56. *Ibid*.
57. Jean M. Kane, "The migrant intellectual and the body of history: Salman Rushdie's 'Midnight's Children'." *Contemporary Literature* 37.1 (1996), p. 94. Academic OneFile. Accessed: 27th June 2013 <http://go.galegroup.com>

6

Literary Representation of the Indian Ethos in Neo-liberal Period

CHAPTER OUTLINE

6.1. Neo-liberal Period

Even though Rajiv Gandhi initiated India to step on to the threshold of twenty-first century, the paradigm shift happened in 1991 when Narasimha Rao adopted the economic liberation policy. It marked the neo-liberal period in India. The opening of the market not only made an impact on the economic matters but also on all domains of personal and social life. The visions and goals, opportunities and approach of the people changed. Globalization brought economic and cultural, material as well as non-material, changes in the Indian society. Some of the major features of the period which affected the ethos of India are analysed under the following headings.

6.1.1. *Economic Development*

Information technology (IT) came as the latest intellectual and cultural invader in India and it coincided with the globalization of 1991.

> The first dimension of undertaking larger projects is having sufficient numbers of employees. At the end of fiscal year 1999 (March 2000), the largest Indian service provider, TCS, had 17,000 employees, and Infosys and Wipro the next largest, had approximately 7000 each. By March of 2006 TCS had 63,000, Wipro had 54,000, and Infosys had 45,000. As of September 2006, TCS had 78,000, Infosys had increased to 66,000, and Wipro had 61,000-plus all three companies had ambitious hiring plans.[1]

Business process outsourcing (BPO) also flourished in India and 2.8 million people depended on it in 2012. The new revolution saved India from the economic crash. IT and globalization formed the sixth major factor that shaped Indian ethos.

India has made remarkable achievements in the spectrum of science and technology. For example, in 2008 India successfully launched the lunar probe, Chandrayaan-I for the first time. In 1998, India went ahead with the Pokharan nuclear tests and asserted itself as one of the superpowers of the world. Boosted with this confidence, India found its own space in the international geopolitics. Identifying the potency of India to become a big power, Washington began to maintain a close relationship and as an external sign, it received Prime Minister Manmohan Singh with full honours in 2005. The improvement in the role of India in international organizations such as G8, G20, and G15 is a sign of the development and the positive evaluation of other countries regarding India. In the third millennium, many speak about the 'Shining India' or 'New India' that is progressing economically. Abdul Kalam set a goal, namely 'Vision 2020.' "India should become a developed nation by 2020. A developed India means, that India will be one of the five biggest economic powers, having self-reliance in national security. Above all, the nation will have a standing in world economic and political forum."[2] Now Indians dream of a developed country.

6.1.2. *Disparity between the Rich and the Poor*

Along with its bright side, India has a dark side too. As socialism declined and capitalism took over, those who had power and opportunity accumulated more wealth. Hence, along with economic development, the disparity between the rich and the poor increased. As a result, new problems emerged in the Indian society. The 'New India' is concerned with the rich and their luxurious problems. "In an increasingly urbanized India, we have little time to hear of the travails of the landless peasant, of the tribal driven out of his home, of forests being denuded, of illegal mining contracts that ravage our hills."[3] The unorganized are rejected; either the politically powerful or the economically prominent are recognized. Because of profit orientation, the rights of the workers are denied. In the name of development, agricultural lands are taken over by the state and handed over to private entrepreneurs.

Development should be holistic and economic progress should not focus only on certain sections of society. It needs to ensure inclusive growth, and more importantly inclusive opportunity creation in the long run. It always has a piecemeal pattern of development in some areas, some sectors, some groups may surge past others—but it must be ensured that it is not always the same pieces moving faster than others.[4] The cities are over populated with the migrants. Development in urban and rural areas should be balanced. The economic inequality endangers the peaceful existence of the country. More than the development of infrastructure in rural areas, the empowerment of villagers is needed; otherwise, they may not be able to explore the benefit of liberalization.

6.1.3. *Corruption*

Corruption and criminalization in politics became detrimental to Indian democracy. The Hawala scandal (1992), the Kargil coffin scam (1999), the Uttar Pradesh food grain scam (2003), the 2G spectrum scam (2010), the Indian coal field allocation scam (2012), and Karnataka Wakf Board land scam (2012) are some of the examples for corruption. Slowly, people became aware of the menace of corruption, so anti-corruption movements became strong in India. The 10th Chief Election Commissioner, T.N. Seshan (in office 1990-96), brought in many measures to abolish the malpractices of election. He prohibited the use of religion, official machinery, liquor, loudspeakers without permission, etc., for election campaigns. The Judiciary also constructively intervened in the situation to guide the Indian democracy according to the spirit of the Constitution. "In the last few years the Supreme Court has, through intense judicial activism, become a symbol of hope for the people of India."[5] Besides, the media have become very vigilant against corruption. For example, Tehelka came with the Match-fixing scandal (2000), and Operation West End (2001). Padma Bhushan Anna Hazare, the social activist, led satyagrahas (2011) for the strict Jan Lokpal Bill against corruption. The crowd moved to the streets in great numbers to protest against corruption. The Lokpal Bill was passed in the Rajya Sabha and in the Lok Sabha on 17 and 18 December 2013 respectively. Corruption became a major evil in Indian society.

6.1.4. *Violence over Non-violence*

Smiling Buddha (1974) and Post Smiling Budda (operation Shakti—1998) were over but 'Smiling Gandhi' and 'Post-Smiling Gandhi' still remain. The historic Buddha stood for *ahimsa* whereas the symbolic Buddha smiles for nuclear bomb. What may/may not be attributed to Gandhiji by his future sons/daughters cannot be predicted! Villainy, terrorism, and communal violence take over the ethos of *ahimsa*. Other than individual incidents, organized groups like terrorist organizations, left wing extremists' groups, separatist movements, and religious fundamentalists' body also instigated violence. The terrorist attacks like the Indian Parliament attack in 2001, Mumbai attack in 2008, and the Pune bombing in 2010 remain nightmares. Along with the externally sponsored terrorism, militant groups like Maoists and Naxalites also take to violence to protest against the system. In turn, instead of solving the issue peacefully the government is becoming an oppressive machinery. Contradictory to this, India has succeeded in conducting elections in Jammu and Kashmir and Punjab in 1996 and 1997 respectively.

In the Neo-liberal period, there is an open clash between religious fundamentalism and secularism. In 1992, Hindu fundamentalists demolished the sixteenth-century mosque in Ayodhya and this led to communal killings. In the Gujarat pogrom of 2002, 1000 Muslims were killed and 20000 became homeless. In the 2008 Orissa communal violence, 100 Christians were murdered, 5600 were displaced. Religious communal violence is an attempt to define Indianness along religious lines. For the fundamental groups, all Indians should follow Hindu religion not the Hindu way of life. In turn Hindus were targeted in the 1993 Bombay bombings, in which 900 people died and 1200 were injured.

The political parties covertly or overtly please various religious groups. "The quality of the secularism of the Indian state and most of the political parties has had varying degrees of weakness. In fact, their secularism has seldom been very sturdy."[6] It is the need of the time to regain the ethos of *ahimsa*. Vempeny proposed religiosity of dialogical liberation as a solution for the peaceful existence of different religions. "All the religions in India have the ideals and potential to cooperate with other religions to build India as a prosperous, progressive, well united, peace-loving and peace making great nation."[7] All, including religious and ethnic groups, should adopt the way of democracy.

6.1.5. *Subaltern Assertions*

The progress of the underprivileged is always a serious concern for India. As per the 2011 census, nearly 20.14 crore people belong to scheduled castes in the country.[8] In spite of the constitutional prohibition, dalit students are still discriminated in the government schools of 38% of villages in India. They are not allowed to enter police stations in 32% of the villages.[9] According to the statistics of the India Rural Development Report of 1992, 43% of the rural population lack land ownership and according to the 1991 census, 64% of the dalits are landless.[10] Poverty among dalits is very common, for instance, half of India's dalit children are undernourished, 21% are severely underweight and 12% die before their 5th birthday.[11] The reports of crimes against dalits are too high. Everyday eleven dalits are beaten, two are murdered, two of their houses are burnt, and three dalit women are raped in India.[12]

Inspite of these atrocities, the condition of the scheduled castes, scheduled tribes, and other backward classes has improved a lot. The lower castes have begun to attain power and the proportion of the members from the high caste to state and central governments has begun to reduce. Uttar Pradesh, Madhya Pradesh and Bihar were ruled by Chief Ministers who belonged to the lower caste. In the Lok Sabha, the strength of the OBCs has grown from less than 5% in 1952 to about one fourth in 2004. The rise of the Scheduled Caste and OBC has made irreversible impact in Indian political and social scenario.[13] The philosophy and social norms of India might be influenced by the high caste but they are no longer able to dictate to the lower castes. The fast shifting of power centres from high caste to low caste is taking place in India. To attain power, casteism becomes a tool. In cities, the caste system is fading away and the class system is gaining prominence.

6.1.6. *Status of Women*

The participation of the lower caste in nation building has improved whereas the condition of women is yet to improve. Indians have glossy words to describe women but their social system subjugates them. In the family as well as in the society, the opportunity first knocks at the door of a male and if he denies, it may or may not come to her. "It is unthinkable that such equality of treatment between a boy and a girl child would ever be thwarted."[14] For example, The Women's Reservation Bill, which proposes to reserve 33 per cent of seats from the total seats of the Lok Sabha and in all State Legislative Assemblies for women, is still hanging in the air. The holistic well-being of women is more essential to establish themselves in the family and in society. "In India, the female construct is always treated as a commodity rather a conscientious person. The kind of attention paid to her physical appearance and activities gain greater significance than the detailed description of her psyche and intellectual potentialities."[15] The neo-liberal period women need equal status, health care, education, employment opportunities, etc., and more freedom from the traditional constraints to construct themselves meaningfully.

6.1.7. *Virtual Representation*

Post-independent Indians live under the shadow of the anti-colonial revolutionaries and their attempts to decolonize the Indian culture. The aftermath of colonialism is filled with ambivalent cultural mood of resistance and acceptance. Panikkar comments that the modern Indian middle class, who were culturally and intellectually influenced by colonialism, dearly embraced the culture of globalization because the renaissance and nationalism aborted the course of history.[16] Hence, the process of de-colonization has to continue vigorously in the neo-liberal period because re-colonization takes place none the less in toneless through globalization. Globalization controls not only the open market but the ontological framework too. It is not passive but can rewrite the yardstick of perception. The eyes of the national consciousness are not able to perceive and critically analyze the impact or meaning of actions.

Culture is interpreted in terms of identity, not in commercial terms but in neo-liberalization phase market value determines it. One is caught in the danger of equalizing culture with commodity. Commoditization of culture in consumeristic society endangers one's identity. In the shadow of the open market, what takes place is westernizing the rest of the space. In the neo-liberal period, the fight is twofold: decolonization and decommodification. Instead of exterminating one's ethos with virtual shadows, continuous reformation of ethos facilitates one to live-fully. If the market determines the value of culture, then identity and meaning may deteriorate. KFC-ization of our culture is the neo-liberal form of colonization and fulfils the prophecy of Macauly: 'English in taste.' Since turning back on globalization is impossible, export Indianness instead of importing the non-Indian.

6.1.8. *Fictional Representation*

The changeover of India to the neo-liberal period constantly redefines the ethos of the people from the 1990s onwards. The nation has been moving in another direction. This is marked by the emphasis on India becoming 'the super power' which is notable through the IT revolution, the growing political role of lower castes and regional parties, economic liberation, etc. At the same time, people have become more worried about corruption and disparity between the rich and poor. Hence, during this period the authors of Indian English fiction deal with a variety of subjects like loss of identity, globalization, suffering of women, corruption, etc., and the phase can be termed as the humanization phase of literature. Some of the novels published during this period are Amitav Ghosh's *The Glass Palace* (2000), *The Hungry Tide* (2005), *Sea of Poppies* (2008), *River of Smoke* (2011); Anita Desai's *The Artist of Disappearance* (2011); Kiran Desai's *The Inheritance of Loss* (2006); Rohinton Mistry's *A Fine Balance* (1995), *Family Matters* (2002); Manju Kapur's *Difficult Daughter* (1998), *Custody* (2011). The fiction of Chetan Bhagat like *Five Point Someone* (2004), *One Night @*

the Call Center (2005), *Revolution 2020: Love, Corruption, Ambition* (2011) have become popular.

Arundhati Roy's *The God of Small Things* (1997) and Aravind Adiga's *The White Tiger* (2008) are selected for the study. *The God of Small Things* won the Booker Prize in 1997 and *The White Tiger* got Man Booker Prize in 2008. The eagle-eyed observations of these novels throw light into various aspects of neo-liberal period of India.

6.2. Analysis of *The God of Small Things* in the Light of the Neo-liberal Ethos

A deep and healthy relationship is a means for self-actualization. Promoting such relationships is one of the characteristics of the ethos of Indian civilization. Compared to other languages, Indian languages have more words to express various types of relationships. In a broader sense, these relationships can be divided into five: with oneself, with others/society, with culture, with nature and with Supreme Reality. These are the various units of one reality and have in-depth relationships between them. In Indian ethos, it is not only a philosophical transcendental interrelationship limited in abstract idea, but also a concrete realization of inter-subjectivity with all beings, which expresses love and concern. Hence, the Indian rishies envisaged the universe as *Vasudhaiva Kutumbakam*—the world itself as a family. It is based on love and is "the expansion of consciousness, which is a comprehensive perception of the universe as teleologically one entity."[17] The whole universe is one family, which has deep inter-relationship and at the same time has independent identity. The relationship is necessary to keep the rhythm of the whole universe. However, forgetting the Dharmaśāstra of relationship, a few persons using intellectual and physical forces have begun to dominate and brought others to the yoke.

The God of Small Things by Arundhati Roy is the story of the victimization of the 'Mombatt' (*GST* 89), who are underprivileged, by 'Laltain' (*GST* 89), who are the subjugators. Laltains make use of all the social structures and institutions such as marriage, parenthood, social relationships, morality, political parties, and police for oppressing the Mombatt who are alone and powerless to fight against this atrocities. Since the story is the saga of a family, it could expose the healthy and unhealthy relationships with oneself, family, society, nature and God. In a nutshell, the novel is the narration of the destructive interventions of a few in personal spaces of others. The hypocritical ethical and moral weapon destroys the peace of certain unarmed people and at large, of *Vasudhaiva Kutumbakam*. A healthy family needs personal freedom and interdependence at the same time. The borderlines between them are so thin. Hence, the proper maintenance of the balance between the two is the sign of a healthy family. There people get space for personal expression and at the same time mutual empowering may take place. So *Vasudhaiva Kutumbakam* is the synchronization of individualism and collectivism, and *The God of Small Things* envisages that it may be realized 'tomorrow' (*GST* 339).

6.2.1. *Individualism versus Collectivism*

The duality of individualism and collectivism helps to understand the differences between attitude and behaviour, silence and voicing, introvert and extrovert, norm and value, reaction and response, emotion and cognition, right and wrong, rejection and acceptance, achievement and failure, stagnancy and change, etc. The distinctions between individualism and collectivism can be summarized in four points. Firstly, the individualists emphasize independence and personal aspects while the collectivist proposes interdependence and group aspects by the collectivists. Secondly, the individualists give importance to personal goals, whereas group goals take precedence for collectivists. Thirdly, the social behaviour of individualists is determined by personal convictions and personal rights, but norms, obligations and duties of the society are the guiding principles for collectivists. Fourthly, the individualists view relationship as rational exchanges, whereas collectivists emphasize the communality of the relationship, even when this represents a disadvantage.[18]

The almost opposing nature of individualists and collectivists causes problems to work together. The collectivists may succumb to the existing norms of the society whereas the individualists may question them and act against or independent of them. This may lead to conflict between the individualist and the society. Society may consider the activities of individualists as deviant behaviour and individualists may review the social rules as meaningless. Triandis went ahead with further research and differentiated horizontal/vertical aspects of individualism and collectivism. Those who accept inequality and social order of the society are classified as vertical dimension. Others who emphasize equality and equal rights are included in horizontal dimension. The psychological terms used to denote individualism is idiocentrism and collectivism is allocentrism.[19] According to the nature of accepting the social order, the members of the in-group can be divided into four and the characteristics are the following:

Vertical individualist (VI):	independent and accepts inequality.
Horizontal individualist (HI):	independent and view others as equals.
Vertical collectivist (VC):	interdependent and accepts inequality or hierarchy of the society.
Horizontal collectivist (HC):	interdependent and perceives all as equals.[20]

The major characters of *The God of Small Things* can be divided according to their characteristics of relationship (Table 6.1). This classification also helps one to understand their behaviour, attitude, and role in the story. The kind of interaction between the people of the same nature and with others can be analyzed from this division for the better understanding of the story from a holistic perspective. It also throws light into the functioning style of the society where collectivism and individualism are influenced by the national culture. The novel highlights the strong thread of relationship between people and the changes in the same.

Table 6.1: The Classification of the Major Characters According to the Nature of Interaction

Classification	Names of the characters
Vertical individualist (VI)	Pappachi, Baby Kochamma, Chacko, Comrade Pillai, Inspector Thomas Mathew (God of Big Things)
Horizontal individualist (HI)	Ammu, Rahel, Velutha (God of Small Things)
Vertical collectivist (VC)	Mammachi, Vellya Paapen, Kochu Maria
Horizontal collectivist (HC)	Estha

6.2.2. *Nationality and Individualism-Collectivism*

The ethos of the nation influences the individualistic and collective nature of the people and controls the general orientation in values and behavioural pattern. Individualism and collectivism are among the set of collective beliefs and values which defines national culture, according to Hofstede's five-dimensional measure of culture. The other factors are uncertainty avoidance, power distance, masculinity-femininity, and long term-short term orientation. Individualism "pertains to societies in which the ties between individuals are loose: everyone is expected to look after himself or herself and his or her immediate family."[21] The individuals stand for their well-being rather than that of the state. The authority should function for the betterment of the individuals and should give personal freedom. In a collective culture people are more attached to the group rather than the personal benefits. "Collective cultures thereby do not usually allow the freedom and independence necessary for organisational members to think creatively and, thereby, fail to cultivate an environment that fosters an innovative spirit."[22] It may negatively affect the personal expressions and self-satisfaction, as in the case of a joint-family. According to this approach, people in a collectivist culture strongly identify with their in-groups such as families, schools, and organization.[23] Since the individualism and collectivism can be seen as a cultural syndrome,[24] Indian ethos can be analysed on the basis of these concepts.

6.2.3. *Individualism and Collectivism in India*

The basic spirit of Indian ethos is collectivism without neglecting individuality. In the traditional Indian society, joint family, tribe, caste, and sect were the various categories of social stratification, which gave social identity to the person and led to self-realization. However, later collectivism got dominance over individualism and individuals lost personal independence. The individual as a single unit had not much to do. The village community took decisions on all types of issues: judicial, criminal, social, fiscal or any other, which may arise in the society.[25] Personal matters like marriage, and child rearing were undertaken by the joint family. According to Herbert Spencer, in joint families, the eldest male had the supremacy to the extent of life and death power over wife and children.[26] The father had full control over the property. The domestic authority was perceived as natural and had religious support. The rights and duties were related to the castes or sex and not to the individual persons. "Even satisfactory terms which mean human rights or equal opportunities are not found in *Dharmasastra* and *Arthasastra*."[27] There was no mention of the fundamental human rights.

The moral life of the person also was determined by the society. At the time of *Grihya Sutras* and the *Dharma Sutras* the individual was controlled by the community. From birth to death everything was fixed and people had to move through the path predetermined by the community. Caste along with the four *ashrams* defined complex duties and functions of each person in each stage. By the Upanishads, even the intellectual level was also pre-determined; so the individual could not question the values, pattern of behaviour or discover new duties. Everything was given to him/her and the person had to fulfill them unquestionably.[28]

Later Buddhism was oriented towards individualism. It rejected ritualistic and magical elements of early Brahmanism and took a less determinative position.[29] The Buddha proposed more rational and psychological approach than collective identity. Later Brahmanism took over and again collectivism got an upper hand over individualism in Indian society. The Bhakti

Movement leaders like Kabir, Tulasidas, Namdev, Tukaram and others tried to move away from the structured system but they could succeed only partially.

The Indian society was not much disturbed by the Muslim invasion because the collective nature of India was not revised by them. Muslims also had an orientation towards collectivism. On the other hand, the European conquest did affect Indians in all aspects of life and they considered eastern civilization as binary to the west and considered the eastern culture as inferior. This brought sharp confrontation with the Indian ethos and shook the collective identity. The response was a mixture of rejection, accommodation, assimilation and aping. It affected all the spheres of life and the individual got more importance. The affirmation of individuality has gone so far that one of the general features of Indian ethos of a comprehensive understanding of the phenomena was challenged. The thoughts and actions are not perceived in their totality. When the Indian collective identity met with Western individual identity all the traditional values related to community, ethics were questioned and the social structure began to change. For example joint family system turned to nuclear family, people began to move out of their ancestral village, etc. According to Max Weber, the joint family system lost its charm as the individual became less content with being bound to the rigid and undifferentiated authority prescribed by the group. On the other hand, people's desire to develop their individuality and to enjoy the fruit of their labour by themselves increased. This led to the disintegration of the joint family and thereby diminished the collective identity.

The Indian democracy also added to the spirit of individualism. It was against the Vedic and medieval spirit of India where people took decisions as a group under a leader. The existence was related to the group. "The notion of 'one man, one vote' has no history in Indian society, but the republican traditions of group society were pervasive."[30] Western imperialism introduced the individual vote and personal rights. One-person one vote directly accepts the individualism in India but it is an ethos which is alien to Indian culture. "Indian individualism as being supported by a democratic and secular society, but also stymied by traditions and socio-economic realities."[31] In addition to this the globalization of 1991 contributed to the promotion of individualism. The increase in opportunities boosted the people to explore the new avenues and to move away from the traditional collectivism, which discouraged individual decisions. Because of the competition in the market, individuals worked hard and aspired to attain higher positions even sacrificing their relationships.

The shift from traditional collective identity to individualist democratic identity created confusion in the value system. The norms of behaviour of the older generation and the younger generation varied and this led to misunderstanding about the deviant behaviour. The moral and ethical grounds of do's and don'ts were questioned and much confusion arouse. Dissatisfaction with the head of the family, and traditional rules led the people to search new systems for family life and opportunities for employment outside the village. "Classes and kinds of people welcomed modernization as industrialization, science and technology. But tension persisted between modern individualistic norms and the traditional group character of Indian society."[32] This created a big gap between the progressives who supported individualism and the conservatives who supported collectivism. Both pleasant and unpleasant incidents related with relationships become the subject matter of writers. *The God of Small Things* is such a novel which gives an account of the changes happening in the Indian society in the structure and practice of relationships.

6.2.4. *The God of Small Things: Search for Individual Identity*

In the traditional Indian society, collectivism got more importance. Therefore, in practice, individuals lack personal freedom and self-satisfaction, everything is determined by the privileged ones of the society to protect their selfish motives. However, the educational revolution, Western invasion and globalization brought a radical shift from collectivism to individualism. Individualism challenged the traditional practices like caste system, marriage, sex, patriarchism, and values. Change creates tension. The radical shift makes awful edginess especially in a large group where most of the members stick to the old working philosophy and few move to the opposite pole. The *God of Small Things* is a story of the transformation of a few members and the apprehension of the larger group. Variations and its aftermath are the connecting thread of the novel.

To expose the abuse of relationships, Arundhati Roy divides the characters generally into Laltain and Mombatt. Laltains who support the inequality and collectivism include Mammachi, Pappachi, Baby Kochamma, Chacko, Pillai, and Inspector Thomas Mathew. Mombatts who stand for equality and individualism are Velutha, Ammu, Rahel, and Estha.

> This novel deals with the universal theme of social consciousness ego confrontation between the "Laltain and Mombatti," class antagonism and class exploitation, exposure of the tyranny and injustice, [...] the "fret and fever" the deserted and the defenceless have to pass through in the police custody and in a class-ridden societal structure.[33]

The social identification of similar values, brings Laltains together and the resistance against them brings Mombatts together. This process can be understood by *The Social Identity Theory* (SIT) published in 1978 by H. Tajfel which is still considered as one of the best theories, even though there are different theories such as self-categorization theory, optimal distinctiveness theory, etc., to explain intergroup relationships of the members of a group.[34] SIT says the internalization of the characteristics of a group leads to the formation of positive social identity and the person tries to enhance the identification, through modification of his/her attitudes and behaviours according to the group norms. The major outcomes of the identification are: self-insight and understanding; downward social comparison; collective self-esteem; in-group cooperation; intergroup comparison and competition; social interaction; and romantic involvement.[35] All who identify with a group have similar meaning and significance. The self-satisfaction through identification, works in Laltains and they try to protect the system.

Conformation to the group may lead to in-group favouritism and conflict with the out-group. In order to get the acceptance of the other members of the in-group or to bring people to the group forcefully or to express revenge to those who resist to conform to the norms of the society, bullying may be used. Bullying is a systematic and intentional abuse of power in the form of physical, verbal, or relative aggression in order to hurt others. This can occur in any human situation where power relationships exist and those with power have opportunities to abuse it.[36] Inspector Thomas, the guardian of law and justice, and Comrade Pillai, Ayemenem's own Crusader for Justice and Spokesman of the Oppressed, come together through social identification. They bully Velutha [horizontal individualist (HI)] who moves against their values. Inspector Thomas accepts the petition of Baby Kochamma, who belongs to the same class [vertical individualist (VI)], but rejects Ammu's (horizontal individualist) plea because she is out of the groups. Chacko, Mammachi and Baby Kochamma who belong to VI group come together to bully Ammu, Estha, Rahel and Velutha who had a different worldview (HI).

Bullying and self-defence take place in neo-liberal India. To a certain extent, the novel is an autobiography. The root of the story evolves from the unpleasant life experience of Mrs. Mary Roy, mother of Arundhati Roy and the scared childhood of the author herself; so the novel is the miniature form of the real situation of India. "The post-sixties India is scanned on micro as well as macro-structural levels. Ayemenem becomes a transforming world-in-miniature that is torn in dissensions: individual as well as collective, emotional as well as instinctive."[37] Roy herself accepts that the problem in relationships in India is too complex to grasp. "To understand history [...] we have to go inside and listen to what they're saying. And look at the books and the pictures on the wall. And smell the smells" (*GST* 52). All the five senses are needed for the holistic comprehension of the situation.

Various modes of subjection or bullying are incorporated in the novel. Individuals can fight with individuals and can win but it is very difficult to fight with a group. In collectivism, the philosophy of the dominating group is considered as normal and the behaviour of individuals are sanctioned on its basis, so the individual who fights for the personal rights may be neglected and considered as deviants. Male chauvinism, unjust caste system, and hypocrisy of communism have collective support. Therefore, the group morally accepts all their actions even if they brutally neglect the human rights. Those who stand for the individual rights are 'the God of Loss, the God of Small Things' (*GST* 220), and The God of Goose Bumps (*GST* 330) but the collective hypocrisy atrociously kill them as they have done something 'unforgivable.' The novel attempts to bring new ethos of relationship based on humanism and individual freedom.

6.2.4.1. Relation to Oneself

According to the ethos of India, human life is a journey, which actively searches for meaning and self-realization. Once collectivism dominates over individualism, many restrictions are imposed on the freedom of the individual. People lose their right to take decisions and become dissatisfied. This is especially so in the life of the woman. Mammachi, the wife of Pappachi, is a victim of such restrictions so 'her own grief grieved her' (*GST* 5). The male superiority complex always haunts Mammachi and there is no space for her to search for identity. She is 'exceptionally talented' but abruptly asked by Pappachi 'to discontinue the violin class' (*GST* 50) only out of 'jealousy' (*GST* 47). The heart breaking sentence which expresses the mind of Mammachi is made by Ammu at the time of the funeral of Pappachi: "Ammu told the twins that Mammachi was crying more because she was used to him than because she loved him" (*GST* 50). The novel distinguishes between real love which is born of heart with satisfaction and respect, and mechanical love born out of law and custom. She passively lives without self-realization and with "scars of old beatings from an old marriage. Her brass vase scars" (*GST* 166).

The character Kalyani, who is a *patidevta* of Pillai, suffers like Mammachi. When Pillai wants to touch Kalyani's 'breast immediately' (*GST* 286), 'she sat on the bed and absentmindedly' (*GST* 286). "A girl forcibly enjoyed by one who does not understand the hearts of girls becomes nervous, uneasy and dejected, and suddenly begins to hate the man who has taken advantage of her."[38] For Pillai she is a tool for sexual enjoyment and she is at his gaze. Another character who lives with dissatisfaction but tries to overcome obstacles is Ammu. The mental agony of the woman who moves away from the 'moral code' of the society is very great. A veshya's affidavit has no validity in the police station and in the society. If the *lakshmanarekha* of the society is broken by anyone, the consequence will be unpredictable. However, at last she had 'no more dreams' (*GST* 42). Every one rejects her and at the end, she 'sat up in the strange bed in the strange room in the strange town' (*GST* 161). She is the emblem of self-sacrifice for not succumbing to the unjust social system. When the dynamic individuals fight against the entrenched social hierarchy, they are forced to carry several crosses.

Rahel belongs to the third generation and she goes with her own convictions. She tries to build-up her individual identity. Rahel has a casual attitude to life, even in marriage. "Rahel drifted into marriage like a passenger drifts towards an unoccupied chair in an airport lounge" (*GST* 18). She challenges the elder generation. "We're divorced." Rahel hoped to shock him into silence (*GST* 130). She breaks the prison of marriage where her grandmother and mother suffered. She even commits incest—a grave sin even in the twenty-first century. She enjoys sex as a free human being. Table 6.2 explains the change in response of women as the relationship changes.

Table 6.2: The Response of Three Generations

First Generation (Mammachi)	Second Generation (Ammu)	Third Generation (Rahel)
1. Collective identity	1. Actively search for self-identity	1. Individualistic
2. Surrendered to husband and son	2. Lack of self-confidence	2. Won over patriarchal system
3. Unprotestingly suffered	3. Suffered yet did not surrender	3. Self confident
4. No self-satisfaction	4. Resisted to subverting marriage system	4. Up hold the individuality & rights

Roy makes use of the epic character Draupadi who is 'strangely angry only with the men that won her' (*GST* 234).

Rahel who breaks the bonds of the society symbolizes Draupadi. The patriarchist is uncomfortable with Draupadi. The Kathakali Men who present the story of Draupadi "took off their make-up and went home to beat their wives" (*GST* 236). The patriarchal society always projects Sita as the role model for women but Arundhati Roy considers Draupadi as the ideal woman who baths 'her hair in fresh blood' (*GST* 235) of Dushasana. This story may create 'madness' (*GST* 235) in those who take Draupadi as the ideal woman who stands against injustice and who wants revenge. Then patriarchism may collapse completely. These women, themselves feel self-confident and live with self-satisfaction.

6.2.4.2. Relationship with the Others/Society

Indian ethos promotes deep relationship in the family and society; and relationships are regulated by various social do's and don'ts which are more conventional than written. The various institutions like caste system, joint family, marriage, and political parties are formed for the well-ordered functioning of the society. However, as time passes, the genuine spirits of these institutions are lost and become oppressive machines. In the collectivism, the privacy of the individual is limited, so society unnecessarily intervened in the personal spheres of individuals. It may affect the smooth functioning of the society and satisfaction of the individuals. "Rahel wondered what he gained by questioning her so closely and then completely disregarding her answers. Clearly he didn't expect the truth from her, but why didn't he at least bother to pretend otherwise?" (*GST* 131). Roy narrates the unjust systems like patriarchism, marriage, caste system, police and Communism, which curtail free social relationships.

6.2.4.2.1. Patriarchism

Married life in India is an expression of collectivism, where not only two individuals are involved but also families, caste, and religion. In the case of arranged marriages the preference of the bridegroom and the bride is sometimes side-lined by other factors. The society considers marriage as sacred, so at any cost couples sacrifice themselves to protect it. For this value, many a time the woman is the sacrificial animal. "Women's position in Indian society has been partly shaped by the ideology of the Indian family. Although the family is theoretically a sanctuary for women, it also has the potential of acting as a prison with a restrictive code of conduct."[39] The novel narrates the anxiety, insecurity, and subjugation in a male dominating society. The melancholy of woman is narrated as a 'relay' and the baton is handed over to the next generation with all its unpleasant experiences. The most selfish attitude of the male is expressed by Chacko, the 'Male Chauvinist Pig' (*GST* 83) that: "What's yours is mine (Chacko) and what's mine is also mine" (*GST* 57).

Through Mammachi, Ammu and Rahel the narrator exposes the trap of marriage and also shows the response of three generations to it. Just like a prisoner, a woman has less opportunity of choice. Marriage is a legalized jail for the woman. The husband takes the role of the police and ill-treats the prisoner who lacks an identity. In marriage, there is no subjectivity for the woman. "[Kalyani] referred to her husband [Mr. Pillai] as *addeham* which is the respectful form of 'he', whereas 'he' called her 'edi' which was, approximately, 'Hey, you!" (*GST* 270). The woman in a cage is either like a pet animal with good food or like a neglected animal in a zoo. Ammu accepts the proposal not out of love but to escape from the marooned life of Ayemenem and the burden of dowry. The marriage function is like decorating a dead body which is taken for cremation.

The woman has no other option but to be in the cage. If they try to break it, the condition becomes pathetic. "She subscribed wholeheartedly to the commonly held view that a married daughter had no position in her parents' home. As for a *divorced* daughter according to Baby Kochamma, she had no position anywhere at all" (*GST* 45). Here, the condition of men is different. Both Ammu and Chacko break the bond of marriage but the approach of the family and the society is entirely different. Chacko gets sympathy out of men's needs (*GST* 168, 238, 295, 313) whereas Ammu is harassed even by the servant. The moral codes for man and woman are different.

In the Indian society marriage is necessary for the survival of women. "The fate of the wretched Man-less woman. The sad, Father Mulligan-less Baby Kochamma" (*GST* 45). For the man, she is a slave in the house and puppet in the society. "They were beaten, humiliated and then made to suffer the envy of friends and relations for having such a wonderful husband and father" (*GST* 180).

In order to prove that the attitude of the Indian male is the problem in the institution of marriage, Roy brings a foreign character, Margaret Kochamma to narrate the Indian patriarchal superiority complex. The Indian wives have to look after their husbands like newborn babies and sometimes it is easier to look after children than their husbands. What Margaret finds is not the character of Chacko but a microcosm of the Indians' nature. Mutual responsibility is necessary for happiness in marriage but Chacko follows the patriarchal lineage of Pappachi. "Margaret Kochamma was happy with Joe. Happier perhaps than she would have been had she not had those wild, precarious years with Chacko. She thought of Chacko fondly, but without regret" (*GST* 249). Patriarchy is the most dehumanizing force and it neglects the identity of women. Patriarchy is beastly, "because certainly no beast has essayed the boundless, infinitely inventive art of human hatred. No beast can match its range and power" (*GST* 236). The various means employed by the patriarchal society to subjugate women are physical and mental force, patriarchal-woman who justifies the patriarchal values, pseudo-patriarchal attitude, and denial of rights.

The first means is physical and mental force. Husbands severely subject their wives to corporal torture. "The Kathakali Men took off their make-up and went home to beat their wives" (*GST* 236). The brutal corporal violence of Pappachi towards Mammachi continues till Chacko twists the hand of Pappachi. Then Pappachi uses mental torture and he does not speak to Mammachi. "In the evenings, when he knew visitors were expected, he would sit on the verandah and sew buttons that weren't missing onto his shirts, to create the impression that Mammachi neglected him" (*GST* 48). The second means used by the patriarchal society is making use of the woman who are already trapped in the patriarchal system. The women themselves become the protectors of masculinity. The step-motherly treatment of Mammachi towards Ammu is an example for this. But she indirectly supports the unethical sexual activities of Chacko "Her tolerance of 'Men's Needs' as far as her son was concerned, became the fuel for her unmanageable fury at her daughter" (*GST* 257). Women are the victims of the same gender who suffer under patriarchism. For example the attitude of Baby Kochamma reveals this. "In the way that the unfortunate sometimes dislike the co-unfortunate, Baby Kochamma disliked the twins, for she considered them doomed, fatherless waifs" (*GST* 45).

The third means, the pseudo-patriarchal attitude, which kills women without noise, can be seen in Comrade Pillai. "Even I cannot persuade her. My own wife. Of course inside the house she is Boss" (*GST* 278). His words lack sincerity but present the woman as boss with a selfish motive. The patriarchal society makes the woman an ideal symbol of virtues such as forgiveness, love, dedication, virginity, and sacrifice and without knowing the hook, women may try their best to practise these virtues. The actions of Pillai betray his words. "He had the easy authority of the Man of the House. He smiled and nodded a greeting to Chacko, but did not acknowledge the presence of his wife or his mother" (*GST* 272). The author says that the attitude of Pillai even to his mother is the same because she too belongs to one category of 'woman'. The fourth means used by the patriarchal society is the denial of rights. For example, even though Ammu is good in learning than Chacko, she is denied the right for higher education and Chacko is sent to Oxford for education in spite of his poor academic performance. The woman cannot attain self-actualization without having rights and duties to empower herself. Even the right over her body is denied.

In Indian ethos, sex is not aversive but sacred. Religious books, mythological traditions, and folk stories narrate incidents where even celestial beings have sexual desires. Hence, Kama is one of the major ends of life. Buddhism is also fully conscious of the inevitable role of sex in human life. "Sex is a key to man's inner being."[40] Indian ethos has a *prema* (love) tradition, against *sringara* (erotic) tradition. The *prema* tradition is based on the mutual respect and relationship where as *sringara* is the patriarchal view where woman is at the gaze of man.

> The love or *prema* tradition in the classical Sanskrit literature [...] where the emotional content in sexual relations is placed higher than physical gratification. Within this love tradition, I include all data from the narrative literature such as *Kathasaritsagara*, *Sukasaptati* and *Brhatkathaslokasamgraha*, in which we find evidence of the celebration of female erotica that subverts the hegemonic masculine, tradition.[41]

Marriage and sex should be born out of love.

However, in modern India the noble rule of sex is violated and the woman is a tool for the man for sexual enjoyment and procreation. *The God of Small Things* turns out to be a powerful protest against the barbaric attitude of men and presents the love tradition on the lines of *sringara* tradition. Mammachi, Kalyani and so on suffer because of the hegemony of the males. Here the woman becomes the object for sexual gratification of man. Woman is not the binary of man. Here the family or the society decides whom to love and have sex with. The social barriers take away the essence of sex, i.e. love. Without love, marriage and sex become a burden. Against the male hegemony Roy narrates the love and sex life of Ammu and Velutha who break the age-old taboos related to sex. About the sexual experience of Ammu and Velutha, Roy writes: "She danced for him. On that boat-shaped piece of earth. She lived" (*GST* 337). Kama is not mere interaction of few physical organs. "Kama is the enjoyment of appropriate objects by the five senses of hearing, feeling, seeing, tasting and smelling, assisted by the mind together with the soul."[42] Ammu and Velutha share "their Love, their Madness, their Hope, their Infinnate Joy" (*GST* 339). Ammu and Velutha are Radha and Krishna who are one, yet they have taken two forms to enjoy the relationship of *lila* but the society brutally kills them. However, Roy makes an attempt to break the uncrossable lines of love laws.

Indian ethos considers the male and the female as complementary to each other. In *Vaisnava* tradition, male gods have a female partner goddess like, Rama and Sita, Narayana and Laksmi, Krishna and Radha and so on. They cannot be separated but come together for creation. The creator is related to god principle and goddess principle. "Vaisnavism, [...] becomes a type of Saktism where the Purna-sakti, or the most complete form of divine feminine energy, is worshiped as the preeminent aspect of divinity, eclipsing even the male godhead in certain respects."[43] Narayana without Laksmi and Krishna without Radha can neither function nor form divine energetic source. "The male and female aspects of divinity are one-equally whole. Male and female Moiety."[44] Estha and Rahel who 'had known each other before Life began' (*GST* 327) are metaphors for Rama and Sita; Narayana and Lakshmi; and Krishna and Rada. Estha cannot exist without Rahel and vice versa because they are 'physically separate, but with joint identities' (*GST* 2). The complementary nature of man and woman is strongly expressed through 'sawdust coated two-egg twins' (*GST* 220).

However, the society separates them. The unjust social system, the 'kuthambalam' (*GST* 234), makes people puppets and they move not by the inner voice but by the taboos. Both the man and the woman are losers and die away without actualizing their potency. The fullness and joy are created not by one alone but together like the *lila* of Radha and Krishna. Estha cannot be separated from Rahel or vice versa. Both are part of one reality. The incest between Estha and Rahel (*GST* 327) who are 'born from separate but simultaneously fertilized eggs' (*GST* 2), can be seen from a transcendental point of view of Samkhya philosophy where the creation is interpreted by the *purusha* and *prakriti*, the two aspects of creation. In gender terms *purusha* is the male principle and *prakriti* is the female principle of creation. The invisible, silent male principle creates life outside of oneself. The visible, dynamic female principle creates life within. Estha and Rahel, the *purusha* and *prakriti*, 'He and She. We and Us' (*GST* 237) are not separate entities but they are two parts of one entity.

6.2.4.2.2. Caste System

The God of Small Things presents the age-old problem of India: the caste system. The touchable always have one voice against the untouchable. "Touchable workers in the factory resented Velutha for ancient reasons of their own" (*GST* 121). No political parties actually serve them but many try to attain power through politicizing untouchability. The communist leader Pillai says against Velutha: 'That Paravan is going to cause trouble for you,' [...]. 'Send him off' (*GST* 278). "The ultimate outcome of the novel is the tragic death of 'untouchable' by the 'touchable boots' at the police station. God is no more in control of 'small things' rather turning him to 'The God of Loss'."[45]

The novel reveals that the caste system not only affected the Hindu community, but all people of India without the exception of religion, place or class. The practice of *Ayitham* existed among the Thomas Christians. The practice of *Ayitham* among Christians is portrayed in the novel. "Pappachi would not allow Paravans into the house. Nobody would. They were not allowed to touch anything that touchables touched. Caste Hindus and Caste Christians" (*GST* 73). About the illicit relation between Ammu and Velutha, Baby Kochamma said: "How could she stand the smell? Haven't you noticed? They have particular smell, these Paravans" (*GST* 257). Before the society, Velutha, the untouchable is *Chappu Thambura* (insignificant creature) (*GST* 343).

However, there is change in the attitude towards the caste system. Vellya Paapen who 'torn between Loyalty and Love' (*GST* 255) accepts untouchability whereas Velutha tries to build-up healthy relationship with the touchables and has schooling. Mammachi considered Velutha as 'filthy coolie' (*GST* 257) and the relationship between Ammu with Velutha 'like animals' (*GST* 257). Whereas Ammu gives the promise of 'Tomorrow' to touch 'the innermost part of her' (*GST* 337) to 'Chappu Thamburan' (*GST* 339). Estha and Rahel enter the forbidden hut and build-up relationship with the untouchable.

6.2.4.2.3. Clench of Democratic Institutions

Democratic India is constituted for the welfare of all the citizens and functions through various systems and structures. If they become corrupt, the true spirit of the Constitution may be endangered. The two prominent institutions among them, mentioned in the novel are the police and the Communist Party. They work in a similar manner not for welfare but for oppression. "They [Inspector Thomas Mathew and Pillai] looked out at the world and never wondered how it worked, because they knew. *They* worked it. They were mechanics who serviced different parts of the same machine" (*GST* 262). They are formed to protect the rights of the weak but become the part of the oppressive machine, which are more powerful than what an individual can fight with. The hegemony of these systems are always justified by the society. So those who go against them loose the 'face' and are judged as 'deviants'. The novel tries to unmask the brutality of the police and the hypocrisy of the Communist Party.

In India, there is only one Constitution but the novel implicitly presents two in practice: one for the Mombatt and another for the Laltain. So Inspector Thomas Mathew, who 'was a prudent man' (*GST* 262) goes to Pillai to select the law for Velutha. The nasty lawbreaker in the novel is Inspector Thomas. The sub-human behaviour of Thomas towards Ammu is provocative. "Then he tapped her breasts with his baton. Gently. Tap, tap. As though he was choosing mangoes from a basket. Pointing out the ones that he wanted packed and delivered" (*GST* 8). He commercialises the female organs like an object in the market and the woman becomes uncomfortable with her own body which eventually leads to suicide. The murder of Velutha in custody shows the brutality and the misuse of power. "India records a high number of violations to the right to life in the form of torture, custodial deaths, killings in fake encounters and deaths through the disproportionate use of firearms."[46] During the period 2005-07 twenty-three autopsies were related to custodial deaths in the Government Medical College, Thrissur in Kerala.[47] The inhuman nature of the police is well-portrayed in the novel.

The utter failure of communism in India is also presented in the novel. 'The ancestral home of Comrade E.M.S. Namboodiripad' is the symbol of decay that happened to the communist party in India. The party holds hands with multinational companies and moves away from its ideologies. The placards with 'Traditional Kerala Umbrella' and 'Traditional Bridal Dowry Box' show that the party immerses in the 'Heart of Darkness' of Kerala tradition instead of changing it. The party tries to complain 'Kurtz and Karl Marx' to greet rich guests' (*GST* 126). The Communist Party 'postponed the revolution for the Time Being' (*GST* 301) when they attained power. The revolution they are prophesying is against the shadows of 'the bourgeoisies' with whom they make all the businesses.

When Namboodiripad becomes Chief Minister they 'annihilate' the students who agitate against our 'People's Government.' 'Surely students aren't People anymore?' (*GST* 67). The students symbolize the entire subaltern groups who are rejected by the society. Roy criticizes the iconic figure E.M.S. Namboodiripad, 'Kerala's Mao Tse-tung' (*GST* 126) and 'Soviet Stooge, Running Dong' (*GST* 69 and 301). "The basic problem, [...] was the task of reconciling a theoretical commitment to forming a Communist Party and establishing its leadership with the given conditions of India."[48] Much has been written about communist socialism but it lacks practice. Comrade Pillai, 'Ayemenem's egg-breaker and professional omletteer' (*GST* 236) is the icon of hypocrisy. "He walked through the world like a chameleon. Never revealing himself, never appearing not to" (*GST* 14). Through the activities of Pillai, Roy unmasks the big chasm between ideology and practice.

At last, the third generation, the globalized youth, throw away the Communist Party which becomes the party of bourgeoisies. Pillai's son changes his own name, which highlights one's identity, slightly for not noticing the political leanings (*GST* 128). The Journey of 'Lenin' to 'P. Levin' is very drastic, which brings about the withering away of the communist movement in India instead of the state.

6.2.4.3. Relationship with Culture

The God of Small Things not only analyses the relationship with oneself and others but also with the native culture. The novel upholds the Indianness and expresses the relationship of the Indians with the myths, folk songs, art, and festivals which are part of ethos of India. Roy builds a strong link between the characters of the *Mahabharata* and the novel. The reticent nature of Estha is compared to that of Karna, "whom the world has abandoned. Karna Alone. Condemned goods. A prince raised in poverty. Born to die unfairly, unarmed [...]" (*GST* 231). The pathetic situation of the underprivileged is glorified. Not only the written tradition but also oral traditions of various ethnic groups are incorporated in the novel. The folk songs which are part of the rich oral tradition are used in the novel. These songs are not merely reputed ones but express the emotions of the suffering of the Mombatts.

Roy also loves vernacular languages and wants to break 'Anglophiles' (*GST* 52). According to her the whole Indians 'were all Anglophiles. They were a *family* of Anglophiles. Pointed in the wrong direction, trapped outside their own history, and unable to retrace their steps because their footprints had been swept away" (*GST* 52). The italicized word 'family' may include all the Indians than the family of Reverend E. John Ipe. The colonial assimilation has made Indians 'Prisoners of War' (*GST* 53). To break the anglophiles, Roy finds a space for vernacular culture and contributes in the process of developing an Indian English. The deliberate distortions and wayward use of the Standard English give Indian colour to the novel. The linguistic acculturation of English helps to express Indian ethos in more emotional and cultural standards. English has been blended itself with the social complex of the country. The words like, *mol*, *mon*, *meen*, *mundu*, *kavani*, *kanji*, *paravan*, *Ammukutty*, *Sundarikutty*, *Velya Pappen*, *Kochamma*, *Idi Appan*, etc., express the native culture. The Indianization is not limited to the use of some words but structure, pronunciation, and spelling. Some of the examples are the following.

(a) Typical Kerala style of conversation:

'*Aiyyo*, RahelMol!' Comrade K.N.M. Pillai said, recognizing her instantly. '*Orkunnilley*? Comrade Uncle?'

'*Oower*, Rahel said' (*GST* 128).

"Oower, oower, oower,' the man said.

His daughter's daughter is this. In Amayrica now' (*GST* 129).

(b) Roy incorporates the speed of the conversation of Malayallees in the novel: 'finethankyou' (*GST* 145); 'pleasetomeetyou' (*GST* 212); 'whatisit' (*GST* 6); 'porketmunny' (*GST* 150); 'mydearjudges' (*GST* 271).

(c) The author tries to imitate the mannerisms of lemon Drink Man by writing as he says: 'ColaFantaicecreamrosemilk' (*GST* 301).

(d) Geographically related simile: 'like a just-caught fish' (*GST* 207); 'Elderly cucumber' (*GST* 20); 'Old boat eyes' (*GST* 204); 'like professional adult gossips in the Ayemenem market' (*GST* 207).

(e) The accent of Malayali English is reproduced in the novel:

'I cometoburyCaeser, not to praise him.

Theevil that mendoo lives after them,

'negoodisoft interred with their bones;' (*GST* 275)

(f) In Malayalam the sound 'w' is absent so Roy avoids the sound: 'vest' (*GST* 271) instead of 'west'; 'vide' (*GST* 271) for wide; 'sod' (*GST* 271) for sword.

(g) In Malayalam vowels and consonants are stressed so 'r' gets stress: 'verrrry sweet' (*GST* 323); Chackosaar (*GST* 271), 'Margaret Kochamma told her to Stoppit. So she Stoppited' (*GST* 141); 'Until Ammu shook her and told her to Stoppit and she Stoppited' (*GST* 300)

(h) Wrong stress: 'A Wake'; 'A Live'; 'A Lert' (*GST* 266).

(i) Literal translation: 'Who Urumban?' (translation of EthuUrumban) instead of 'Who is Urumban?' (*GST* 177); 'His daughter's daughter is this.' (*GST*); 'He's standing first in class' (*GST* 275); 'Lenin Mon, tell Comrade Uncle the one Pappa taught you' (*GST* 274).

The novel also expresses the noble relationship of Indians with art forms, "The Kathakali Man is the most beautiful of men. Because his body is his soul. His only instrument" (*GST* 230). It is his whole life, "To the Kathakali Man these stories are his children and his childhood" (*GST* 229). However, in the materialistic world people forget the spiritual side of the art forms: "Their turning to tourism to stave off starvation. On their way back from the Heart of Darkness, they stopped at the temple to ask pardon of their gods. To apologize for corrupting their stories" (*GST* 229). In the globalized India, Kathakali is a means to exploit the tourist. Art is no more a means for *Moksha* or self-satisfaction but a commodity for sale.

6.2.4.4. Relationship with Nature and Supreme Reality

Human relationship with nature and God are also scrutinized in *The God of Small Things*. According to the ethos of India, nature is not just for livelihood but the whole life is wedded to it. Indians have a strong affiliation with the ancestor's place. The novel starts with the vivid narration of the beautiful village of Ayemenem. 'Red bananas ripen. Jackfruits burst' (*GST* 1). However, the industrialization polluted nature. "Some days he walked along the banks of the river that smelled of shit, and pesticides bought with World Bank loans. Most of the fish had died. The ones that survived suffered from fin-rot and had broken out in boils" (*GST* 13). The luxurious life is also, a part of pollution. "Gulf-money houses built by nurses, masons" (*GST* 13). In Indian ethos, nature is the visualization of the unseen reality.

Even though the word 'god' is not used with a metaphysical view, it has a humanistic perspective. The compassionate attitude towards the underprivileged is the real god concept in the novel.

The words 'god' and 'small' are used ironically. The real and everlasting 'Love' is turned into small by the oppressive 'Big God.' 'God' of small things is human centred.

6.2.5. *Education as Means*

The story takes place at Ayemenem in the District of Kottayam, Kerala. The place has been selected not only because it is the native place of Roy but also due to the educational factors. Kottayam, the *aksharanagari* (city of letters) is the first district in India that achieved 100% literacy in 1989. In 1813, English education commenced in the Old Seminary and in 1817 higher education was introduced by the Church Missionary Society in CMS College for the first time in South India. In 1846 a Sanskrit school, which is the first in India where the rich and poor, high caste and low caste sat together for education, started at Mannanam near Aymanam by the Carmelites of Mary Immaculate (CMI).

Hence, such a powerful story could take place only in a place where a social revolution was brought about through education. All these educational factors led to a radical change in the society, especially among Christians. "The Christian presence in Kerala's educational scenario seems much more effective and consequential."[49] The Western influence also caused the questioning of the traditional practices in India especially of Syrian Christian Community in Kerala. "In the social life of the St. Thomas Christians the influence of the Portuguese is very conspicuous."[50] This influence is obvious while Arundhati Roy mentions, "before three purple-robed Syrian Bishops murdered by the Portuguese were found floating in the sea" (*GST* 33). The education enabled people to question the age-old practices in their own community. For example, in 1986 Mary Roy, the mother of Arundhati Roy won the law suit against The Travancore Succession Act 1916 and Cochin Succession Act 1921 which denied the right of daughters to have a share of father's property. Roy realises that education is the most powerful tool to overcome or to question the Laltains and their exploitation.

The first injustice done to Ammu is the denial of her right to education. "Pappachi insisted that a college education was an unnecessary expense for a girl" (*GST* 38). At the end, she fails to handle her difficulties positively. The novelist gives the reason very emphatically. "Because Ammu had not had the kind of education, nor read the sorts of books, nor met the sorts of people that might have influenced her to think the way she did. She was just that sort of animal" (*GST* 180). Books make people. Ammu's childhood is filled with the 'Bear stories' so "In her version, Father Bear beat Mother Bear with brass vases. Mother Bear suffered those beatings with mute resignation" (*GST* 180). Rahel attains higher education and she faces her life situations with confidence. She is moved by her inner voice and asserts herself. Even though Baby Kochamma is a villain for the twins, she always asserts herself and finds her own engagements. She becomes a Roman Catholic, tries to become a nun, and gets the degree from America, which shows that above collective identity, she attempts to build upon individual identity.

Malayallies especially the Christian community gave much importance to education and they established schools and colleges for the society. Even the low caste was allowed to learn in their school. Mammachi sent Velutha to school which was started by her father-in-law for the Untouchables. "He [Velutha] had been educated by her family, in the Untouchables' school started by her father, Punnyan Kunju" (*GST* 261). The novelist has used education as powerful means to revolt against Laltains.

In short, Mammachi suffers but Rahel is liberated; Pillai holds communism but Lenin moves away; Vellya Paapen is untouchable but Velutha touches 'the innermost part' (*GST* 337) of the upper caste. The novel is an eye-opener to building up integrity and empathy in relationship which is the essence of *Vasudhaiva Kutumbakam.* The concept of *Vasudhaiva Kutumbakam* is different from 'global village', which arises out of the IT revolution and globalization. Through globalization, there is no growth in consciousness but only in economic and technological interconnection. "But the fact remains that there is little evidence of a radical change in human consciousness. [...] And these policies aid and abet models of development, which can sustain themselves only on the inevitable corollary of deprivation elsewhere."[51] The society, which is based on exploitative relationship, cannot be called as *Vasudhaiva Kutumbakam*. The novelist wants to twist the negative elements in the relationship among Indians such as patriarchism, caste system, unjust social system, polluted nature, etc., and says: 'I never want this to happen again,' [...] 'Ever' (*GST* 48). Pappachi's twisted hand is a metaphor. 'Liberating spirit' is the key element of the novel and; Ammu and Velutha are the great martyrs for it. Human beings should actively search for meaning in their own unique ways by relating to oneself, others/society, culture, nature and god. The extreme form of collectivism and individualism endangers either personal identity or interrelation. However, they should go hand in hand to build-up a *Vasudhaiva Kutumbakam* which *The God of Small Things* envisages.

6.3. Analysis of *The White Tiger* in the Light of the Neo-liberal Ethos

The White Tiger by Arvind Adiga is a journey into the heart of darkness and light of Indian ethos especially against the backdrop of globalization. The words darkness and light are used fifty and seventy times respectively and the narrator 'sings louder the only truth' (*WT* 16) even though he is 'not a philosopher nor a poet' (*WT* 8). To emphasize the objectivity of the 'truth' which is turned upside down from the Prime Minister's facts (*WT* 15) he says "I am in the light now, but I was born and raised in Darkness" (*WT* 14) and he uses the word 'truth' thirteen times. It describes the truth about Laxmangarh, which represents villages; truth about Ganges, which symbolizes all the religions; truth about Delhi, which stands for all the cities; and truth about Bangalore, which denotes the globalization. So it brings a holistic understanding of Indian ethos and portrays the *adharma* in all spheres of life.

In his adventurous journey of life, he finds out two castes which exist in India: "Men with Big Bellies and Men with Small Bellies" (*WT* 64) and he discovers two destinies which Indians have: 'eat—or get eaten up' (*WT* 64). These two unquestionably contradictory images, which create horror, show the imbalance in the personal and social lives in India. "Delhi is the capital of not one but two countries—two Indias. The Light and the Darkness both flow into Delhi" (*WT* 251). The novel emotionally narrates the aftermath of the imbalance, which ultimately disturbs the cosmic order, with the vision to re-establish *dharma* so that a 'new India' (*WT* 318) can be formed.

6.3.1. *Cosmic Order*

To move in accordance with the cosmic order, the principle of the universal movement, is sum total of all religions, ethics, and moral teaching. The thought and behaviour of human beings should be in tune with the rhythm of the cosmic order, which regulates the operation of the entire universe. In order to protect the cosmic order, Indian civilization developed *Dharmasastra*, which gives guidelines for all endeavours of human beings. K.V.R. Aiyangar says that

> *Dharmasastra* is a comprehensive code to regular human conduct in accordance with the unalterable scheme of Creation, and to enable everyone to fulfill the purpose of his birth. [...] Among the duties that it lays down are both self-regarding and altruistic, those to the living and to the dead, to those who are alive and those who are yet to be born."[52]

The *Dharmasastra* has been controlling the personal and social life of Indians and it becomes the underlying principle of the Indian ethos.

The individual life is meaningful only when it fulfills the objectives of life set by the Supreme Self, which dwells in each being. The seers of ancient India broadly codified these aims under four headings: *Dharma* (righteousness), *artha* (wealth), *kama* (desire), and *moksha* (liberation). They are together called *Purusharthas*. *Purusha* means personal and *artha* means objective or pursuit. These *purusharthas* are not separated from one another and they should be persuaded in a balanced manner for the holistic development of the individual and society. Of course, according to the stages of life and social roles the priority may change. The undue importance to one *purushartha* may affect the personal, family, social and ecological life. The balance is attained through *ekatvam* (oneness) which unites the four goals for the self-realization whenever this oneness is lost in the individual life, it may affect the cosmic rhythm and lead to darkness. *The White Tiger* narrates the darkness of India which is created through the imbalance in *purusharthas*.

6.3.2. *Purusharthas* in *The White Tiger*

Even though *purushartha* is an age old concept, at every point of time in Indian civilization, it is powerful enough to guide the lives of individuals and the morality of the society. *The White Tiger* is an attempt to establish proper balance between *purusharthas* so it highlights the deviations in all the fields of *dharma*, *artha*, *kama* and *moksa*. The novel is the voice of the voiceless. Through the novel the silent majority gets a roaring voice over the rich minority. Kapur emphatically says, "every scene, every phrase, is a blunt instrument, wielded to remind Adiga's readers of his country's cruelty."[53] The novel envisages to re-create the *ekatvam* in the globalized India.

The novel acknowledges the greatness of India too. For the narrator Gautama Buddha who shaped the nation's history (*WT* 18) and found enlightenment (*WT* 18), Gandhiji who led the people from darkness to light (*WT* 136) and the god of gods (*WT* 310), and Mother Ganga who is the daughter of the Vedas, and breaker of the chain of birth and rebirth (*WT* 15) are ideals. They uphold the real ethos of India but 'the great socialist' who represents all the corrupted politicians, the entrepreneur who stands for material exploiters and the police who represents the corrupt government employees together mutilate the spirit of India. So 'the half baked' Indians lost their mother at the banks of Ganga like Balram's (*WT* 18). India reduced Gandhiji to a sandalwood statue for gifts without Gandhism (*WT* 5). India without Gandhiji is zero.

6.3.3. *Artha*

Artha is one of the goals of life in Indian civilization. *Artha* means goal, worldly objective or wealth and it is one of the oldest words in Indian culture inherited from Eastern Iran.[54] Later it got the meanings like material property, social value and economic value of life, then added among *purusharthas*. Here under the heading *artha*, the researcher includes all the material activities of individuals, social system, political system and all the functions of state. *Artha* as a moral value makes the society free from exploitation, as a political value brings political consciousness among the citizens, and as an economic value equips everyone to attain material goals. In short, it stands for harmony, justice and growth.

The White Tiger gives a good account of how the practice of *artha* takes place in neo-liberal India. It vividly portrays the exploitation of the poor by the rich with the support of the unjust social and political system. The two powerful and apt images used in the novel to convey the big chasm between the rich and poor are 'Big Bellies and the Small Bellies' (*WT* 64) and the terrific motives of the people are shown by saying: "And only two destinies: eat—or get eaten up" (*WT* 64). Under the following headings such as socialism, the flight of the oppressed, Indian democracy, death of villages, and globalization the injustice in the area of *artha* can be summarized.

6.3.3.1. Socialism

In 1947, India woke up to freedom at midnight with the great mission to serve the country, which "means the service of the millions who suffer. It means the ending of poverty, ignorance, disease and inequality of opportunity."[55] With this socialistic perspective, India began its journey and the word 'socialist' was incorporated in the preamble of the Indian Constitution by the Forty-second Amendment in 1976.

The novelist paradoxically presents the practice of socialism in India. 'The Great Socialist' is used as an allegory to mean all the corrupted politicians who make great speech about socialism. 'Lohia Universal Free Hospital' stands as a monument of the corruption and hollowness of the government welfare policies. It is written in front of: 'Lohia Universal Free Hospital' proudly inaugurated by The Great Socialist a holy proof that he keeps his promises (*WT* 48). Contrary to this inscription, the working condition of the hospital is pathetic. The doctors are appointed on the basis of 'open auction' (*WT* 49) which may go up to 'four hundred thousand rupees' (*WT* 49) and money goes to 'the great socialist' (*WT* 49). Balram's father passes away in the very hospital, which is built for the poor, due to the lack of medical treatment. Economic, social, political, and judicial corruption leads to injustice against the voiceless. The novel harshly attacks the inequality in economic distribution and becomes the voice of the voiceless.

6.3.3.2. The Flight of the Oppressed

Politicians, bureaucrats, and socially privileged groups together oppress the underprivileged group and *The White Tiger* is the cry of the oppressed, which echoes for generations. The lifelong sufferings and hardships of the poor are reflected in their body. "A rich man's body is like a premium cotton pillow, white and soft and blank. Ours are different. [...]. The story of a poor man's life is written on his body, in a sharp pen" (*WT* 27). Balram, the poor is the hero of the novel and his hardships during his odyssey of life is the story of the novel. He calls the story of his life, 'The Autobiography of a Half-Baked Indian' (*WT* 10).

Balram begins his life without name. 'She lies in bed and spews blood. She's got no time to name me.' 'And your father?' 'He's a rickshaw-puller, sir. He's got no time to name me' (*WT* 13). The underdogs are nameless, which means, they have no identity as Indians. The death of the nameless poor on the road by Pinky also reflects the same. The behaviour of the landlords towards the servant is cruel and there is no professional dignity. "The rich don't have drivers, cooks, barbers, and tailors. They simply have servants" (*WT* 68). The dogs get better treatment than the servants. In India certain spaces are not opened for the underprivileged who are the children of the street. "Is There No Space for the Poor in the Malls of New India?" (*WT* 148). The human being is valued not based on what s/he has but the very being. But in the consumeristic world, priorities are different.

> In today's Indian society everyone is judged by the position he or she occupies in the hierarchical scale. In the past, the caste hierarchy was prescriptive, positioning individuals in the social scale as a consequence of their birth. Today, various additional factors determine one's position in society. What was started in 1947 by the new rulers has caught the imagination of future generations of the powerful as well.[56]

When the sole aim of life is to become successful executives, people forget altruism and offer fellow-beings as the sacrificial victims for the goal.

6.3.3.3. Indian Democracy

The welfare of the poor was neglected because of the corrupt democratic system. "We all live in the world's greatest democracy. What a fucking joke" (*WT* 170). In the novel, the grave sins of Indian democracy are exposed in its nakedness. Representation through election is the basis of a democratic country and the voters portrayed in the novel speak about elections as 'the worst disease' (*WT* 98) in the country 'like eunuchs discussing the Kama Sutra' (*WT* 98) and "people make talk and talk about things that they have no say in" (*WT* 98). Balram's father "has seen twelve elections—five general, five state, two local" (*WT* 100). Balram is an eligible voter (*WT* 102) like his father. Ironically both of them have not votėd or "have not seen the inside of a voting booth" (*WT* 102). If someone turns to oppose the Great Socialist, the politicians will, 'hit him and the policeman stamped on his face' (*WT* 102) and they 'made his Benaras that day' (*WT* 101). The poor are cheated at the time of election by different promises. Yet Indians "entrust the glorious Parliamentary democracy [...]. That's the whole tragedy of this country" (*WT* 10). There is no system to evaluate the performance of the elected members after their election victory.

The most agonizing part of corruption is that, the police who have to protect the justice of the poor, stand for injustice. The duties of the police are to 'knock the rickshaw-puller down'

(*WT* 102), 'writing slogan on the wall outside the temple' (*WT* 35) for 'THE GREAT SOCIALIST!', and 'slap boy's belly' (*WT* 310). They make false charges against people who stand against politicians and ignore the howling of the innocent. "A man on a bicycle getting killed—the police don't even have to register the case. A man on a motorbike getting killed—they would have to register that. A man in a car getting killed—they would have thrown me in jail" (*WT* 309).

6.3.3.4. Death of Villages

Without the culture and spirit of Indian villages, Indian ethos cannot be completed. "From time immemorial the village has been a basic and important unit in the organization of Indian social polity."[57] The Indian villages are painted colourfully and many have a romantic vicw about them. However, apart from the natural beauty, Adiga points to the reality about the poor who are in darkness. "Ha! Electricity poles—defunct. Water tap—broken. Children—too lean and short for their age, and with oversized heads from which vivid eyes shine, like the guilty conscience of the government of India. Yes, a typical Indian village paradise" (*WT* 19-20).

Urbanization, modernization, and globalization have been leading to the death of villages of India. Even the growing commodification and commercialization of natural resources in agriculture itself creates a serious crisis for hundreds of millions of villagers whose lives are critically dependent upon the availability and sustainability of these resources. They make decisions regarding the consumption of resources, lifestyle and social functioning and all are linked to the symbiotic relationship between them and nature. However, by the entry of multinational companies, there has not only been unlimited rapacious exploitation of national resources, but there has also been a loss of commons, an increase in the pollution of life sustaining bodies and increasing focus on export-bound cash crop production.[58] The lifestyles of villagers are inter-twined with the land and once the village landscape is changed, they are like fish out of water. For livelihood, the villagers migrate to urban areas. The villagers who move to towns are also not safe and the dark side of India exists both in cities and villages. "These poor bastards had come from the darkness to Delhi to find some light—but they were still in the darkness" (*WT* 138). India cannot exist by forgetting her villages. Gandhi says: "If the village perishes India will perish too. It will be no more India."[59]

6.3.3.5. Globalization

Globalization is a hope and a trap. The reforms opened job opportunities, foreign consumer goods, banking facilities, shopping malls, foreign trade, and capital flow. It also helped to increase Indian's GDP from 5.6 of 1980-91 to 6.4 in 2001, and 2002-07 it was 8.0. At the same time, the growth brought by the liberalization policy could not benefit everyone. Due to the desirable and undesirable consequences of globalization, the gap between the people increased. "A relationship between liberalization, corrupt lifestyles, the criminalization of the poor, growing civil strife including caste 'wars,' commercialization of expectations and the resultant cultural disarray and breakdown of civil society is slowly becoming clear."[60] *The White Tiger* presents Bangalore as the icon of globalization with its light and dark sides. For the poor, Bangalore is like the old wine in new bag. "When you come to Bangalore, and stop at a traffic light, some boy will run up to your car and knock on your window" (*WT* 6). Bangalore gives birth to a new brahminic 'class of people, named entrepreneur' (*WT* 319). The novel portrays the grim reality of corrupted entrepreneurs, who have economic success stories through murder, bribery, the unjust police system, and inaccessibility of the poor. To create a just society in the epoch of globalization, India should move away from corruption. Entrepreneurs turn impossible into possible with the help of corrupt bureaucrats. "To break the law of his land—to turn bad news into good news—is the entrepreneur's prerogative" (*WT* 58). The narrator ironically reads the inscription in front of Vidhan Soudha: 'GOVERNMENT WORK IS GOD'S WORK' (*WT* 297). Ironically even the Vidhan Soudha is not free of corruption and injustice.

Globalization also leads to virtual imperialism. Bangalore stands for new colonizers' capital because bangalorians work according to their masters' convenience. Now Bangalore becomes 'A small bit of America in India' (*WT* 204). Even in the 21st century, colonization continues in its attractive form. Life's rhythm is determined by the American timing because Indian slaves work for them. In spite of these trades, globalization may not lead to the real interaction of culture with mutual respect and may not intrude into each other's space.

> It is Western, particularly, North American culture which is being termed as a global culture. All other cultures are termed 'ethnic', which is a replacement of the term 'native' of the colonial days. The term 'ethnic', like the term 'native', carries a sense of backwardness and something not in keeping with the acceptable trend. Thus, for all practical purposes, 'globalization,' is westernization or, to be more precise, Americanization.[61]

Pinky Madam and Mr. Ashok are examples of the rootless people of the globalized world. Cultural expatriation, which can be called in positive terms hybridity, is common. People caught between two cultures and those who have floating cultural identity imitate foreign culture and consider them as a mark of social standard. Mimicking the colonizer becomes a part of Indian lifestyle. The novelist tries to Indianize English by the use of certain Indian words freely to express Indian sensibility such as, *namastes,* daal, paan, gulabjamuns, laddoos, Om, pooja, dosa, chapattis, lassi, mandala, etc.

Today, the sign of the elite class in India is the ability to speak English in its American form not in British form. Mr. Ashok speaks English like Americans, so he is a baked Indian whereas Balram speaks 'piJJA', maal, etc., and fails to answer to some general knowledge so he is a half-baked Indian. Indians send their children to English medium schools. "He goes to a good school here in Bangalore—an English school. Now he speaks English like a rich man's son. He can say 'pizza' the way Mr. Ashok said it. (And doesn't he love eating pizza—that nasty stuff?)" (*WT* 204). The real attitude of the narrator towards the mimicking of the master's life style is: "I hate that whole fucking Bangalore attitude" (*WT* 46).

One of the major reasons for these inequities is the unequal distribution of *artha*. The government has to play a pivotal role for the welfare of all. For Kautilya "the state or government has a crucial role to play in maintaining the material well-being of the nation and its people."[62] The novel sets forth the critical failures related to *artha* and tries to reset the priority of values. The early part of the 21st century Indian ethos may be controlled by *artha*. However, according to Indian ethos, *artha* is not the end of human life but liberation is the ultimate aim.

6.3.4. *Kama*

According to Indian ethos, *kama* which is generally translated as 'desire' is another aim of life. It is the aesthetic as well as sensuous value of life. "Kama as an intrinsic value refers to the pursuit of pleasure, pursuit of sex and pursuit of aesthetic experience."[63] It is also a means to develop Bhakti in the mind of a devotee towards the personal god (deity). However, it usually refers to sexual pleasure and Indian ethos recommends rightful gratification of sexual desire. Along with *dharma*, *artha* and *moksha, The White Tiger* also unfolds the sexual abuses in the Indian society. Women are the victims of this animal entertainment and they become a commodity to be 'picked' from the market as any other commodity. "The girls would not be safe on buses or trains anyway. The men of this city, frankly speaking, are animals" (*WT* 298). Due to poverty, exploitation, and family problems women take up prostitution as a profession. The girl who starts her life without name and does sex work makes the confession to Balram (*WT* 234). Vatsyayana, the author of *Kamasutra* condemns those desires which are not sanctified on moral and social grounds.[64] The body of a woman is used commercially to catch the attraction of the consumers. The magazines use "catchy cover—a woman in her underwear was lying on a bed, cowering from the shadow of a man" (*WT* 124). Sexy literature is also popular with the public. This does not evoke noble aesthetic thoughts but erotic desires in its ugliness.

Kama also stands for deep relationship which is an element of Indian ethos, between persons and families. Despite that, the relationships in the family and society are reduced considerably. Mr. Ashok and Pinky are victims of such relationship problems. Since the globalized world is under so much pressure to make profit there is no importance for relationships. 'I'm not a sentimental man,' (*WT* 12). Against this impersonal trend, the novel presents a family with deep attachments, which forgets fellow beings. "I saw the silhouettes of the slum dwellers close to one another inside the tents; you could make out one family—a husband, a wife, a child—all huddled around a stove inside one tent, lit up by a golden lamp. The intimacy seemed so complete—so crushingly complete" (*WT* 188). This cordial relationship is the real ethos of India.

Pragmatic philosophy orients people for progress but should not lose the holistic view of life. Nevertheless, today philosophy gives much consideration to economic developments. 'I'm a man of action and change' (*WT* 5). The corporate world lacks true friendship, only competition exists. "When the work is done I kick them out of the office: no chitchat, no cups of coffee. A White Tiger keeps no friends. It's too dangerous" (*WT* 302). The one who sits next to you with a smiling face may be an enemy. "The Indian entrepreneur has to be straight and crooked, mocking and believing, sly and sincere, at the same time. So: I'm closing my eyes, folding my hands in a reverent *namaste*" (*WT* 8-9). Hypocrisy may destroy the authenticity in life. The novel exposes all kinds of abuses in relationship including those of man and woman. "The new generation, I tell you, is growing up with no morals at all" (*WT* 316). Mutual respect and love which are sidelined by the cooperative sector are a major part of Indian ethos. Indians are more collective than individualistic.

6.3.5. *Dharma*

Dharma is inextricably linked with the ethos of India and the entire personal, social, ecological, and spiritual life is guided by it for ultimate liberation. "This [dharma] term and the notions underlying it clearly constitute the most central feature of Indian civilization down the centuries, irrespective of linguistic, sectarian, or regional differences. In a special way, the centrality of *dharma* to the understanding of Indian religions has been recognized by all scholars."[65]

Franklin Edgerton tries to give an all-encompassing definition to *dharma*: "*Dharma* is propriety, socially approved conduct, in relation to one's fellow men or to other living beings (animals, or superhuman powers). Law, social usage, morality, and most of what we ordinarily mean by religion, all fall under this head."[66] For modern reformists *dharma* is not mere laws but values which guide moral uprightness. Their focus was on *sanatanadharma* (universal norms) and *varnasramadharma* (*dharma* related to each one's varna). In short, *dharma* interprets the cosmic order and is a touchstone for human beings to coordinate all the aspirations and activities to empower the cosmic balance.

The White Tiger narrates how Indians have moved away from *dharma* in its normative sense which includes practice of religious rituals, family life, social system, state administration, and moral principles. It is made clear while the narrator speaks about his early period at Laxmangarh, where he was born and brought up, the place was near Bodh Gaya, where Lord Buddha was enlightened. Balram says that Indians have lost the true spirit of all religions including Buddhism. "I thought there was no need to offer a prayer to the gods for him, because his family would be offering very expensive prayers all along the Ganga for his soul. What can a poor man's prayers mean to the 36,000,004 gods in comparison with those of the rich?" (*WT* 316-17). Not the rituals but *dharma* liberates the people. The reflection of *dharma* in the novel can be studied under four headings: religion, inequality, environmental consciousness, and re-establishment of *dharma*.

6.3.5.1. Religion

Religion plays a vital role in upholding *dharma* and it has contributed much in shaping the life of Indians. It tries to build-up a holistic view of life including material achievements, mental maturity, intellectual growth, moral uprightness and spiritual insight. So in Indian ethos, philosophy, religion, and science cannot be separated and it is enriched with deeper insights.

"We live in a glorious land. The Lord Buddha received his enlightenment in this land. The River Ganga gives life to our plants and our animals and our people. We are grateful to God that we were born in this land" (*WT* 34).

However, in the course of time, the real spirit of religion was perverted and became ritualistic. 'Nothing would get liberated here' (*WT* 18). So, it makes meaningless interventions in the life of Indians and the novelist humorously says 'that I too should start off by kissing some god's arse' (*WT* 8). Once the religion as a moral force loses its true spirit, the whole society may move to unjust social system where human beings have no meaning. Religions help one to see the indwelling spirit (atman) of the ultimate reality in human beings. If they fail to see the *atman*, they become mere commodities. Religion should enforce altruism and foster *daan* (giving) like *Vidya Dāna* (sharing of knowledge), *Bhu Dāna* (donation of land) *Anna Dāna* (giving food), and *Go Dāna* (donation of a Cow) to the poor and the needy. But today religion has lost its humanistic face.

The distorted philosophies and images of religions made by the upper caste give religious sanctions for the oppression. The favourite gods in the darkness, like Hanuman (*WT* 19) and Balram (*WT* 14) are faithful servants. They are given by the upper caste to the underprivileged for being faithful to their masters and to remain in rooster coop for being butchered. Balram, also, sarcastically narrates the superstitions like, the number 786 would flash against the black screen (*WT* 8), marriage brings more rain (*WT* 190), body and mind get cured when one penetrate a virgin (*WT* 193); lose of faith in God may lead to the death of buffalo (*WT* 186), etc. The religion, which is meant to facilitate liberation, becomes a means for oppression.

The politicians make use of religious identity for their selfish benefits. The novelist draws a parallelism between gods and politicians. "It's true that all these gods seem to do awfully little work—much like our politicians—and yet keep winning reelection to their golden thrones in heaven, year after year" (*WT* 8). The fundamentalism of modern politicians is also, echoed in the novel. In the true Indian ethos the ultimate God is one and the same. 'Truth is one, though the wise call it by different names.' But today 'the Muslims have one god, the Christians have three gods, and Hindus have 36,000,000 gods' (*WT* 8). Religion touches every area of life even in selecting the role models like Gavaskar or Azharuddin (*WT* 70). Though the Constitution guarantees freedom of religion as a fundamental right, for the poor it is not affordable and they are compelled to 'hide religion' (*WT* 110) "just to get a job and feed his starving family, he claimed to be a Hindu! And took the name of Ram Persad" (*WT* 109). Against this, Adiga upholds the value of Indian secularism without giving any priority to any religion or any god but sarcastically presents everyone. "Making a grand total of 36,000,004 divine arses for me to choose from" (*WT* 8).

The relationship between people of different religions has deteriorated in India, where tolerance and religious harmony were once the very spirit of the nation. The Ganges has lost its meaning. So Balram leaves it and continues his pilgrimage in search of a new meaning. Once he breaks the rooster coop, he "pulled out all the stickers of the goddess, and threw them on Mr. Ashok's body" (*WT* 286). As Dr. Thomas Manickam CMI says, "Discovering a shareable sensitivity of the religious consciousness of the people of other religions, other than one's own, living in close neighbourly relationship and interaction with each other in the same cultural milieu, is an urgent concern in inter-religious dialogue and life as well."[67] The narrator never rejects religions but tries to make them more scientific and humanistic.

6.3.5.2. Inequality

Inequality among the citizens is a visible sign that *Adharma* prevails in all spheres of life. Since *adharma* has increased, the difference between the privileged and underprivileged is widening. In "India is two countries in one: an India of Light, and an India of Darkness" (*WT* 14). *The White Tiger* narrates the various types of inequalities that exist in India. India of the dark consists of the farmers, lower castes, villagers, slum dwellers, and so on, and India of the light includes landlords, the privileged, entrepreneurs and so on. The division is not limited to the economic realm but social, political, and religious values.

The inequality and the gap between the rich and the poor are powerfully conveyed through the statement: "The dreams of the rich, and the dreams of the poor—they never overlap, do they? See, the poor dream all their lives of getting enough to eat and looking like the rich. And what do the rich dream of? Losing weight and looking like the poor" (*WT* 225). The poor starve for food while the rich lead a luxurious life.

'The capital of the glorious nation' (*WT* 118) is divided into two: Dark Delhi and light Delhi. The dark Delhi consists of "thousands of people who live on the sides of the road in Delhi. They have come from the Darkness too—you can tell by their thin bodies, filthy faces, by the animal-like way they live under the huge bridges and overpasses [...]" (*WT* 120). Opposed to this, one can see "The seat of Parliament, of the president, of all ministers and prime ministers. The pride of our civic planning. The showcase of the republic" (*WT* 118). Without equality, peaceful and lasting progression is a mirage.

6.3.5.3. Environmental Consciousness

Dharmasastra deals with the relationship not only between human beings but also with nature and human beings. In the Indian ethos environment is considered as the manifestation of the ultimate reality and to exploit nature out of greed is injustice. "They saw the universe as organized on the ecological unity of consciousness. Whether it is a city, a forest or a village, the apparently varied and diverse economies were hung together by consciousness that experienced at every step the underlying unity."[68] The earth is considered as mother and it illumines and protects the life of all (*WT* 15). Indian ethos urges to nurture and protect trees, plants, etc., however today out of greed, human beings pollute the environment without any respect to it. It is an assumed truth for all the Indians that the Ganges is a holy river but today, "I urge you not to dip in the Ganga, unless you want your mouth full of feces, straw, soggy parts of human bodies, buffalo carrion, and seven different kinds of industrial acids" (*WT* 15).

Before the environmental degradation, the consciousness of persons pollutes first. The external pollution is the by-product of the inner impurity. "I haven't been back to see the Ganga since then: I'm leaving that river for the American tourists!" (*WT* 18). America stands for exploitation and consumerism. Without considering the need to protect nature, human beings seek comfort. The rich is playing with the life of the future. The environmental issues are not solved even in New Bangalore and the city is becoming a concrete jungle. "There is construction everywhere. Piles of mud everywhere. [...] The entire city is masked in smoke, smog, powder, cement dust. It is under a veil. When the veil is lifted, what will Bangalore be like? Maybe it will be a disaster" (*WT* 317-18). The environmental crisis is material as well as spiritual which needs immediate attention. Protection of nature is the basis for the establishment of *Dharma*.

Dharma is violated and *adharma* becomes the pragmatic principle. The inequalities between the rich and the poor, the ritualistic religions and polluted environment show that Indians have moved away from the guiding principle of *dharma*. *Dharma* alone can guarantee mutual respect, sharing of material property, and caring for the weak including nature which are essential for a meaningful and peaceful survival of human beings.

6.3.5.4. Re-establishment of *Dharma*

Adiga presents the prevailing imbalance of *purusharthas* in India through the ineffective education system, sexual abuse, child labour, unjust policy system, corrupted political system, in disciplined bureaucrats, exploiting economic system, hollowness of government welfare schemes, and unholy religions. The condition of the poor is getting worse in villages as well as in cities. "These people were building homes for the rich, but they lived in tents covered with blue tarpaulin sheets, and partitioned into lanes by lines of sewage. It was even worse than Laxmangarh" (*WT* 260). The novel uses the image of rooster coop to express the unjust system where the majority is exploited by the minority.

More than the suffering, the narrator takes pity on the underprivileged for their passive and submissive attitude to the discriminatory system. Adiga severely criticises the unassertive nature of the deprived. "The roosters in the coop smell the blood from above. They see the organs of their brothers lying around them. They know they're next. Yet they do not rebel. They do not try to get out of the coop" (*WT* 175). The most pathetic situation is that even though the poor know that they are exploited by the rich, they have not moved against them. Balram asks a question "Why doesn't that servant take the suitcase full of diamonds? He's no Gandhi, he's human, he's you and me" (*WT* 175). He gives an image as the answer that the servant is in the rooster coop. Government itself is in dilemma and seeing no other means to come out of the unjust social system, but the promotion of revolution "that's why the government of India publishes [Murder Weekly] and sells it on the streets for just four and a half rupees so that even the poor can buy it" (*WT* 125).

Adiga calls for a radical paradigm shift in the unfair social functions in religious, political, economical, democratic, bureaucratic systems and calls for revolution for the same. "Speak to me of civil war, I told Delhi. [...] Speak to me of blood on the streets, I told Delhi" (*WT* 221). However, like Arjuna who was confused about his *svadharma* as a *Ksatriya*, common people are in confusion. Balram expresses this dilemma very clearly. "An Indian revolution? No, sir. It won't happen. People in this country are still waiting for the war of their freedom to come from somewhere else" (*WT* 303-04). As Arjuna fought in the *kurukshetra* war to establish *dharma*, each person has to stand on his feet and establish his/her rights. *The White Tiger*, the story of Balram who changes his destiny in the democratic India, is a challenge before each person. He transforms himself into Ashok.

In order to attain the balance of *purusharthas*, Krishna in *Bhagavad Gita* says: "Do engage yourself in action that is necessary; activity is indeed better than non-activity."[69] Krishna justifies Arjuna's act of fighting based on certain reasons. Firstly, it is an indispensable act to establish *dharma* to keep the social order. Secondly, fulfilling one's *dharma* which is the *Karmayoga*, (the path of action) is a means to attain *moksha* which is the ultimate aim of life. Thirdly, it is necessary to fulfill the *dharmic* obligation to the society. Finally, these actions should be out of selflessness or without attachment to attain *moksha* since the attachment to the action and expectation of fruits bond one to the world. The killing of Mr. Ashok, the crucial moral question in the novel can be read as an allegory as the *Kurusetra* war in the *Bhagavad Gita*. Munna, whose destiny is to be a sweet-maker, fights in the battlefields of Laxmangarh, the dark village; Delhi, the crazy city; and Bangalore, the entrepreneur's city. A constant war is taking place between good and evil, order and disorder, justice and injustice, greed and generosity, luxury and substance, and submission and progress in the democratic country. This continuous fight takes place not only outside but also within oneself. This conflict helps human beings to advance in social, intellectual, economical, political, and personal levels. Only through this war Munna is transformed to Ashok Sharma. Thus the narrator justifies his act of murder.

Rooster Coop stands for ignorance (*avidya*). Though people have the potency within themselves, because of ignorance they are not liberated. "You were looking for the key for years/But the door was always open!" (*WT* 253, 267). *Avidya* (ignorance) is the root cause of every evil. Appearance and experience take one away from the reality. Hence without transcendental intuition one cannot be out of *maya*. Bijayananda Kar says: "right knowledge (*vidya*) consists only in knowing something, as it.... To take something as something else is *adhyasa*."[70] *Adhyasa* means misconception or mistaken notions and it is the root cause of all the problems. People behave as if they are liberated and it is their destiny. "The error in *maya* is not the appearance as such but the forgetfulness that the appearance is appearance."[71] The wealthy traps the disadvantaged and will have no escape from the slavery. "My life had been written away. I was to go to jail for a killing I had not done. I was in terror, and yet not once did the thought of running away cross my mind. Not once did the thought, I'll tell the judge the truth, cross my mind. I was trapped in the Rooster Coop" (*WT* 177). The narrator of *The White Tiger* wants to destroy ignorance "One night, will they all join together—will they destroy the

Rooster Coop?" (*WT* 305). The narrator calls for a new ethos for the poor.

Balram is a symbol of one's self (*atman*). The conflict takes place within each person and 'the coop is guarded from the inside' (*WT* 194). In order to attain good, each person should come out of the ignorance which is a hindrance to self-realization. Balram quotes the poem: 'They remain slaves because they can't see what is beautiful in this world' and commend, 'That's the truest thing anyone ever said' (*WT* 40). Balram does only his *dharma* nothing more or less. He kills his master to come out of Rooster Coop for the welfare of the society as Arjun killed all his relatives. Human beings have the right to protect one's right and find a space for development. Balram wants to live like a man and it is a birth right. "All I wanted was the chance to be a man—and for that, one murder was enough" (*WT* 318). The novel represents the eternal force or the *paramathman*, which dwells within each person i.e. the atman. 'We saw a white tiger in a cage' (*WT* 278). Ultimately man ought to be liberated from the rebirth. The dark Ganges represents the misleading rituals, teachings which are not able to liberate the atman. "The villagers are so religious in the Darkness" (*WT* 90). Human beings are moved by distorted views and philosophy.

The family of Mr. Ashok stands for the challenges before each person to fulfill one's *dharma* which is everywhere. "Even here, in the weight machine of a train station, they try to hoodwink us. Here, on the threshold of a man's freedom, just before he boards a train to a new life, these flashing fortune machines are the final alarm bell of the Rooster Coop" (*WT* 248). But without fear one should do one's duty. The jobless, landless, marginalized farmers, exploited, and others are to take decisive decisions in their life for being free to fulfill one's *dharma*.

> The supernatural only operates in history and human societies through the mediation of human beings in so far as these consciously enter into contact with the transcendent reality of the pure Good who is God. In a certain sense, therefore, it is the capacity of men and

> women who love justice and struggle for it which in a democracy represents the best warranty of right and freedom. In this sense, right may at times depend on force.[72]

People who do their *dharma* are the instruments of god. "I think the Rooster Coop needs people like me to break out of it" (*WT* 320). If the white tiger can make the revolution everyone can make it.

The train to Bangalore is the chariot taken to liberation and it is a life long journey. 'It was a long trip by train' (*WT* 197). Each radical step in life is compared to a shift of train. 'He boards a train to a new life' (*WT* 248). The statement 'transfer myself from train to train' (*WT* 292) shows the continuous transformation happening within each person. People are afraid to make changes in life. The gap between the trains is a challenging time. 'The train station is a dangerous place' (*WT* 293). The transformation from Munna to Ashok Sharma is a hazardous journey. One has to pass through Munna—Balaram Halwai—to White Tiger—Ashok Sharma.

6.3.6. Moksha

The achievement of *moksha* takes place in the day to day life of human beings. *Moksha* which is the spiritual and transcendental value of life, means liberation, emancipation and salvation. "It is a state of pure bliss, a value par excellence.... It is not a mere communication-existence with people, it is rather an inter-existence."[73] In the modern period *moksha* means liberation and freedom in this world rather than looking towards a world yet to come. Once the individual and the society become humane, *moksha* is realized on earth. *Moksha* is a state where the individual lives with a transformed spirit.

The White Tiger is a novel that calls for liberation. 'I've made it! I've broken out of the coop!' (*WT* 320). The novel envisages a just society and finds its expression in the uplifting of the deprived. The New India has the freedom of 'choice' which is lacking 'in the darkness' (*WT* 121). "A handful of men in this country have trained the remaining 99.9 percent—

as strong, as talented, as intelligent in every way—to exist in perpetual servitude; a servitude so strong that you can put the key of his emancipation in a man's hands and he will throw it back at you with a curse" (*WT* 176). Such an India is not liberated but Balram's odyssey liberates himself. *Dharma* leads to liberation: *Moksha*. India is moving to a new epoch where Bangalore is becoming the centre. Bangalore is a new myth: the *moksha* of India. New Bangalore symbolizes a liberated India and "it makes [the new generation] happy to see a chandelier" (*WT* 117) as a morning star which symbolizes hope. Bangalore is an allegory for meaningful existence with freedom. "That is the difference between this India and that India: the choice" (*WT* 306). It is a state of Being than a place.

Balram's life is an analogy for the rise of the underdogs of India in the 21st century. The liberated Balram is his 'own master' (*WT* 231) for he is actively involved in the worldly affairs without attachments. The attitude of Balram towards the family stands for his detachment from everything and aims for the highest goal. For self-realization Balram breaks his relationship with his own family and Mr. Ashok's family. The relationship should not become bondage but a facilitating factor for *moksha*. "Only a man who is prepared to see his family destroyed—hunted, beaten, and burned alive by the masters—can break out of the coop" (*WT* 176-77). Balram is not tied to material gains. He moves to detachment. "After three or four years in real estate, I think I might sell everything, take the money, and start a school—an English-language school—for poor children in Bangalore" (*WT* 319). Balram urges to attain the stage of *nishkama karma*. Even though the blood of the master immerses Balram in the corrupt Indian system and the master's money becomes the capital, he tries to come out of the unjust system. The final 'Ha' before having children says that he does not want a new generation participation in the corrupted system, but a new generation of 'White Tigers'. "A school full of White Tigers, unleashed on Bangalore!" (319). Balram synthesizes both Vedic and non-Vedic thoughts and follows the path of activism (*pravrtti*) and the path of renunciation (*nivrtti*)[74] which are complementary to develop the integrated personality of liberation.

The analysis can be concluded with the following paragraphs. The continuous religious establishment of *dharma* is an inexorable in-built mechanism for human existence, and it can be called as *avathara*. It keeps the rhythm of nature and well-being of all without any discrimination. When *adharma* ascends, the unity of life disintegrates. In order to regain the integrity, nature takes its own means. All the measures that prevail in the universe to uphold *dharma* are included in *avathara*.

Adharma has shot up in globalized India and "the rich always get the best things in life, and all that we get is their leftovers" (*WT* 233). *The White Tiger* is an *avathar* in the form of a novel to reestablish *dharma*. The novel upholds a deep commitment to equality and tries to bring all Indians on to a common platform. The integrity of a person lies in *dharma*, *artha*, *kama* and *moksha* that balances the rhythm of all life including the sacred and the secular. The novel envisages a society based on equality and justice. It is a force to make the people realize the *adharma* in society and fight against it. "*The White Tiger* should make every right thinking citizen read the signs of the times and be socially conscious of the rights and duties of each one, irrespective of caste, creed or economic status, to prevent create people like Ashok and Balram in our society."[75]

In the modern world, empowering a democratic way of life is the best tool for the elimination of social inequality, which gives to each person without discrimination, the freedom to attain the *purusharth* as in a balanced manner. There exists the basic conditions for justice, such as (a) equity in the powers and capacities of persons; (b) cooperation largely based on reciprocal advantage; and (c) a situation where all parties are in a condition of moderate scarcity. Justice prevails in a society where there must be enough reciprocity around for all people to find some balance of reciprocal advantage.[76] In order to establish social justice, the post-independent India adopted democracy and urged people to establish JUSTICE, LIBERTY, EQUALITY, and FRATERNITY, The novel acknowledges the strength of the Indian constitution. The constitution envisages: "Any boy in any village can grow up to become the prime minister of India" (*WT* 35). India has succeeded a lot in fulfilling the dreams of the founding fathers of the post-independent India. Yet it has to go a long way to establish a just society. The novel narrates the dark side of India in neo-liberal period to liberate it. First and foremost the fight should start from within to win over one's own mind against injustice, committing oneself and then stand for social justice. "I am in the Light now" (*WT* 313).

Notes

1. Rafiq Dossani, *India Arriving: How this Economic Powerhouse is Redefining Global Business* (New Delhi: 2008), p. 119.
2. A.P.J. Abdul Kalam, *India 2020: A Vision for the New Millennium.* Y.S. Rajan (ed.) (New Delhi: Penguin Books, 1998), 269-70.
3. Somnath Batabyal, "New Delhi's Times: Creating a myth for a City." Bharati Chaturvedi (ed.) *Finding Delhi: Loss and Renewal in the Megacity* (New Delhi: Penguin Group, 2010), p. 110.
4. N.K. Singh, *Not by Reason Alone: The Politics of Change* (New Delhi: Penguine Group, 2009), p. xvi.
5. P.N. Bhagwati, "*Judicial Activism in India.*" Accessed: 19th March 2014. <law.wisc.edu/m/4mdd4/gargoyle_17_1_3.pdf> p. 8.
6. Bipan Chandra, *Communalism in Modern India.* 1984 (New Delhi: Har-Anand Publications, 2008), p. 347.
7. Bandhu Ishanands Vempeny, "Western Secularism and Religion-Centered Indian secularism: An Indian Alternative to Western Secularism." Antony Kalliath and Raj Irudaya (ed.) *Indian Secularism: A Theological Response* (Bangalore: Indian Theological Association, 2010), p. 159.
8. B. Sivakumar, "Half of India's dalit population lives in 4 states." Web: 2ed May 2013. Accessed: 18th March 2014. <http://timesofindia.indiatimes.com/india/Half-of-Indias-dalit-population-lives-in-4-states/articleshow/19827757.cms>.

9. Human Rights Watch. "Hidden Apartheid: Caste Discrimination against India's Untouchables" Web: 13th February 2007. Accessed: 18th March 2014 <http://www.hrw.org/reports/2007/02/12/hidden-apartheid>.
10. Dionysius Rasquinha, *Towards Wholeness from Brokenness: The Dalit Quest* (Delhi: ISPCK, 2013), p. 16.
11. "Dark India: Dalit in India Facts and Figures." Accessed: 18th March 2014 <http://darkindia.wordpress.com/dalit-in-india-facts-and-figures/>.
12. *Ibid.*
13. Christophe Jaffrelot, "The Paradoxical Democratisation of Indian Democracy." Christophe Jaffrelot (ed.) *India Since 1950: Society, Politics, Economy and Culture* (New Delhi: Yatra Books, 2012), p. 69.
14. Balmiki Prasad Singh, *India's Culture: The State, the Arts, and Beyond* (India: Oxford University Press, 2011), p. xxxv.
15. T. Sai Chandra Mouli and Jaydeep Sarangi. *Indian Women's Writings in English* (Delhi: Gnosis, 2008), p. v.
16. K.N. Panikkar, *Colonialism, Culture and Resistance.* 2007 (New Delhi and Oxford: Oxford University Press, 2009), p. 12.
17. M. Sivaramkrishna, *Hindu View of Life: A Contemporary Perspective* (Bangalore: Dharmaram Publications, 2001), p. 169.
18. Alvin Hwang, Anne Marie Francesco, and Eric Kessler, "The relationship between individualism-collectivitsm, face and feedback and learning processes in Hong Kong, Singapore, and the United States." *Journal of Cross-cultural Psychology* 34.1 (2003), pp. 72-73.
19. *Ibid.* p. 73.
20. Star Soh and Frederick T.L. Leong, "Validity of vertical and horizontal individualism and collectivism in Singapore: Relationships with values and interests." *Journal of Cross-cultural Psychology* 33.1 (2002), p. 3.
21. Boonghee Yoo, Naveen Donthu and Tomasz Lenartowicz. "Measuring Hofstede's Five Dimensions of Cultural Valuesat the Individual Level: Development and Validation of CVSCALE." *Journal of International Consumer Marketing* 23. Web: 1st May 2011. Accessed: 8th November 2013. p. 194 <http://ehis.ebscohost.com.ulm.idm.oclc.org>.

22. Kwasi Dartey-Baah, "The Cultural Approach to the Management of the International Human Resource: An Analysis of Hofstede's Cultural Dimensions." *International Journal of Business Administration* 4.2 (2013), Accessed: 8th November 2013. <www.sciedu.ca/ijba>.
23. Drew Nesdale and Mikako Naito, "Individualism-Collectivism and the Attitudes to School Bullying of Japanese and Australian Students." *Journal of Cross-cultural Psychology* 36.5 (2005), pp. 537-38.
24. Micheller Nelson and Sharon Shavitt, "Horizontal and Vertical Individualism and achievement values: A Multimethod Examination of Denmark and the United States." *Journal of Cross-cultural Psychology* 33.5. (2002), p. 440.
25. G.R. Madan, *Western Sociologists on Indian Society: Marx, Spencer, Weber, Durkheim, Pareto* (Bombay: Allied Publishers Private Limited, 1979), p. 49.
26. *Ibid.*, p. 43.
27. Vinayaka P. Bhatta, "Human Rights and Dharmasastra." V.N. Jha (ed.) *Dharmasastra and Social Awareness* (Delhi: 1996), p. 62.
28. J.N. Farquhar and H.D. Griswold, *The Religious quest of India* (Oxford: Oxford University Press, 1922), p. 48.
29. *Ibid.*, p. 100.
30. Asha Mukherjee, "Gandhi and The Problem of Modernity: A Point of Departure." Asha Mukherjee & et al. (ed.) *Civil Society in Indian Cultures: Indian Philosophical Studies* I. Cultural Heritage and Contemporary Change Series III b, South Asia, Vol. 6. (Washington: 2001), p. 7.
31. Kathleen Waller, "Redefinitions of India and Individuality in Adiga's *The White Tiger*." CLCWeb: *Comparative Literature and Culture* 14.2 (2012) Web: 2012. Accessed: 5th November 2013. <http://go.galegroup.com/>.
32. Asha Mukherjee, "Gandhi and The Problem of Modernity: A Point of Departure." Asha Mukherjee & et al. (ed.) *Civil Society in Indian Cultures: Indian Philosophical Studies* I. Cultural Heritage and Contemporary Change Series III b, South Asia, Vol. 6. (Washington: 2001), p. 7.
33. Meenu Dubey, "Graphic Scrutiny of Subaltern in Arundhati Roy's The God of Small Things." Amar Nath Prasad, and Bithika

Dasgupta Sarkar (ed.) *Arundhati Roy: A Critical Elucidation* (New Delhi: Sarup Book Publishers, 2010), p. 138.

34. Dora Capozza and Rupert Brown, "Introduction: Social identity theory in retrospect and prospect." Dora Capozza and Rupert Brown (ed.) *Social Identity Process* (London: Sage Publications, 2000), p. vii.
35. Kay Deaux, "Models, Meanings and Motivations." Dora Capozza and Rupert Brown (ed.) *Social Identity Process* (London: Sage Publications 2000), p. 12.
36. Drew Nesdale and Mikako Naito, "Individualism-Collectivism and the Attitudes to School Bullying of Japanese and Australian Students." *Journal of Cross-cultural Psychology* 36.5 (2005), p. 537.
37. Ashwini Kumar Vishnu, "The God of Small Things: A Note on Roy's Sociological Imagination." Amar Nath Prasad and Bithika Dasgupta Sarkar (ed.) *Arundhati Roy: A Critical Elucidation* (New Delhi: Sarup Book Publishers, 2010), p. 129.
38. *The Kama Sutra of Vatsyayana*. Richard Burton and F.F. Arbuthnot (Trans.) (Great Britain: Wordsworth Classics, 1996), p. 82.
39. Niveditha Menon and Michael P. Johnson, "Patriarchy and Paternalism in Intimate Partner Violence: A Study of Domestic Violence in Rural India." Kamal K. Misra and Janet Huber Lowry (ed.) *Recent Studies on Indian Women* (Jaipur: Rawat Publications, 2007), p. 172.
40. L.P.N. Perera, *Sexuality in Ancient India: A Study Based on the Pali Vinayapitaka* (Colombo: The Postgraduate Institute of Pali and Buddhist Studies, 1993), p. 249.
41. Shalini Shah, *Love, Eroticism and Female Sexuality in Classical Sanskrit Literature: Seventh-Thirteenth Centuries* (New Delhi: Manohar, 2009), pp. 165-66.
42. *The Kama Sutra of Vatsyayana*. Richard Burton and F.F. Arbuthnot (Trans.) (Great Britain: Wordsworth Classics, 1996), p. 11.
43. Steven J. Rosen, "Introduction." Steven J. Rosen (ed.) *Vaisnani: Women and the Worship of Krisha* (Delhi: Motilal Banarsidass Publishers, 1996), p. 2.
44. *Ibid.*
45. Prashant Subhash Mothe. "Arundhati Roy's The God of Small Things: Focusing on Marginal Gender." Patel M.F. (ed.)

Indian Women Novelists Critical Discourses (Jaipur: Aavishkar Publishers, 2010), p. 22.

46. Hithesh T.S. Sanker and Praveenlal Kuttichira, "Custody Deaths in Kerala: A Study from Post-mortem Data in Thrissur Medical College." *Economic & Political Weekly,* xlvil. 12 (2012), p. 24.
47. *Ibid.*
48. Shashi Joshi, *A History of the Indian Communists: The Irrelevance of Leninism* (India: Sage Publications, 2011), p. 385.
49. Cyriac Thomas, "Christian Contribution in Nation Building." *Journal of St. Thomas Christians* 14.1 (2003), p. 176.
50. Jose Porunnedom, "Meeting of Two Laws: Influence of Western Missionaries on St. Thomas Christian Church." *Journal of St. Thomas Christians* 13.4 (2004), p. 151.
51. M. Sivaramkrishna, *Hindu View of Life: A Contemporary Perspective* (Bangalore: Dharmaram Publications, 2001), p. 171.
52. K.V.R. Aiyangar, *Some aspects of the Hindu view of Life According to Dharmasastra* (Baroda: Oriental Institute, 1952), p. 62.
53. Akash Kapur, "The Secret of His Success." *New York Times.* Web: 7th November 2008. Accessed: 10th November 2013 <http://www.nytimes.com/2008/11/09/books/review/Kapur-t.html?_r=0>.
54. Hartmut Scharfe, "Artha." Sushil Mittal and Gene Thursby (ed.) *The Hindu World* (London: Routledge, 2004), p. 249.
55. Jawaharlal Nehru, "Tryst with Destiny." Accessed: 1st September 2013 <http://www.svc.ac.in/files/TRYST%20WITH%20DESTINY.pdf>.
56. G.J.H. Admin. "Is there something called Indianness?" Web: 30th January 2011. Accessed: 4th September 2013 <http://www.ghadar.in/gjh_html/?q=content/there-something-called-indianness>.
57. S.C. Dube, "*Indian Village*" (Bombay: Allied Publishers, 1965), p. 1.
58. Smitu Kothari, "Whose independence? The social impact of economic reform in India." *Journal of International Affairs* 51.1 (1997), p. 85. <http://ehis.ebscohost.com>.

59. M.K. Gandhi, "Rebuilding Our Villages." Bharatan Kumarappa (ed.) (Ahmedabad: Navajivan Publishing House, 1952), p. 3.
60. Smitu Kothari, "Whose independence? The social impact of economic reform in India." *Journal of International Affairs* 51.1 (1997), p. 85. <http://ehis.ebscohost.com>.
61. Ashgar Ali Engineer, "Globalization, Islam and Threat to Diversity." *Globalization Stepping into the One World* (Chennai: Ramakrishna Math, 2000), pp. 94-95.
62. Kautilya, *The Arthashastra*. L.N. Rangarajan (ed.) (New Delhi: Penguin Books, 1992), p. 13.
63. A.C. Sarangi, "Four Purusarthas and Their Role in Society." V.N. Jha (ed.) *Dharmasastra and Social Awareness* (Delhi: Indian Books Centre, 1996), p. 120.
64. *Ibid.*
65. Patrick Olivelle, "Preface." *Dharma: Studies in its Semantic, Cultural and Religious History*. Patrick Olivelle (ed.) (Delhi: Motilal Banarsidass Publishers, 2009), p. vii.
66. Franklin Edgerton, "Dominant Ideas in the Formation of Indian Culture." *Journal of the American Oriental Society* 62.3 (1942), pp. 151-56. Accessed: 22nd October 2013. <http://www.jstor.org/stable/59413>.
67. Thomas Manickam, "Biblical Hermeneutics: An Indian Approach," *Indian Interpretations of the Bible*, Augustine Thottakara cmi (ed.), (Bangalore: Dharmaram Publications, 2000), pp. 115-16.
68. M. Sivaramkrishna, *Hindu View of Life: A Contemporary Perspective* (Bangalore: Dharmaram Publications, 2001), p. 177.
69. *The Bhagavad Gita* III.8. *Nitya Chaitanya Yati* (Tran.) (New Delhi: D.K. Printworld, 1993), p. 86.
70. Bijayananda Kar, *Indian Theories of Error* (Delhi: Ajanta Publication, 1990), p. 98.
71. M. Sivaramkrishna, *Hindu View of Life: A Contemporary Perspective* (Bangalore: Dharmaram Publications, 2001), p. 80.
72. Maria Clara Bingemer, "War, suffering and detachment: Reading the Bhagavad Gita with Simon Weil." Catherine Cornille (ed.) *Song Divine: Christian Commentaries on the Bhagavad Gita*. (Leuven: Peeters, 2006), p. 77.

73. A.C. Sarangi, "Four Purusarthas and Their Role in Society." V.N. Jha (ed.) *Dharmasastra and Social Awareness* (Delhi: Indian Books Centre, 1996), p. 121.
74. S.R. Goyal, *Fundamentals of Pauranika Hinduism* (Jodhpur: Kusumanjali Book, 2009), p. 152.
75. A.J. Sebastian, "Poor-Rich Divide in Aravind Adiga's *The White Tiger*". *Journal of Alternative Perspectives in the Social Sciences* 1.2 (2009), p. 244. EBSCOhost Research Database. Accessed: 3rd August 2013 <http://ehis.ebscohost.com.ulm.idm.oclc.org/>.
76. Kai Nielsen, *Globalization and Justice* (America: Humanity Books, 2003), p. 234.

7

Parallelisms of Indian Ethos in Indian English Novels of Different Phases

CHAPTER OUTLINE

Indian ethos is continuously being moulded by the new notions emerging from the historical events. This change can be seen in the study on the refurbishment of Indian ethos in Indian English novels of different time span. The pre-independent, post-independent, de/re-democratization and neo-liberal periods made their impressions on the Indianness and Indian English novels imbibed a lot from each period. The novels, in turn contributed their part in shaping and guiding the Indian society in its proper ethos. The theme, style, and characterization vary from time to time in the novels to protect the ethos and identity of the nation.

The pre-independent phase was a time of the formation of a collective dream and the attempt to realize the same. Indians began to visualize a united and sovereign nation. The aspiration inspired the crowd to sacrifice themselves for the mother land. Ernest Renan, the nineteenth-century French scholar, argued that it is the 'will' which makes a nation. A nation is 'amoral consciousness,' a community with a common memory—a people which has suffered together.[1] The collective aim got dominance over individuals to attain freedom for the nation. The social reformation and nationalism were the major thrust of the age. The spirit of the common man is narrated in the novels of the time. For example, in *Kanthapura,* the villagers are the real heroes. Out of nationalism the writers took efforts for Indianization by maintaining fidelity to the traditions and customs. The social awakening went along with nationalism and the reformers emphasized the Indian ethos of respecting every human being. Irrespective of religion and nationality, Indian ethos teaches all beings to love each other. The novels like *Untouchable*, sympathized with the underprivileged ones of the society. "*Untouchable* is not only a problem novel but also one of protest, attacking the social evil of untouchability."[2] The suffering of the untouchable was terrifying. For example, Bakha was publically harassed for touching a high caste (*UT* 38). The social reformers toiled a lot to bring equality between all human beings.

In the post-independent phase people became more anxious to materialize the obtained chance to build-up the nation.

Herculean efforts were made to satisfy the personal, regional and national interests. The period emphasized secularism, socialism and unity of the nation. One of the great achievements was the completion of the Constitution. Compared to many Asian and African countries, India constituted and implemented a qualitative constitution within the limited time frame. For the future generations, the constitution is a concrete means to know the ethos of India and is a guide to mould it.

During the period, writers became more realistic about nationalism and they gave hope to people at the time of crisis. At that time, expectations were high but the growth of the nation was limited. Hence the people lost their trust in leaders and frustrations were expressed. Power and money began to control the politicians. In *Waiting for Mahatma*, Mr. Natesh who represents politicians reveals his insincerity through his hypocritical behaviour. "[Mr. Natesh], had effected a few alterations in his house, such as substituting Khaddar hangings for the gaudy chintz [...] and had taken down the pictures of hunting gentry, vague gods and kings. [...] and substitute pictures of Maulana Azad, Jawaharlal Nehru, Sarojini Naidu" (*WM* 33). The poor people become disappointed and marginalized in the governance of the state. They began to lose faith in democracy. Yet the writers made efforts to inspire people to have faith in democracy. The novels expressed the longing for a leader like Gandhiji and urged to wait for the growth of the young nation. "The most striking feature of the first years of Indian independence was an absence. It was the absence of the man whom we all called (though he rejected the phrase) the Father of the Nation, the Mahatma (Great Soul another term he detested) Gandhi."[3] No one could replace Gandhiji to build the nation and whenever there was a pitfall, many lamented the absence of Gandhiji. In 1963, Rajagopalachari wrote in *Swarajya*, "All things that Gandhiji wanted to be done are forgotten. And the very opposite of what he wanted are being done."[4] Along with R.K. Narayan, Indians were waiting for the second coming of Mahatma. Religious fundamentalism and regionalism were the major hindrance of the unity. Jawaharlal Nehru, was often worried about the 'fissiparous tendencies' that could undo the nation and he could observe the tendency both in governmental and non-governmental organizations.[5] Opposing to these threats, *Train to Pakistan* gives prime importance to ethnic consciousness in the identity formation. Promoting Indian consciousness facilitates the nurturing of harmony and thereby brings unity among the diversified elements in India.

In the de/re-democratization phase the cry of the people resounded louder than ever and the leaders could not satisfy them. The clouds of conflicts and reactions came together and ended in State Emergency. The decline and restoration of Indian democracy was not only limited to emergency but many other factors too, like economic and political factors. All these situations are portrayed in Indian English Novels of the period. The novels of the period have more personalized language and thoughts in a refined way. They openly criticize the government and leaders for mismanagements. For instance *Great Indian Novel* narrates the pitfalls of Indira Gandhi through the character Priya Duryodhani. The political and economic disappointments were reflected in the novels. For the writers, socialism seemed to be a failure not because of the ideological defects but because of the execution. Gandhiji, remarked before independence itself, "Only truthful, non-violent and pure-hearted Socialists will be able to establish a Socialistic society in India and the world."[6] To achieve a socialist society, one of the essential requirements is a leader who follows the force of the soul. But the nation could not attain the dream of the socialists of post-independent period. The regionalism also became a destructive factor against the smooth functioning of the democracy. "Language marchers demanded the partition of the state of Bombay along linguistic boundaries—the dream of Maharashtra was at the head of some processions, the mirage of Gujarat led the others forward" (*MC* 231). Indian English novels could comprehend the situations in their wholeness.

In the neo-liberal period, India made remarkable economic growth and began to explore the human resources. "More than half of all Indians are currently under the age of twenty-five. With the youngest working population on the planet,

India has the potential to become the world's factory. Get it right and it could become its chief provider too."[7] Along with economic progress, Indian English novels also progressed. In the neo-liberal phase, authors had at most freedom and they gave importance to regional cultures. Malayalee culture plays a significant role in the novel, *God of Small Things*. The writer has taken liberty to make use of the vocabularies, idioms, proverbs, and rhythm of speech from the regional *bhashas*. Subaltern characters are conscious of the rights. Instead of flight from adversities, they are ready to fight for the same. For instance, Ammu and Velutha the characters of *God of Small Things* break the laws of love. Another feature of the period is the widening gap between the rich and the poor. "India's economic growth rate may be riding high, but many millions of its citizens continue to live unresplendent lives dulled by poverty. Likewise 'New India' has a presumptuous ring to it, as if the Old had upped and gone."[8] The labour unions and socialist parties sided with the entrepreneurs and ignored the rights of the poor. Acquisition of land in Nandigram led to violence and the killing of fourteen people in 2007. The writers are well aware of the disparity between the rich and the poor. "However, displaying their usual genius for town planning, the rich of Delhi had built this part of Gurgaon with no parks, lawns, or playgrounds—it was just buildings, shopping malls, hotels, and more buildings. There was a pavement outside, but that was for the poor to live on" (*WT* 225). Later, to provide just and fair compensation for landowners, the Central Government brought out the Land Acquisition Act and it came into force on 1st January 2014. The entrepreneurs who manipulate the governance of the state for their selfishness, know 'the time to smile,' 'sip the hot coffee,' and keep paying and paying the fucker (*WT* 310). The positive and negative forces which tried to control India are well portrayed in the novels. The Indianness and the Indian history shaped the novels, so the major shifts in the novels can be compared with the changing nature of India. The major areas where one can find parallelisms in Indian English novels of different periods are given below. In addition to this, the unique features of each period and their reflections in the novels are analyzed here.

7.1. Nation Building

One of the major objectives of Indian English novels has been nation construction and they have played a major role in the promotion of nationalism. The efforts taken by writers to arouse attachment to the land and the sense of brotherhood/sisterhood among Indians, are remarkable. At the time of pre-independence Indians began to revitalize the ethos of the nation and anchored their identity on it. "Nationalism is the most powerful force of the twentieth century [...]. It is an expression of love as well as of hate."[9] The self-awareness facilitated the Indians to move away from the perspectives of the colonizer and define their identity based on Indianness. During the phase, Indian English novels insulated the spirit of nationalism for the freedom struggle. *Kanthapura* is an embodiment of Indian nationalism. At the end of the freedom struggle, "there's neither man nor mosquito in Kanthapura" (*KA* 259). It is a story of radical transformation of the overt and covert nature of people with nationalistic spirit. "Nationalism is not at all accidental: its roots are deep and important, it was indeed our destiny."[10] In order to nurture nationalism, Raja Rao makes use of socio-religious ethos of India with a political agenda. All the major decisions of the time like, Civil disobedience, Dandi march, non-tax payment campaign, Non-Cooperation Movement, Satyagraha, and socialistic influence are reflected in the novel. It is also a subaltern history of independence since it narrates the great sacrifice of women, villagers and so on. The struggle for freedom was unusually spiritual and it reflected in Indian English novels of pre-independent period. The novel is not limited to mere political objectives but the realization of life. The novel never aims at any tangible gains but a higher meaning of life, which Gandhiji persuaded.

> For a creative visionary such as Rao, a nation is neither an intellectual nor a political make up of a people's imagination [...], gathered together to garner

some political profits. For Raja Rao and with him to other earlier generation Indian writers, a nation is an emotional, spiritual, religious, catholic, and a visionary identification of a people for the attainments of higher goals in life. For Moorthy in the novel, nation is like 'a thousand-pillared temple.'[11]

Indian ethos is based on a holistic perspective of life including, material, social, and spiritual elements.

The challenges of India were different in the post-independent age and they shadowed in Indian English novels too. The economic developments, religious harmony, upholding integrity, and keeping unity were the major themes of the period to build-up a new nation. *Train to Pakistan*, aimed to nurture communal harmony within the country and with Pakistan, which was a vital need for the peaceful existence. Partition is not a finished product. "Partition is at the heart not only of the great regional conflicts...[but] it is also an important component or factor in a whole series of religious-cum-political conflicts reaching down to the present time."[12] The novel attempts to heal the wounds of the partition and promotes nationalism. National identity above religious identity was also a prerequisite of the time. Actually, Indians possess such an ardent attachment to the land and the native village. "Another identity is a tense emotional belongingness to the village which gave separate religious identities."[13] Without blaming any particular community, the novel portrays the chronicle of the horror that accompanied the partition of India. "A thousand charred corpses sizzling and smoking while the rain put out the fire" (*TP* 112). The novel begins with the indication that the total rhythm of nature and symphony of the social life was going to collapse. "The summer of 1947 was not like other Indian summers. Even the weather had a different feel in India that year" (*TP* 10). The sacrifice of Jugga and life inside Nimmo, urge every Indian to love Pakistanis, the brothers and sisters of Indians.

Another dimension of post-independent India was revealed in *Waiting for the Mahatma*. It gives nostalgic feeling of the independent struggle, to motivate the independent people to face the obstacles of nation building. Sriram, the protagonist lacked the true spirit of nationalism but for a beautiful lady, he took part in the freedom struggle. However, gradually he was inspired by Gandhiji and consumed the true national spirit which the post-independent Indians required. He assimilated the true spirit of India. "He is not influenced by anything else except what is called Indianness. He writes about beliefs, habits, rituals and customs of the Indian people, and is satisfied with it."[14] The novel is about a hero and heroine from a common flock who contributed to the freedom struggle of India. "R.K. Narayan's Malgudi mirrors the time and image of India as a whole. It is not microcosm but macrocosm which combines the old and the new, tradition and modernity, the mood of the novelist and that of the contemporary world."[15] The aim of the novel is to give confidence and optimism to the common people to have faith in the development of India. By bringing different points of view of laypersons it acts as an eye opener to the leaders.

In India, the democratic catastrophe reached its peak in 1975 when State Emergency was declared and the phase is named de/re-democratization phase. There might be a number of justifying reasons for the need of the emergency, yet it was a direct violent-war against democracy. Therefore Indian English novels responded to the situation in the de/re-democratization phase. *The Great Indian Novel* rejects all forms of authoritarianism, including colonialism and emergency. The brutality of colonial rule is recorded in the novel. The novel, also gently and sharply expresses protest against the misuse of power by Indira Gandhi. "Questioning the sanity of the victor is the only course open to any civilization defeated by forces it cannot understand" (*GIN* 369). At the same time, the novel realistically presents the political and economic indiscipline. The politics of protest was the working principle and the functioning of the government endangered by the irresponsibility of the trade union leaders. "But I still believed that the political chaos in the country, fuelled by Drona's idealistic but confused uprising which a variety of political opportunists had joined and exploited, could have led the country nowhere but to anarchy" (*GIN* 369). The novel mourns for India which could not find an alternative for those who threatened democracy. "An India where a Priya

Duryodhani can be re-elected because seven hundred million people cannot produce anyone better, and where her immortality can be guaranteed by her greatest failure [...]" (*GIN* 412-13). The novel stands for a proper democratic government.

One of the most celebrated Indian English novels of the period is *Midnight's Children*, which also reflects the chaos of the State Emergency. "Midnight's Children was his first major attempt in fiction to address the 'betrayal' of India by its government. [...] For Rushdie maintains that the promise of India has not been eradicated, even if it has been repeatedly betrayed."[16] The Nehruvian 'ideal India' did not exist during emergency. "The gradual disintegration of the Midnight Children's Conference [...] was already well under way. When novelty wears off, boredom, and then dissension, must inevitably ensue" (*MC* 352). The true condition of India is well allegorized here. The fundamental rights were taken away and oppositional leaders were arrested. The personal history of Aadam Sinai was merged with the emergency. "[...] at the precise instant of India's arrival at Emergency, he emerged. There were gasps; and, across the country, silences and fears. And owing to the occult tyrannies of that benighted hour" (*MC* 586). The reality is distorted by emergency. The novel is a historical text which goes against the distorted history books by the authoritarian rulers. "Rudolf Bader writes that Rushdie's 'ultimate motive' in Midnight's Children is 'to save the present through the preservation of the past' (*MC* 76). It is thus a book of memory, an attempt at 'the chutnification of history...the pickling of time'"[17] (*MC* 548). It is a diary of the common flock.

The novel attempts to revive democracy, which should be of the people, by the people, and for the people. All kinds of deformities of India were attributed to Aadam Sinai who had elephantiasis. "He was the true great-grandson of his great-grandfather, but elephantiasis attacked him in the ears instead of the nose—because he was also the true son of Shiva-and-Parvati" (*MC* 587). The nostalgia of the freedom struggle and innocence of the great leaders of renaissance were the themes of the novels of de/re-democratization period. Even though the novels of the period set apart ample space to narrate the failures of the Indian dream, they work towards a true democracy. They are not pessimistic but optimistic about India. The novels seem to be filled with pessimism, but the intention is to correct the deviant behaviours of the nation to attain the aspirations of the freedom fighters.

During 1990s globalization appeared to be a strange phenomenon for Indians. But it was welcomed with hope and anxiety. On the one hand, India moved to the new policy with the desire to overcome the economic crisis and to develop a self-reliant economy. On the other, it created apprehensions about neo-imperialism and imposition of hegemonic culture. Hence, after de/re-democratization the attention of all shifted to the impact of globalization and anxiety about the upcoming events due to privatization and liberalization. The neo-liberal waves on Indianness are replicated in Indian English novels too. *The White Tiger* is about the emerging pros and cons of multinational globalization. It presents Bangalore, the Silicon valley of India, as a new myth and hope for the new generation. 'A new Bangalore for a new India' (*WT* 318). At the same time, it is a prophetic novel which warns against corruption, disparity between the rich and the poor, degradation of values, and imperialism. "In the present era of globalization and integration of markets, the lifestyle of people is changing dramatically. The recent phenomenon of unrestrained consumption and display of wealth by certain classes in India may create a counter image of 'self-indulgent Indians'."[18] If precautions are not taken "it may well turn out to be nothing" (*WT* 320). *The God of Small Things* cautions against commodification of Indianness. "Next to the bottle there was a list of all the Paradise products and a Kathakali dancer with his face green and skirts swirling" (*GST* 46). The culture and values are sold out in the consumeristic world.

> To the contemporary minds, however, the issue to think the perception of a national identity having eroded and expanded beyond its margins, or the practices of literary writing having outlived the erstwhile pedagogical, intellectual or ideological points of viewing a historical frame of reference, particularly the transition from pre-

independence, Gandhian and Nehruvian conception, even of Tagore and Aurobindo, to a new, politically hybrid, economically unstable and socially and ethnically explosive nationshood.[19]

The neo-liberal Indian English novels are the critical space to evaluate whether the developments go with the interest of the nation.

7.2. Gandhian Epoch

Gandhism is the consciousness of India and Sabarmti is the centre of Indian soul. Its impact on Indian ethos cannot be neglected as many creative writers of different era, were inspired by Gandhism. The focus and mode of presentation varies with persons and time. *Kanthapura* is a Gandhian purana. It eternalizes Gandhiji through mythologizing and divinizes him by considering him as an *avathar*. Murthy, the protagonist is a shadow of Mahatma and Kanthapurians found realization in Gandhiji. Out of the steadfast love towards Gandhiji and faith in Gandhism, they sacrificed themselves for the nation. Gandhiji lived in the hearts of Indians. "[Gandhiji] did not descend from the top; he seemed to emerge from the millions of India, speaking their language and incessantly drawing attention to them and their appalling condition."[20] *Waiting for the Mahatma* presents Gandhiji in more a realistic and humanistic manner. Sriram was moved not by Gandhiji but by the beautiful girl, Bharati. "Sriram wanted to go and assure the girl on the grandstand that he fully and without the slightest reservation approved of her outlook and habits. [...] He seized the chance at the end of the meeting" (*WM* 24). Since Bharati was a disciple of Gandhiji, Sriram internalized Gandhism slowly. Mahatmaji added: "Remember that she is your guru, and think of her with reverence and respect, and you will be all right and she will be all right" (*WM* 72). At last, Sriram became a new man: a new Gandhian of post-independent India. It is a call for each Indian to become a Gandhian to solve the crisis of pre-independent India.

In later ages, Gandhiji is presented idealistically and Gandhism is reflected as more theoretically than by the pragmatic philosophy for life. Tharoor writes, "Mahatma Gandhi was the kind of person it is more convenient to forget. The principles he stood for and the way in which he asserted them are easier to admire than to follow."[21] He presents Gandhiji in *The Great Indian Novel* as 'impossible to imitate' (*GIN* 47) and satirizes some of his behaviours. At the same time, the novel accepts the greatness and contribution of Gandhiji. "Gangaji's greatest achievement was that he made the people at large feel they had a stake in the struggle for freedom" (*GIN* 371). May be as a reaction to emergency, *Midnight's Children* did not want to project any human-god in Indian democracy. "The clearest indication of Rushdie's unwillingness or inability to produce heroic models, according to this argument, is the bizarre absence of Mahatma Gandhi from Midnight's Children."[22] The novel acknowledges the power of Gandhiji to mobilize people for the national cause. The greatest failure of modern India is that it could not give birth to a second Gandhi.

The White Tiger, the novel of the twenty-first century, is about New Delhi and New Bangalore without Gandhiji. The novel ironically presents Gandhiji and kept his principles away from practical life. "A school where you won't be allowed to corrupt anyone's head with prayers and stories about God or Gandhi' (*WT* 318). The big chasm between the way of life of Indians and that of Gandhiji is portrayed but it also acknowledges that only Gandhiji can guide Indians to light (*WT* 137). The various depictions of Gandhiji in Indian English novels of different time-zone concur that there is no India without Gandhiji and quest for Gandhiji still continues. The most striking feature is that throughout independent India Gandhiji has been acclaimed. From *Waiting for the Mahatma* to *The White Tiger,* Gandhism is praised but the focus alters. The novels satirize the modern Gandhians who take the side of the rich and lack the virtue of renunciation. In his address to the United Nations General Assembly, Nehru said "Though we in India have failed in many ways in following his advice, something of his message still clings to our minds and hearts."[23]

He is a powerful symbol of Indian ethos. Gandhiji is always an inspiration for the people of all the ages.

7.3. Identity Formation

Even though it may be emotionally provoking, realistically it is impossible to regain the Indian ethos that prevailed before colonization. "For all its magnificent antiquity, and historical depth, contemporary India is unequivocally a creation of the modern world. The fundamental agencies and ideas of modernity—European colonial expansion, the state, nationalism, democracy, economic development—all have shaped it."[24] Along with colonization the Western ideologies had a tremendous influence on the Indian ethos in the modern era. There have been a lot of efforts taking place to refurbish Indianness according to present time without losing its identity. More than anything else, it is high-priority to empower Indians to be rooted in the national ethos. At this venture, Indian English novels took a leading role in the identity formation process of India. Some of the means used for Indianization are working on Indian themes, glorifying the civilization, celebrating the achievements, idealizing personalities, criticizing the evil practices, using vernacular vocabulary, adopting Indian style of writing, breaking the standard rules of English, and introducing code mixing. Through these tools, they made self-assertion at different stages of history.

Before independence, Indian English novels tremendously attempted to decolonize the Indian minds. *Kanthapura* which promotes the greatest legacy of India in the Puranas, is the best example for the same. Puranas reflect the way of life of Indians. "M.K. Naik says, 'the Puranas are a blend of narration and description, philosophical reflection, and religious teaching. The style is usually simple, flowing, and digressive, and exaggeration is the keynote or most accounts of happenings and miracles. There is much to correspond to this in *Kanthapura*."[25] Raja Rao made a revolutionary endeavour to bring Indianness in his novel. He wrote in the introduction of *Kanthapura*: "The tempo of Indian life must be infused into our English expression."[26]

Rao internalized the rhythm of Sanskrit. The efforts continued with many other writers like, R.K. Narayan, Mulk Raj Anand and their peer group. "[Narayan] is an exporter of ethos of South Indian Hindu middle class families in the background of Malgudi. Malgudi is not a place but an experience of soil and soul of India."[27] Narayan borrowed from South Indian language and culture. The writers transcribed the Indian life with its fine distinctions to Indian English novels.

1980s witnessed quintessential progress in Indianization.

> One can find several similarities between many of the Indian novels written in English and published in the 1980s and 1990s, namely a renewed focus on national history, a self-conscious transformation of English into an "Indian" language, and a distinctly postcolonial translation of postmodernism and canonical realism into a variety of "nativized" literary styles.[28]

Indian English writers got confidence for adapting more to the regional sensibility in the novels. Manjit also says, "[In 1980s] a decisive shift in theme, tone and architectonic marks an explainable relation of Indian fiction in English to its literary counterparts across the rest of the post-colonial world."[29] With the publication of *Midnight's Children,* there began a new style of chutnification in Indian English novels. Rushdie chutnified language, and history to preserve the Indianness. He attempted to accept both "Tai-for-changelessness opposed to Aadam-for-progress" (*MC* 124). More than purity of language, heteroglossia is found in Indian English novels to localize the work. *The Great Indian Novel* adapts the epics with modern political history of India. A perfect blending of two yugas! "The tone, language, and allusions used by Tharoor are influenced by and directed towards a particular literary tradition that might be called standard Indo-English."[30] The novel takes one to the heart of Indianness. The West also began to accept the Indianized English novels.

Indian English novels are also immensely vigilant with the future of Indian identity. Not only the influence but also colonization itself carries on with new subtle forms. "If the power of the empire of capital was taking on ever more global and imperial dimensions, what could this possibly mean for those at its receiving end, those in a global South who were increasingly unable to defend themselves against the 'free global market' as projected upon them by the US, the IMF, the WTO: what else could it be if not recolonization?"[31] During the neo-liberation time, the hegemony of recolonization has been experienced. Colonization moved to post-colonization and next to re-colonization. The colonization process happened like a spiral model. "The fact that the continuing reality of economic subordination to the advanced capitalist centres from whence the colonial empires originally sprang was soon well enough known to often earn the term itself the critical qualifiers 'false' (as in 'false decolonization')."[32] In the midst of re-colonization, *The White Tiger* gives a warning against virtual imperialism and speaks about the American masters (*WT* 298). The novel narrates the uprooted lives of Mr. Ashok and Pinky Madam. Bangalore stands for the capital of new colonizers.

Indian English novels strive to redefine the reality through the contextualization of the works. The writers from the beginning to till neo-liberal period struggled to understand India from different perspectives such as spiritually, historically, aesthetically, culturally, politically, economically, and racially. The flow of Indianness in history stands parallel to the history of Indian English novels.

7.4. Fostering Pluralism

Pluralism is the core value and working principle of Indian ethos. Indian English novels also reflect the spirit of pluralism for appealing to the next generation. *Kanthapura* carries rich diversities of a village. C.D. Narasimhaiah remarked about the novel, "One hadn't thought until one read this novel that a village could offer such opportunities for observing human nature in its rich diversity."[33] The Kanthapurians transcended all the diversities for the freedom of India. Raja Rao quotes Kabir,

> The road to the City of Love is hard, brother,
> It's hard,

Take care, take care, as you walk along It. (*KA* 89)

The integrity of diversities is not merely a religious matter but something that includes all aspects of life, the complementary nature is reflected. For example, in India religion and nationalism went hand in hand. They were not contradictory but joined together to nurture the lives of Indians.

> If identity can be explained as a sense of association and identification with a bigger defining force, then one can safely assert that people's imaginings of identity in India during the 1930s were largely associated with the nation as defined through its culture and religion. Religion was indeed, a bigger defining force during the period.[34]

Temple was the centre of all the activities of kanthapurians. Even their imagination of the nation is associated with the temple. "We'll build a thousand-pillared templc, [...] and each one of you be ye pillars in it, and when the temple is built, [...] we shall invoke the Mother to reside with us in dream and in life. India then will live in a temple of our making" (*KA* 169). The word 'temple' is used around 102 times in the novel. The temple is not only for worship but also used for national purpose. The inter-relatedness of different realms of human life can be seen here. "[Moorthy] will fast for three days in the temple" (*KA* 87). For Indians, the whole life is related with land and god. "In fact, there was nothing beyond nation and religion to which these people could relate themselves. Nation and religion provided them ultimate answers to their both sacred and profane questions."[35] Kanthapurians felt secure with Kenchamma "We said there is but one safe place and that is the temple sanctum" (*KA* 215). Peaceful pro-existence is the dominant pattern of Indian ethos.

In the course of time, the national integration amidst cultural mosaics was destroyed and this resulted in the tragedy of partition. As a result, building up the religious harmony became one of the major challenges before India and the Indian English novels took up the challenge in the post-independent India. They promulgate the religious harmony as the part of Indian ethos. *Train to Pakistan* promotes pro-existence of faiths, beliefs, and rituals of different religions. "Do not taunt us like this, Captain Sahib. We are brothers and will always remain brothers" (*TP* 156). They prayed together and had freedom to go to any place of worship of any religion. "Everyone is welcome to his religion. Here next door is a Muslim mosque. When I pray to my Guru, Uncle Imran Baksh calls to Allah" (*TP* 49). The spirit of the Indian Constitution is not negation but a positive approach to religions. Indian secularism can be called Nirguna-infinite approach, i.e. there is faith in God but not promoting any particular approach to the infinite or God. It can be called sectarian free nation.

India presents a supreme reality without material form, so that any citizen can attribute any form to god and can profess it. Here, religions have nothing to do with the function of the nation. On the contrary, many times the principle was violated. Hence, the latter Indian English novels gave profound seriousness for cultivating pluralism and multi-voice among Indians. *Great Indian Novel* blames the British for their divide and rule policy. "At the twilight hour, the Raj realized what it had done. *Divide et impera* had worked too well. A device to maintain the integrity of British India had made it impossible for that integrity to be maintained without the British" (*GIN* 210). Later the role of the British was taken by fundamentalists and attempted to destroy the harmony of Indian pluralism. In response to this *Midnight's Children* envisaged unity in diversity with equal recognition to all ethnic groups like the various elements in a pickle and *chutnification* is the process mentioned in the novel for the unity. The *chutnification* allegorized the pro-existence of Indian pluralism. Midnight's Children National Conference represents the pluralism of Indian society. "Reality can have metaphorical content; that does not make it less real. A thousand and one children were born; there were a thousand and one possibilities [...] they can be seen as the last throw of everything antiquated and retrogressive in our myth-ridden nation" (*MC* 201). Tolerance and mutual respect are the basic values which facilitate the functioning of pluralism among the people. However the 'prejudices of their parents' destroyed the unity. "Children, however magical, are not immune to their parents; and as the prejudices and world-views of adults began to take over their minds, I found children from Maharashtra loathing Gujaratis, and fair-skinned northerners reviling Dravidian 'blackies'; there were religious rivalries; and class entered our councils" (*MC* 353). Inter-relatedness configures the basic ethos of the nation.

In the neo-liberal period 'pluralism' and 'religion' did not get the prime attention. But even so, *God of Small Things* also presents a harmonious society where the Syrian Christian family goes to Ayemenem temple to watch Kathakali performance (*GST* 192). The novel draws images from Hindu religion and flock traditions of Kerala. For instance, Estha is compared to Karna in *Mahabharata*. The Ayemenem temple is sacred for the Christian author. The temple removes "the humiliation of the Hart of Darkness" (*GST* 229). Thus, the religious centres become means to preserve the culture of the land. In short Indian English novels always promoted social harmony based on plurality and fought against chauvinistic movements. Here the fact emphasized is: being an Indian means being a pluralist.

7.5. Social Reformation

Every society has its own strength and weakness; India too, had its negatives in the form of caste system, distress of women, economic disparity between rich and poor, etc. Caste system which started for the smooth functioning of the society is a part of Indian culture. The practice of caste system does not belong to Hinduism alone but its shadows can be seen in other religions too, like Islam and Christianity. *The Great Indian Novel* speaks about caste system in the Muslim community. "The Muslims of India were no more cohesive and monolithic a group than any other in the country" (*GIN* 133). Though the Church was against caste system, it prevailed in the Christian Community as a vestige of the old tradition. The Act ix, Decree: iii of Synod of Daimper says:

> The Synod being informed, that in some parts when any one of the baser sort do but touch the Cisterns of Christians, that Christians do *Disempolear* or Purify them, by performing certain Ceremonies...[the Synod] with great rigour command those that make the said

> *Disempoleamento* or purification,...to be thrown out of the Communion of the Church, and to be denied Casture...and to be punished with the Penalties....[36]

God of Small Things narrates the caste system in Christianity. Indian English novels focused on social reformation without fail and they emphasized the dignity of life which is the real spirit of Indian ethos. "The significance of the worth of humanity here goes beyond the simple assumption that human life is valuable. It constitutes a philosophical precept which defines the ultimate good in existence as human life."[37] Caste consciousness should be replaced by universal brotherhood/sisterhood consciousness for the well-being of all the beings.

Although, the pre-independent period was much focused on freedom struggle, social reformation got its prime concern. The well-known novel of pre-independent period, *Untouchable* was fully focused on the suffering of Bakha, the representative of lower caste. Anand dedicated himself for the upliftment of the weaker sections of the society. "Humanism became indistinguishable part of his [Anand] personality."[38] Anand brought the wretchedness of the low caste to the attention of the world. For him art is to improve the quality of life. "Anand's quest now is above all for art, for 'a truly humanist art', but art nonetheless, an art that will 'help raise the untouchables, the serfs, the coolies and other members of the society to human dignity and self-awareness."[39] Rao's *Kanthapura* also visualized a casteless society. "If Truth is one, all men are one before it" (*KA* 123). It proclaims the equality of humanity.

After independence, the fight against untouchability continued especially by including provisions in the Constitution. Immediately after independence there was not much difference in the social system. "Despite the best intentions of Gandhi and the Indian Constitution, India is still run very much along caste lines, although growing numbers of exceptions are being made for the talented or enterprising."[40] Slowly the backward sections of the Indian society established their political power. *The Great Indian Novel* narrates the formation of caste-based parties. "The 'backward classes', the 'backward castes' or the 'backward strata of society', they rapidly acquired for their party the sobriquet 'the Backward Front'" (*GIN* 405). The disharmony that prevailed in Indian society is allegorized in *Midnight's Children*. "Brahmins began to feel uneasy at permitting even their thoughts to touch the thoughts of untouchables" (*MC* 352).

In the neo-liberal period the untouchables began to assert themselves and actively participated in the Indian politics to attain power. "The changing temper of the Dalit communities of India in our times is perhaps the most explosive and the most heartening development in contemporary politics within the country."[41] Bakha in *Untouchable* was illiterate and passive in attaining the rights but Velutha in *The God of Small Things* was educated and dared even to make love with a 'touchable.' Though the 'touchable boots' (*GST* 305) killed Velutha, Balram in *The White Tiger* murdered Mr. Ashok, the touchable. Balram who was from the lower caste had begun his life with 'nameless' and 'birthday-less' but attained high social status by becoming an entrepreneur. The novel narrates the shift from caste system to class system. "These days, there are just two castes: Men with Big Bellies, and Men with Small Bellies" (*WT* 64). The power of religion has been replaced with money. "Caste and religion didn't matter any longer in today's world" (*WT* 185). Hence, the effort for equality among all persons should be continued.

Another subaltern group which obtained ample space in Indian English novels is women but the transformation in the society is slow. The suffering and upcoming of women are focused in *Kanthapura* in a different framework than the expected role of women in patriarchal society. Kenchamma, the goddess, represents the unlimited power and potency of women. Through three widows, namely Achakk, Rangamma, and Ratna, the author redefines the identity and function of women in Indian society. Even in the midst of tribulations, the women lead the Kanthapurians to the greatest realization of life. *Train to Pakistan* also presents the wretched life of women. Nimmo represents the suffering of all the women in India who suffer at the time of war, riots, etc. "Beybey, I have Jugga's child inside me. If I go to Pakistan they will kill it when they know it has a Sikh father" (*TP* 152). *Midnight's Children* also says about a miserable incident: "soldiers entering women's hostels without knocking; women, dragged into the street" (*MC* 497). The hopeless lives of women have to be enlightened.

In the neo-liberal age, women began to profess their rights to a certain extent. *God of Small Things* is a classic novel, which unfolds the suffering of women who belong to three generations and their responses. Even though, Ammu could not succeed, she fought against Age-old Indian society of patriarchal dominance and supremacy. Whereas, Rahel violated the taboos of the society, even incest as a protest against all kinds of oppression. Neo-liberal period represents a radical liberation of women. The pan-subaltern identity is much acclaimed in modern Indian society and it is boosted by Indian English novels.

7.6. Economic Reformation

After the great triumph of independence, India planned its economy with much expectations dreaming from 1947 onwards. It envisaged the welfare of all with the ideological support of socialism. Nehru the sculpture of modern India also followed the same. "We must not forget that Nehru too was the product of a certain society and age. The spirit of the times offered socialism as the answer."[42] So the government which envisaged economic equality, gave importance to public sector with the view to build-up a just society. The hope of the people was reflected in the novels of post-independent period. *Waiting for the Mahatma* presents a group of people with passion to construct a better economy. "The trouble is that things are still disorganized. But I blame no one" (*WM* 177). In post-independent period, India faced burdensome responsibilities of nation building. Apart from the expectations, Indian economy collapsed and could not meet the basic needs of the people. Socialism seemed a failure.

> The mixed economy ended in combining the worst features of socialism and capitalism—the 'controls' of socialism with the 'monopolies and lobbies' of capitalism—and we got the worst of both worlds. The 'controls' suppressed growth by subduing the innovative

> energies and animal spirits of capitalism. Nor did the mixed economy deliver social justice and welfare, which at least the socialist countries did.[43]

However, the policies could not lead the nation to development to a certain extent and the economic crisis increased as the days passed. The novels after 1970s sharply criticized the economic policy of the government. *The Great Indian Novel* found fault with nationalization of banks and other impractical measures of the socialists.

> There Drona's son became a one-man ginger group, loudly advocating a more socialist direction to party policy. The more the party elders explained why his proposals, could not immediately be adopted, the more Ashwathaman insisted upon them, the Prime Minister encouraging him with her silence, and sometimes with her support. (*GIN* 344)

Instead of facing the hardships, socialism is used as a tool to arouse people emotionally for vote. *Midnight's Children* says that 'money-and-poverty' are the controlling 'principle' of India and 'Midnight's Children National Conference could not become a 'third principle' (*MC* 339). The non-constructive attitude of the trade unions was also projected in *God of Small Things* by Arundhati Roy who turned against communism. The placard in Pillai's house had the slogan 'Work is Struggle. Struggle is Work' (*GST* 268) which laughs at the insincere attitude of the unions.

Indian economy has been a journey from socialism to liberalism. It is reflected in Indian English novels of neo-liberal period. In the midst of global hegemony, Indian English novels have a greater role to play in guiding the nation to the future with its Indianness. *The White Tiger* is a story based on the 'New Bangalore', which is the hope of the new generation. It is a story of entrepreneurs. "I'm always a man who sees 'tomorrow' when others see 'today.' The whole world will come to Bangalore tomorrow" (*WT* 319). Neo-liberalism is accepted with constant vigilance to imperialism. "[...] to avoid the danger of being swallowed up by faceless globalization. In the post-colonial world borders are becoming increasingly insignificant and cultural purity is a misnomer."[44] The regional cultures are marginalized and gradually without force they may vanish from the face of the earth. "Neither you nor I speak English, but there are some things that can be said only in English" (*WT* 3). Indian English novels are conscious about the re-colonization happening behind globalization. The dangers of disparity between rich and the poor, corruption, underdevelopment of rural area, and migration to cities are cautioned in *The White Tiger*. "Capitalism for the rich, socialism for the poor"[45] is the economic policy of the present time.

> In other words, with money as an exclusive determinant of success, the corollary would be that anything is available for a price, for, in short, the dollar. Perhaps, the odd picture of plenitude alongside scarcity creates insecurity which clutches at the nearest straw, ironically, available through the very methodology that created the plenitude/scarcity syndrome, in the first place.[46]

Cosmopolitan consumerism gets prominence in globalization. Hence, the novel warns against the upcoming danger of the class inequality because of the unequal distribution of income. The novel is a fusion of the benefits and scourges, opportunities and deficiencies of globalization. These shifts in economic and cultural outlook are well highlighted in the novels of neo-liberal phase.

In short, Indian English novels are pregnant with Indian ethos of each period so the replication of every incident in Indian history is vastly reflected in them. The Indian history should be created and recreated, interpreted and reinterpreted for understanding Indian ethos. "There is no return to the past, to the beginning, for, there are no 'beginnings'; there is only a constant renewal of our sources of desire and memory, search and discovery, a ceaseless encounter with new points of recognition within representation, a linking in the chain of being and becoming."[47] They narrate personal, political, and socio-economic life of the natives in Indian style. The influence of vernacular language, native culture, regional themes, etc., can be seen in the novels and through these experiments, the writers could express Indianness of each period. The novels promote

Indianness in the changing circumstances. Since Indian history is governed by multiple factors, it is a complex phenomenon and thus difficult to understand the cause and effect. The power centres have a decisive role in manipulating them. Hence, the novels have their great role in purifying socio-political malpractices in India. They took the side of the marginalized and wrote a different history from their perspective. They are the watch dogs of the Indian democracy and rights of the subaltern groups. The novels attempt to present the critical evaluation of the incidents of each period to facilitate the society to be firm in its identity so there is continuity in the history of Indian English novels.

Notes

1. William Pfaff, "Nationalism and Identity." *The Way: Contemporary Christian Spirituality*. January 1994, pp. 12-13.
2. P. Rajendra Karmarkar. "Reality and Realism: An Unorthodox Reading of Anand's *Untouchable*." *Journal of South Asian Literature* 31.1 & 2 (1996), p. 114.
3. Shashi Tharoor, *India: From Midnight to the Millennium* (India: Penguin Books, 1997), p. 16.
4. Anand Amaladass, "Rajaji's Contribution to the Process of Nation Building." Anand Amaladasss (ed.) *Political Thinkers of India* (Chennai: Satya Nilayam Publications, 1998), p. 77.
5. Rafiq Dossani, *India Arriving: How this Economic Powerhouse is Redefining Global Business* (New Delhi: 2008), p. 10.
6. M.K. Gandhi, "Socialism of My Conception." Anand T. Hingorani (ed.) (Bombay: Bharatiya Vidya Bhavan, 1957), p. 3.
7. Oliver Balch, *India Rising: Tales from a Changing Nation* (London: Faber and Faber, 2012), p. 6.
8. *Ibid.*
9. William Pfaff, "Nationalism and Identity." *The Way: Contemporary Christian Spirituality*. January (1994), p. 6.
10. *Ibid.*, p. 12-13.
11. H.S. Komalesha, "History, Colony, Nation and Nationalism: Revisiting Raja Rao and His Kanthapura." Jaydeep Sarangi (ed).

Raja Rao: The Master and His Moves (New Delhi: Authors Press, 2007), p. 65.

12. Gerald James Larson, *India's Agony Over Religion* (New York: State University Press, 1995), p. 182.
13. Grishma Manikrao Khobragade, "Reflection of Multiculturalism in Khushwant Singh's Train to Pakistan." *Galaxy: International Multidisciplinary Research Journal* II.II. Accessed: March 2013. http://www.galaxyimrj.com/V2/n2/Grishma.pdf
14. Ashok Kumar Jha, *R.K. Narayan: Myths and Archetypes in His Novels* (Delhi: B.R. Publishing Corporation, 2000), p. 93.
15. Lalji Misra, "Gandhian Consciousness: A Study in the Novels of R.K. Narayan." M.K. Bhatnagar (ed.) *New Insights into the Novel of R K Narayan* (New Delhi: Atlantic, 2008), 104 -12, p. 105.
16. John J Su, "Epic of Failure: Disappointment as Utopian Fantasy in *Midnight's Children*." *Twentieth Century Literature* 47.4 (2001), p. 545. Academic OneFile. Accessed: 29th June 2013. <http://go.galegroup.com>.
17. Marc C. Conner, "*Midnight's Children* and the Apocalypse of Form." *Critique: Studies in Contemporary Fiction* 38.4 (1997), p. 289. Academic OneFile. Accessed: 25th June 2013 <http://go.galegroup.com>.
18. Balmiki Prasad Singh, *India's Culture: The State, the Arts, and Beyond* (India: Oxford University Press, 2011), p. xxxiii.
19. Manjit Inder Singh, *The Critical Space: Studies in Literature, Theory, Nationalism and Deaspora* (New Delhi: National Publishing House, 2005), p. 2.
20. Jawaharlal Nehru, *The Discovery of India* (1946) (Delhi: Oxford University Press, 1994), p. 358.
21. Shashi Tharoor, *India: From Midnight to the Millennium* (India: Penguin Books, 1997), p. 17.
22. John J Su, "Epic of Failure: Disappointment as Utopian Fantasy in *Midnight's Children*." *Twentieth Century Literature* 47.4 (2001), p. 545. Academic OneFile. Accessed: 29th June 2013. <http://go.galegroup.com>.
23. B.R. Nanda, "Gandhi and Nehru: An Intertwined Legacy." Hiranmay Karlekar (ed.) *Independent India: The First Fifty Years* (Delhi: Oxford University Press, 1998), p. 32.

24. Sunil Khilnani, *The Idea of India 1997* (London: Penguin, 2004), p. 5.
25. K. Ratna Shiela Mani, "A Critique of Raja Rao's Art." Jaydipsinh K. Dodiya (ed.) *Perspectives on Indian English Fiction* (New Delhi: Sarup & Sons, 2006), p. 10.
26. Raja Rao, "Foreward" in *Kanthapura*. 1983 (New Delhi: Oxford University Press, 2005), p. vi.
27. Lalji Misra, "Gandhian Consciousness: A Study in the Novels of R.K. Narayan." M K Bhatnagar (ed.) *New Insights into The Novel of R K Narayan* (New Delhi: Atlantic, 2008), p. 105.
28. Neelam Srivastava, "Languages of the nation in Salman Rushdie's *Midnight's Children* and Vikram Seth's *A Suitable Boy*." *ARIEL* 36.1-2 (2005), p. 207. Academic OneFile. Accessed: 22nd June 2013. <http://www.http://go.galegroup.com/>.
29. Manjit Inder Singh, *The Critical Space: Studies in Literature, Theory, Nationalism and Deaspora* (New Delhi: National Publishing House, 2005), p. 219.
30. Uma Parameswaran, "Shashi Tharoor." Emmanuel S. Nelson (ed.) *Writers of the Indian Diaspora: A Bibliographical Critical Source Book* (New Delhi: Rawat Publications, 2010), p. 434.
31. John S. Saul, *Decolonization and Empire: Contesting in Rhetoric and Reality of Resubordination in Southern Africa and Beyond* (New Delhi: Three Essays Collective, 2007), p. 7.
32. *Ibid.*, p. 6.
33. K. Ratna Shiela Mani. "A Critique of Raja Rao's Art." Jaydipsinh K Dodiya (ed.) *Perspectives on Indian English Fiction* (New Delhi: Sarup & Sons, 2006), p. 8.
34. H.S. Komalesha, "History, Colony, Nation and Nationalism: Revisiting Raja Rao and His Kanthapura." Jaydeep Sarangi (ed.) *Raja Rao: The Master and His Moves* (New Delhi: Authors Press, 2007), p. 54.
35. *Ibid.*
36. James Hough, *The History of Christianity in India: From the Commencement of the Christian Era*. Vol. II (London: R.B. Seeley & W. Burnside, 1839), p. 670. Accessed on 8th March 2015. <https://archive.org/details/historychristia02houggoog>.
37. Suijit S. Dulai, "Practice before Ideology: Mulk Raj Anand's Untouchable." *Journal of South Asian Literature* 27.2,

(1992), p. 195. Accessed: 1st May 2013 <http://www.jstor.org/stable/40874125>.

38. S. Sen & J.K. Chopra. *Untouchable: Mulk Raj Anand* (New Delhi: Unique Publishers, 2007), p. 58.
39. Suijit S. Dulai, "Practice before Ideology: Mulk Raj Anand's Untouchable." *Journal of South Asian Literature* 27.2, (1992), p. 189. Accessed: 1st May 2013 <http://www.jstor.org/stable/40874125>.
40. Bruce Palling, *India: A Literary Companion* (London: John Murray, 1992), p. 122.
41. Ravinder Kumar, "Democracy: From Consolidation to Fluidity." Hiranmay Karlekar (ed.) *Independent India: The First Fifty Years* (Delhi: Oxford University Press, 1998), p. 14.
42. Gurcharan Das, *India Unbound: From Independence to the Global Information Age*. 2000 (New Delhi: Penguin Books, 2007), p. 99.
43. *Ibid.*, p. 98.
44. D. Maya, "Raja Rao's Fiction: Cultural Reassertions in the Context of Globalisation." Jaydeep Sarangi (ed.) *Raja Rao: The Master and His Moves* (New Delhi: Authors Press, 2007), p. 21.
45. Gurcharan Das, *India Unbound: From Independence to the Global Information Age*. 2000 (New Delhi: Penguin Books, 2007), p. 85.
46. M. Sivaramkrishna, *Hindu View of Life: A Contemporary Perspective* (Bangalore: Dharmaram Publications, 2001), p. 166.
47. K. Satchidanandan, "Literature: Signing in Different Scripts." Hiranmay Karlekar (ed.) *Independent India: The First Fifty Years* (Delhi: Oxford University Press, 1998), p. 370.

8

Conclusion

The research pinpoints that novels of the land should carry the 'smell of the soil.' Such works transfer ethos of the native from one generation to the next and to people across the globe. The process not only facilitates to endure the culture but also builds up personal and social identity which is necessary for meaningful and united existence of an individual and a nation. Inherited ethos, one of the primary elements of nationalism, unifies people. Hence for an integrated India, all creative works including Indian English novels have to exhibit Indianness. Therefore the studied topic, namely 'refurbishment of Indian ethos in selected fictions of some Indian English writers' is relevant to the present and future generations. The researcher analysed the novels from various periods to see how Indian ethos is portrayed in them.

After defining ethos and the elements of Indian ethos, the study commences with the pre-independence which is the initial period of the study. The main thrusts of this phase were social awakening and nationalism. The analysis on *Untouchable* and *Kanthapura* indicates that Indian English novels added confidence and zest to attain independence and empower the underdogs. Bakha, the central character of *Untouchable* represents the hardships of the down trodden and the spirit of pre-independent period to create a welfare nation. The novel promotes the subaltern class in search of identity and free from the colonialism of 'in-group' as well as 'out-group'. It is an epitome of the ethos of humanism of the Indian renaissance. *Kanthapura* which is the embodiment of nationalistic consciousness is the hallmark of pre-independent ethos. The novel fights back with 'English' against the colonizer who taught the language to the colonized. It attempts to depersonalize the Englishness of English and remould it with Indianness. The novel embeds with the pre-independent spirit of 'narrative resistance' and the soul force of the novel is Gandhism, which is depicted as the *avatar* of Indianness. The Gandhian legend touched the heart as well as spirit of the people so it became the spiritual power for self-realization. The ethos of pre-independent period can be well extracted from these novels.

The second period which is called the post-independent, highlights a time of confusion and lack of resource. Just after independence, the Indians who were in a jubilant mood had the spirit of hope and aspiration. However, when they met with the harsh realities of nation building the positive attitude underwent fluctuation. The pessimism began to indulge them. At this juncture Indian English novels like *Train to Pakistan* and *Waiting for the Mahatma* played a crucial role in creating optimistic minds and became a platform for expression. The themes of the novels were intertwined with the crisis of political, social, cultural, psychological, economical and moral realms of Indians. They intend to stimulate the morale of people and to remind the leaders about their commitment. The novels also carry on with the effort for cultural decolonization because the English continued to sway the minds of Indians even after the day of independence. The novels gave ample importance to indigenization. *Train to Pakistan* attempts to build-up brotherly relationship with different sects of people as well as with Pakistan. It is against the growing trend of regionalism and sectarianism. Keeping besides the view of the power centres, the novel takes an impartial yet realistic narration of the partition in the eyes of villagers. *Waiting for the Mahatma* empowers the people with the hope to build-up the nation. The incidents and characters are from the quotidian life of Indians. The novel upholds Gandhian *marga* as a means for holistic development. It is the history of Indian independence from below, in other words it is a subaltern perspective of independence.

De/re-democratization which is the third period begins with the State of Emergency in 1975. It is the culmination of the failure of Indian democracy. Paradoxically, by emergency all become aware that democracy could not sustain without conscious effort. Hence, it is a stage of questioning the inimical actions against democratic ethos of India and conscious effort like ironic expressions, to protect the freedom. Indian English novels, like *The Great Indian Novel* and *Midnight's Children* of the period are covert attempts to remove ambivalent attitude to the negative forces against democracy and integrity of India. They actively participate in the promotion of democracy. The political ferment and turmoil of Indian democracy are the major themes of the novels and become the outburst of emotion of the longing for democracy. They express the urge of Indians to preserve and protect the freedom in all scenarios. *The Great Indian Novel* upholds the ancient and modern richness of great India. It is a mock-epic against the ruling class through the rediscovery of India in the light of the *Mahabharata*. It is a thought provoking novel to reestablish the ethos of *dharma* in democracy. *Midnight's Children* manifests extensive experimentation for indigenization. With the novel it becomes unquestionable that India which has unique literatureness with various languages, incorporated English as one among the languages to express the same Indian literatureness. Indians befriended with the English to express Indianness. Nativization of English commences with Raja Rao and culminates in *Midnight's Children*. Indian English novels of the period acted as double-edged sword to criticize the persons and situations which caused chaos in Indian democracy. They narrate the de-democratized practices and suggest corrective measures to re-establish the Indian democracy. Both the novels, *The Great Indian Novel* and *Midnight's Children* are the fictional reworking of the history, to unfold the untold truths which cannot say otherwise.

The fourth period, namely the neo-liberal begins in 1991 when India adapted the liberal economic policy. The principle of 'leaving the control to the market' affected all the realms of life. The novels of the time express the afterglow of the unexpected economic development of liberalization and the trauma of indirect subjection of neocolonialism. The spirits of the novels are the de-hegemonization of the globalization and prepare Indians to counter the neo-colonialism. *God of Small Things* is the expression of the unjust relationship of the human beings of the age. The novels attempt to give centre stage for the marginalized such as woman and the untouchable. *The White Tiger* throws light on the social condition due to urbanization, industrialization and globalization. Along with the economic progression it narrates the economic disorder such as corruption. The market generates a bundle of inequality. The trauma of neo-colonialism and skeptical attitude towards globalization are the concern of the novels of the period. They make introspection in the midst of so-called economic progression and highlight the domestic problems of the voiceless. For instance, the village dwellers are forced to relocate themselves mentally and physically. In addition to this, the novels are irresolutely rooted in Indianness.

The study facilitated to expose the Indianness in the selected Indian English novels. The novels play a vital role in constructing the pan-Indian identity. For instance, *Kanthapura* tries to inculcate national identity by identifying the struggle for independence with ancient Indian history, English with regional *Bhashas*, and Gandhiji with gods. The novels do function in two ways. On the one hand, they attempt to free Indians from the mental servitude which may lead to racial shame and self-rejection, to the colonized. The novels sow the seeds of Indianness in the minds of the colonized for decolonizing them. On the other hand, through upholding the eminence and identity of India, the novels attempt to free the colonizer from the prejudice about the colonized. The research has made known that the novels undertook the mission of the proclamation of the greatness of Indianness to the globe. As a result Indian ethos got a visibility among the global audience.

The researcher also found that Indian English novels promoted nationalism and reinforced democracy. While *Kanthapura* wrote for independence and coached against 'white man's burden,' *Midnight's Children* and *The Great Indian Novel* fought against the corrupt Indian political and economic situation. At the time of crisis after independence, *Waiting for the Mahatma* could give an optimistic outlook to go ahead to face the challenges as a new nation. *The God of Small Things* warns against commodification of Indian heritage. *The White Tiger* which calls the attention of the society towards the danger of corruption is an alarming novel. The values like secularism, social harmony, and equality are the underlying principles in Indian English novels.

Further, the thesis brings to light the role played by Indian English novels in maintaining 'the unity in diversity', which is one of the core values of Indian ethos. Since English functions as a link language, the novels erase cultural alienations of different regions from Kanyakumari to the Himalayas. The novels are located in various states of India, for example *Kanthapura* in Karnataka, *Train to Pakistan* in Punjab and *The God of Small Things* in Kerala. They give voice not only to the main-stream Indian culture but also to remote villages. Ethnic minorities get ample space in the novels, since the novels promoted multi-culturalism. The regional cultures reach out to other Indian cultures via the novels. The novels acted like a bridge between different regional cultures with the outlook of a united India. Along with the heterogeneity of India, Indian English novels build up a unified Indian ethos.

Besides, Indian English novels played a decisive role for the social awakening of India. The novels like *Untouchable* and *The God of Small Things* are crusaders of the suffering. The touchstone of Indian English novels is humanism and the novels fight for the revival of a just society based on Indian ethos. They heartbreakingly narrate the wretchedness of the underdogs of the society. The subaltern theme always got a prominent place in the novels. *Kanthapura* and *Waiting for the Mahatma* are re-reading of Indian independence struggle from the perspective of the subaltern. The exploitation of the oppressed by the hegemonic power of capital in the modern times, too, is poignantly narrated in *The White Tiger*. The novels played a vital role in bringing change in the sorrow of the downtrodden and liberating the customs from the clutches of social evils.

The analysis of the selected novels proves that the English in Indian English novels is no longer a tool of the colonizer but it faithfully carries Indianness. The Indian writers have not just been following the view of the colonizer but they critically analysed the situation and Indianized English to express their ethos to the world. The novels have taken noticeable shifts in the usage, spelling, idioms, turn and style of the colonizer's English. By the Indianization of English, the novels reformed English to such an extent that Indians can express their sensibility through it. Furthermore, the novels become defenders of Indian culture against cultural neo-imperalism in the cultural clash. Here English is used against the colonizer through various methods like code switching and code mixing. The study exposes such shifts in the nature of the language in the novels. Thus, the thesis is a spark to kindle the light of Indianness in the life of a reader.

The thesis is not merely an intellectual exercise about the past writings but a visionary analysis oriented to the future. In a hybrid world, one should be firmly embedded to national ethos to nurture one's identity. Otherwise the neo-imperialism may uproot the person and draw to cultural assimilation of the colonized people. For instance, in the analysis of *The White Tiger* the thesis is about cultural expatriation. The relevance of *swadeshi* movement with timely interpretation is relevant in the coming age of globalization. Enhancement of universality based on nationality and individuality is important for one to become a meaningful citizen of the nation. The research has facilitated to torch the unpredictable paths of the future for not falling into the danger of neo-imperialism.

The research also envisages how people can keep Indianness according to the changing circumstances. The study clearly shows the various means used by different generations to protect the ethos of the land. In addition to this, the thesis becomes a guideline to the future writers to see how Indian English novels affirmed the Indianness and to follow the paths to keep away from the overrun of the hegemonic power of capital. The upcoming novels also uphold Indianness and stand for the national cause according to the signs of time.

In short, the researcher could find out that Indian English novels attempt to decolonize the Indian minds which were under the yoke of the colonizer and uphold the Indianness. The novels took birth from Indian ethos and proclaim the same. The researcher could see that the eight novels which were selected for the research faithfully express the Indianness and various elements of Indian ethos are also included in them. The characters are born from the Indian soil. The style, story, setting and plot are Indian in essence. The myths, traditions, customs, stories, and usages got space in the novels. Indian English novels give collective and personal imagination for the existence of India and provide triumphant optimism in the time of crisis. Since Indian culture is a fascinating equilibrium of miscellany, one element is enough to form desynchronization in the rhythm. It is difficult to unify the various cultures to hold on to a powerfully built India. So Indian English novels have a decisive role to play to refurbish the Indian ethos according to the signs of time.

Bibliography

Primary Source

Adiga, Aravind. *The White Tiger*. 2008 (New Delhi: Harper Collins, 2009). (In the text the book is abbreviated 'WT').

Anand, Mulk Raj. *Untouchable*. 1935 (New Delhi: Penguin Books, 2001). (In the text the book is abbreviated 'UN').

Narayan, R.K. *Waiting for the Mahatma*. 1955 (New Delhi: Penguin Books, 2001). (In the text the book is abbreviated 'WM').

Rao, Raja. *Kanthapura*. 1938 (New Delhi: Oxford University Press, 2005). (In the text the book is abbreviated 'KA').

Roy, Arundhati. *The God of Small Things* (New Delhi: IndiaInk, 1997). (In the text the book is abbreviated 'GST').

Rushdie, Salman. *Midnight's Children*. 1981 (London: Vintage Books, 2013). (In the text the book is abbreviated 'MC').

Shashi, Tharoor. *The Great Indian Novel* (New Delhi: Penguin Books, 1989). (In the text the book is abbreviated 'GIN').

Singh, Khushwant. *Train to Pakistan*. 1956 (Chennai: Orient Longman, 2007). (In the text the book is abbreviated 'TP').

Secondary Source

Ahmed, Talat. *Literature and Politics in the Age of Nationalism: The Progressive Writers' Movement in South Asia*, 1932 -56 (New Delhi: Routledge, 2009).

Aiyangar, K.V.R. *Some aspects of the Hindu view of Life According to Dharmasastra* (Baroda: Oriental Institute, 1952).

Alam, Javeed. *India: Living with Modernity* (Delhi: Oxford University Press, 1999).

Ali, A.N.M. Irshad. "Kinship and Marriage among the Assamese Muslims." Imtiza Ahmad (ed.), *Family, Kinship and Marriage among Muslims in India* (New Delhi: Manohar, 1976).

Amaladass, Anand. "Rajaji's Contribution to the Process of Nation Building." Anand Amaladass (ed.) *Political Thinkers of India* (Chennai: Satya Nilayam Publications, 1998).

Ambedkar, B.R. "Gandhism: The Doom of the Untouchable." Valerian Rodrigues (ed.), *The Essential Writings of B.R. Ambedkar* (New Delhi: Oxford University Press, 2002).

———. "The Indian Constitution Defended and Interpreted." Ramachandra Guha (ed.), *Makers of Modern India* (New Delhi: Penguin Books, 2010).

———. *Pakistan or The Partition of India* (Bombay: Thacker & Communication, Ltd, 1946).

Anand, Mulk Raj. "Afterword: Cultural Self-Comprehension of Nations" Gobinda Prasad Sarma (ed.), *Nationalism in Indo-Anglian Fiction* (New Delhi: Sterling Publishers, 1978).

Ananda, Staff. *Myth, Symbol and Language: A Modern Perspective with Reference to India and her Religions* (New Delhi: Aryan Books International, 1998).

Anne, Vaugier-Chatterjee. "Sikhs: Between Integration and Separatism." Christophe Jaffreloted (ed.) *India Since 1950: Society, Politics, Economy and Culture* (New Delhi: Yatra Books, 2012).

Ashcroft, Bill. *Post-Colonial Transformation* (London: Routledge, 2001).

Badrinath, Chaturvedi. *The Mahabharata: An Inquiry in the Human Condition* (New Delhi: Orient Longman, 2006).

Baer, Ben Conisbee. "Shit Writing: Mulk Raj Anand's *Untouchable*, the Image of Gandhi, and the Progressive Writers." *Modernism/Modernity* 16.3 (2009).

Bahadur, Diwan and K.S. Ramaswami Sastri. "The Puranas" Suniti Kumar Chatterji (ed.), *The Cultural Heritage of India: Language and Literatures,* Vol. 5 (Calcutta: The Ramakrishna Mission, 1978).

Bajaj, J.K. "Chowdhary Charan Singh and the Politics of Independent India." Anand Amaladass (ed). *Political Thinkers of India* (Chennai: Satya Nilayam Publications, 1998).

Balch, Oliver. *India Rising: Tales from a Changing Nation* (London: Faber and Faber, 2012).

Bankart, C. Peter & et al. "On the path of the Buddha: A Psychologists' Guide to the History of Buddhism." Kathleen H. Dockett & et al. (ed.) *Psychology and Buddhism: From Individual to Global Community* (New York: Klumer Academic/Plenum Publishers, 2003).

Batabyal, Somnath. "New Delhi's Times: Creating a Myth for a City." Bharati Chaturvedi (ed.) *Finding Delhi: Loss and Renewal in the Megacity* (New Delhi: Penguin Group, 2010).

Bayly, Susan. *Caste, Society and Politics in India from the Eighteenth Century to the Modern Age.* Vol. IV.3 (Cambridge: Cambridge University Press, 1999).

Beniwal, Anup. *Representing Partition, History, Violence and Narration* (Delhi: Shakti, 2005).

Bhagwati, P.N. "*Judicial Activism in India.*" Accessed: 19th March 2014. <law.wisc.edu/m/4mdd4/gargoyle_17_1_3.pdf>.

Bhatt, Bansidhar. *Ahimsa: In the Early Religious Traditions of India* (Rome: Centre for Indian and Inter-religious Studies, 1994).

Bhatta, Vinayaka P. "Human rights and dharmasastra." V.N. Jha (ed.) *Dharmasastra and Social Awareness* (Delhi: 1996).

Bhattacharjea, Ajit. *Jayaprakash Narayan: A Plitical Biography* (Delhi: Vikas Publishing House, 1975).

Bhattacharjya, Mithun. "Spatial Fixity and Postcoloniality—the Issue of Language in Indian Writing in English." *Language in India* 12.4 (2012).

Bingemer, Maria Clara. "War, Suffering and Detachment: Reading the Bhagavad Gita with Simon Weil." Catherine Cornille (ed.) *Song Divine: Christian Commentaries on the Bhagavad Gita* (Leuven: Peeters, 2006).

Bipan, Chandra. *India since Independence* (New Delhi: Penguin Group, 2008).

Biswas, Sravani. "The Dialogic Imagination in R.K. Narayan's *Waiting for the Mahatma*: A Bakhtinian Analysis." M.K. Bhatnagar, *New Insights into The Novel of R K Narayan* (New Delhi: Atlantic Publishers and Distributors, 2008).

———. *A Study of R K Narayan's Novels: A Celebration of the Carnival* (New Delhi: Atlantic Publishers and Distributors, 2010).

Broomfield, J.H. "The Regional Elites: A Theory of Modern Indian History." Thomas R. Metcalf (ed.) *Modern India: An Interpretive Anthology* (America: The MacMillan Company, 1971).

Burton, Stein. *The History of India* (Oxford: Oxford University Press, 1998).

Capozza, Dora and Rupert Brown. "Introduction: Social identity theory in retrospect and prospect." Dora Capozza and Rupert Brown (ed.) *Social Identity Process* (London: Sage Publications, 2000).

Chacko, Sam. "Defining Indianness." Web: 14th September 2010. Accessed: 4th September 2013. <http://geography.about.com/od/indiamaps/a/Defining-Indianness.htm>.

Chandra, Bipan & et al. *India's Struggle for Independence* (New Delhi: Penguin Books, 1989).

Chordiya, Deepa P. "Taking on the tone of a Bombay talkie: the function of Bombay cinema in Salman Rushdie's Midnight's Children" *ARIEL*. 38.4 (2007). Academic OneFile. Accessed: 27th June 2013 <http://go.galegroup.com>.

Conner, Marc C. "Midnight's Children and the Apocalypse of Form." *Critique: Studies in Contemporary Fiction*. 38.4 (Summer 1997). Academic OneFile 25 June 2013. <http://go.galegroup.com>

Corse, Sarah M. *Nationalism and Literature: The Politics of Culture in Canada and the United States* (Cambridge: Cambridge University Press, 1997).

Danker, Frederick William (ed.). *Greek-English Lexicon of the New Testament and other Early Christian Literature* 3rd ed. (Chicago: The University of Chicago Press, 2000).

Dartey-Baah, Kwasi. "The Cultural Approach to the Management of the International Human Resource: An Analysis of Hofstede's Cultural Dimensions." *International Journal of Business Administration* 4.2 (2013) Accessed: 8th November 2013. <www.sciedu.ca/ijba>.

Das, Gurcharan. *India Unbound: From Independence to the Global Information Age*. 2000 (New Delhi: Penguin Books, 2002).

Das, M.N. "Political Thought of Jawaharlal Nehru." *The Spirit of India*. Vol. II. Indira Gandhi Abinandan Samiti (New York: Asia Publishing House, 1976).

Datta, Bibhutibhusan. "Vedic Mathematics." Priyadaranjan Ray and S.N. Sensibilityed, (eds.) *The Cultural Heritage of India* (Calcutta: The Ramakrishna Mission Institute of Culture, 1986).

Datta, K.K. "Our Cultural Renaissance and Nationalism." Indira Gandhi Abinandan Samiti, *The Spirit of India*. Vol. II (New York: Asia Publishing House, 1976).

Davi, Hardiman. *Gandhi in his Time and Ours* (Columbia: Columbia University Press, 2003).

David, Ludden. "India's Development Regim." Nicholas B. Dirksed (ed.) *Colonialism and Culture* (USA: The University of Michigan, 1992).

Deaux, Kay. "Models, Meanings and motivations." Dora Capozza and Rupert Brown (eds.) *Social Identity Process* (London: Sage Publications, 2000).

Deshpande, C.R. *Transmission of The Mahabharat Tradition* (Simla: Indian Institute of Advanced Study, 1978).

Deva, Indra and Shrirama. *Society and Culture in India* (New Delhi: Rawat Publications, 1999).

Devaraja, N.K. *The Mind and Spirit of India* (Delhi: Motilal Banarsidass, 1967).

Devi, Moirangthem Linthoingambi. "Multiculturalism and Conflict in Khushwant Singh's *Train to Pakistan.*" *Journal of Literature, Culture and Media Studies.* III.5-6 (2011). Accessed 31st May 2013.

Dirks, Nicholas B. "Introduction." Nicholas B. Dirks (ed.) *Colonialism and Culture* (United States of America: The University of Michigan Press, 1992).

———. *Castes of Mind: Colonialism and the Making of Modern India* (New Delhi: Permanent Black, 2002).

Diwakar, R.R. "*Satyagraha—Some Reflections.*" Indira Gandhi Abinandan Samiti. *The Spirit of India.* Vol. II (New York: Asia Publishing House, 1976).

Dossani, Rafiq. *India Arriving: How this Economic Powerhouse is Redefining Global Business* (New Delhi: Amacom, 2008).

Dube, S.C. "*Indian Village*" (Bombay: Allied Publishers, 1965).

Dubey, Meenu. "Graphic Scrutiny of Subaltern in Arundhati Roy's *The God of Small Things.*" Amar Nath Prasad and Bithika Dasgupta Sarkar (ed.) *Arundhati Roy: A Critical Elucidation* (New Delhi: Sarup Book Publishers, 2010).

Dulai, Suijit S. "Practice before Ideology: Mulk Raj Anand's Untouchable." *Journal of South Asian Literature*, 27.2 (1992), Accessed: 1st May 2013 <http://www.jstor.org/stable/40874125>.

Dumont, Louis. *Homo Hierarchicus: The Caste System and its Implications*. Mark Sainsbury (Trans.) (Great Britain: Vikas Publications, 1966).

Edgerton, Franklin. "Dominant Ideas in the Formation of Indian Culture." *Journal of the American Oriental Society* 62.3 (1942). Accessed: 22nd October 2013. <http://www.jstor.org/stable/59413>.

Elst, Koenraad. *Decolonizing the Hindu Mind* (New Delhi: Rupa & Co., 2001).

Engineer, Ashgar Ali. "Globalization, Islam and Threat to Diversity." *Globalization Stepping into the One World* (Chennai: Adhyaksha Math, 2000).

Farquhar, J.N. and H.D. Griswold. *The Religious Quest of India* (Oxford: Oxford University Press, 1922).

Gail, Omvedt. *Dalits and the Democratic Revolution: Dr. Ambedkar and the Dalit Movement in Colonial India* (New Delhi: Sage Publications, 1994).

Gandhi, Indira. *Two alone, Two together: Letters between Indira Gandhi and Jawaharlal Nehru 1922-1964*. Sonia Gandhi (ed.) (New Delhi: Penguin Books, 2005).

Gandhi, M.K. "Rebuilding Our Villages." Bharatan Kumarappa (ed.) (Ahmedabad: Navajivan Publishing House, 1952).

———. *Socialism of My Conception*. Anand T. Hingorani (ed.) (Bombay: Bharatiya Vidya Bhavan, 1957).

Goicoechea, Maria. "The Post Human Ethos in Cyberpunk Science Fiction," *CLC Web* 10.4 (2008), Accessed 2nd April 2012. <http://docs.lib.purdue.Education/clcweb/vol10/iss4/9>.

Goyal, S.R. *Fundamentals of Pauranika Hinduism* (Jodhpur: Kusumanjali Book, 2009).

Gupta, Rameshwar. "The Gandhi in Narayan." Ram Atma (ed.) *Perspectives on R.K. Narayan* (Ghaziabad: Vimal Prakashan, 1981).

Györke, Ágnes. "Rushdie's Postmodern Nations." *The AnaChronisT* 15 (2010), p. 135. Ebscohost. Accessed: 5th July 2013 <http://ehis.ebscohost.com.ulm.idm.oclc.org>.

Hardiman, David. *Gandhi in his Time and Ours* (Columbia: Columbia University Press, 2003).

Harper, Douglas. "Ethic" Web page 2001, Accessed: 2nd April 2012. <http://www.etymonline.com/indexphp? allowed in <frame=0&search=ethos&searchmode=none>.

Hasan, Mushirul. "Partition Narratives: Introduction." *The Partition Omnibus* (New Delhi: Oxford University Press, 2002).

Heffernan, Teresa. "The Nation in Salman Rushdie's Midnight's Children." *Twentieth Century Literature* 46.4 (2000). Academic OneFile. Accessed: 1st July 2013 <http://www. http://go.galegroup.com/>.

Herald, Deccan. "Defining Indianness: Multiple Voices." Assessed: 4th September 2013. <http://www.deccanherald.com/content/171602/defining-indianness.html>.

Hogan, Patrick Colm. "Midnights Children: Kashmir and the Politics of Identity." *Twentieth Century Literature* 47.4 (2001). Academic OneFile. Accessed: 22nd June 2013 <http://www. http://go.galegroup.com/>.

Hough, James. *The History of Christianity in India: From the Commencement of the Christian Era*. Vol. II (London: R.B. Seeley & W. Burnside, 1839). Accessed on 8th March 2015. <https://archive.org/details/historychristia02houggoog>.

Human Rights Watch. "Hidden Apartheid: Caste Discrimination against India's Untouchables" Web: 13th February 2007. Accessed: 18th March 2014 <http://www.hrw.org/reports/2007/02/12/hidden-apartheid>.

Husai, S. Abid. *The National Culture of India* (India: Asia Publishing House, 1961).

Hwang, Alvin, Anne Marie Francesco, & Eric Kessler. "The relationship between individualism-collectivism, face and feedback and learning processes in Hong Kong, Singapore, and the United States." *Journal of Cross-cultural Psychology* 34.1 (2003).

Irma, Taavitsainen & Gunnel Melchers. "Writing in nonstandard English: Introduction." Irma Taavitsainen and et al. (ed.)

Writing in Nonstandard English (USA: John Benjamins Publishing Company, 1999).

Jaffrelot, Christophe. “The Paradoxical Democratisation of Indian Democracy.” Christophe Jaffrelot (ed.) *India Since 1950: Society, Politics, Economy and Culture* (New Delhi: Yatra Books, 2012).

Jain, Pankaj. *Dharma and Ecology of Hindu Communities* (USA: Ashgate Publishing Company, 2011).

Janmejay, Choudhury. “Gandhi’s Padayatra in Orissa and Upliftment of Harijans.” *Orissa Review,* January (2011).

Jha, Ashok Kumar. *R.K. Narayan: Myths and Archetypes in His Novels* (Delhi: B.R. Publishing Corporation, 2000).

Jones, W.H. Morris. “India’s Political Idioms.” Thomas R. Metcalf (ed). *Modern India: An Interpretive Anthology* (America: The MacMillan Company, 1971).

Joshi, P.C. “Culture and Cultural Planning in India.” *Economic and Political Weekly* 18.50 (1983). <http://www.jstor.org/stable/4372774>.

Joshi, Shashi. *A History of the Indian Communists: The Irrelevance of Leninism* (India: Sage Publications, 2011).

Kakar, Sudhir. “Indian-ness: So what really makes Indians Indian?” Web 2nd April 2007. Accessed 4th September 2013. <http://www.littleindia.com/nri/1730-indian-ness.html>.

Kalam, APJ Abdul. *India 2020: A Vision for the New Millennium.* Y.S. Rajan (ed.) (New Delhi: Penguin Books, 1998).

Kane, Jean M. “The migrant intellectual and the body of history: Salman Rushdie’s Midnight’s Children.” *Contemporary Literature* 37.1 (1996). Academic OneFile Accessed: 27th June 2013. <http://go.galegroup.com>.

Kapur, Akash. “The Secret of His Success.” *New York Times.* Web: 7th November 2008. Accessed: 10th November 2013 http://www.nytimes.com/2008/11/09/books/review/Kapur-t.html?_r=0.

Kar, Bijayananda. *Indian Theories of Error* (Delhi: Ajanta Publication, 1990).

Karmarkar, P. Rajendra. "Reality and Realism: An Unorthodox Reading of Anand's *Untouchable*." *Journal of South Asian Literature*. 31.1 & 2 (1996).

Kautilya. *The Arthashastra*. L.N. Rangarajan (ed.) (New Delhi: Penguin Books, 1992).

Khilnani, Sunil. *The Idea of India*. 1997 (London: Penguin, 2004).

Khobragade, Grishma Manikrao. "Reflection of Multiculturalism in Khushwant Singh's *Train to Pakistan*." *Galaxy: International Multidisciplinary Research Journal* 2.2. Accessed: March 2013. <http://www.galaxyimrj.com/V2/n2/Grishma.pdf>.

Khosla, Gopal Das. "Stern Reckoning: A survey of the Events leading up to and following the partition of India." *The Partition Omnibus* (New Delhi: Oxford University Press, 2002).

Komalesha, H.S. "History, Colony, Nation and Nationalism: Revisiting Raja Rao and His Kanthapura." Jaydeep Sarangi (ed.) *Raja Rao: The Master and His Moves* (New Delhi: Authors Press, 2007).

Kortenaar, Neil Ten. "Postcolonial ekphrasis: Salman Rushdie gives the finger back to the empire." *Contemporary Literature* 38.2 (1997). Academic OneFile. Accessed: 25th June 2013 <http://go.galegroup.com>.

Kothari, Smitu. "Whose independence? The social impact of economic reform in India." *Journal of International Affairs* 51.1 (1997). <http://ehis.ebscohost.com>.

Kotturan, George. *Ahimsa: Gautama to Gandhi* (New Delhi: Sterling Publishers, 1973).

Krishna, Daya. "India's Intellectual Tradition: An Overview" Daya Krishna (ed.) *India's Intellectual Tradition: Attempts at Conceptual Reconstructions* (New Delhi: Indian Council of Philosophical Research, 2003).

Kumar, K.S. Anish. "Deconstructing the Power Structure: A Contemporary Reader's Response to Raja Rao's

Kanthapura" Jaydeep Sarangi (ed.) *Raja Rao: The Master and His Moves* (New Delhi: Authors Press, 2007).

Kumar, Raj. *Encyclopaedia of Untouchables Ancient, Medieval and Modern* (Delhi: Kalpaz Publications, 2008).

Kumar, Ravinder. "Democracy: From Consolidation to Fluidity." Hiranmay Karlekar (ed.) *Independent India: The First Fifty Years* (Delhi: Oxford University Press, 1998).

Lakshmi, D. Samrajya. "Subtlety, Mockery and Dharma in Shashi Tharoor's *The Great Indian Novel.*" *Language in India*. Web: 2nd February 2009. Accessed: 2nd April 2014. <www.languageinindia.com>.

Larson, Gerald James. *India's Agony Over Religion* (Delhi: Oxford University Press, 1997).

Lohia, Rammanohar. *Marx, Gandhi and Socialism* (Hyderabad: Navahind, 1963).

Lyon, Peter. "The First Great Post-Colonial Stage: India's Tryst with Destiny." James Mayall and Anthony Payne (eds.) *The Fallacies of Hope: The Post-Colonial Record of the Commonwealth Third World* (UK: Manchester University Press, 1991).

Madan, G.R. *Western Sociologists on Indian Society: Marx, Spencer, Weber, Durkheim, Pareto* (Bombay: Allied Publishers Private Limited, 1979).

Mahajan, Sucheta. *Independence and Partition: The Erosion of Colonial Power in India* (New Delhi: Sage Publications, 2000).

Mani, K. Ratna Shiela. "A Critique of Raja Rao's Art." Jaydipsinh K. Dodiya (ed.) *Perspectives on Indian English Fiction* (New Delhi: Sarup & Sons, 2006).

Manickam, Thomas. "Biblical Hermeneutics: An Indian Approach," *Indian Interpretations of the Bible*, Augustine Thottakara CMI (ed.), (Bangalore: Dharmaram Publications, 2000).

Manusmrti Book: III/55. J. Duncan M. Derrett (Tran & Notes) *Bharcui's Commentary on the Manusmrti* Vol. II (Wiesbaden: Franz Steiner Verlag Gmbh, 1975).

Mark, Mossman. "Salman Rushdie's Midnight's Children: National Narrative as a Liminal Voice." *The Midwest Quarterly* 41.1 (1999). Academic OneFile. Accessed: 22nd June 2013 <http://www.http://go.galegroup.com/>.

Maya, D. "Raja Rao's Fiction: Cultural Reassertions in the Context of Globalisation." Jaydeep Sarangi (ed.) *Raja Rao: The Master and His Moves* (New Delhi: Authors Press, 2007).

Mazumader, Vina. "Women: From Equality to Empowerment." Hiranmay Karlekar (ed.) *Independent India: The First Fifty Years* (Delhi: Oxford University Press, 1998).

Mehta, G.L. *Understanding India* (New York: Asia Publishing House, 1959).

Menon, Niveditha and Michael P. Johnson, "Patriarchy and Paternalism in Intimate Partner Violence: A Study of Domestic Violence in Rural India." Kamal K. Misra and Janet Huber Lowry (ed.) *Recent Studies on Indian Women* (Jaipur: Rawat Publications, 2007).

Milbert, Isabelle. "Building the Economy: 1947-1980." Christophe Jaffreloted. *India Since 1950: Society, Politics, Economy and Culture* (New Delhi: Yatra Books, 2012).

Misra, Lalji. "Gandhian Consciousness: A Study in the Novels of R.K. Narayan." M.K. Bhatnagar (ed.) *New Insights into the Novel of R.K. Narayan* (New Delhi: Atlantic Publishers and Distributors, 2008).

Mitra, Sisirkumar. *The Vision of India* (Calcutta: Culture Publishers, 1947).

Momin, A.R. "Interface of Cultural Identity Development: Cultural Pluralism, National Identity and Development, The Indian Case." Web page. Accessed: 4th September 2013. (New Delhi: Indira Gandhi National Centre for the Arts, 1996), <http://ignca.nic.in/ls_03016.htm>.

Moon, Penderel. "Divide and Quit: An Eyewitness Account of the Partition of India." *The Partition Omnibus* (New Delhi: Oxford University Press, 2002).

Mossman, Mark. "Salman Rushdie's Midnight's Children: National Narrative as a Liminal Voice." *The Midwest Quarterly* 41.1 (1999), p. 66. Academic OneFile. Accessed: 22nd June 2013 <http://www.http://go.galegroup.com/>.

Mothe, Prashant Subhash. "Arundhati Roy's *The God of Small Things*: Focusing on Marginal Gender." M.F. Patel (ed.) *Indian Women Novelists Critical Discourses* (Jaipur: Aavishkar Publishers, 2010).

Mouli, T. Sai Chandra and Jaydeep Sarangi. *Indian Women's Writings in English* (Delhi: Gnosis, 2008).

Mukherjee, Asha. "Gandhi and The Problem of Modernity: A Point of Departure." Asha Mukherjee & et al. (ed.) *Civil Society in Indian Cultures: Indian Philosophical Studies* I. Cultural Heritage and Contemporary Change Series III b, South Asia, Vol. 6. (Washington: 2001).

Naik, M.K. *Raja Rao*. 1972 (Madras: Blackie & Son, First Published in Twayne's World Authors Series, 1982).

Nanda, B.R. "Gandhi and Nehru: An intertwined Legacy." Hiranmay Karlekar (ed.) *Independent India: The First Fifty Years* (Delhi: Oxford University Press, 1998).

Narasimhaiah, C.D. "National Identity in Literature and Language: Its Range and Depth in the Novels of Rajo Rao," K.L. Goodwin (ed.) *National Identity*. (US: Heinemann, 1970).

Narayan, Jayaprakash. "A Plea for Political Decentralization" (1959). Ramachandra Guhaed (ed.) *Makers of Modern India*. 2010. (New Delhi: Penguin Books, 2012).

Nehru, Jawaharlal. "Letter to Indira Gandhi, dated 4th December, 1937." Sonia Gandhi (ed.) *Two alone, two together: Letters between Indira Gandhi and Jawaharlal Nehru* (1922-1964) (New Delhi: Penguin Books, 2005).

Nehru, Jawaharlal. "Tryst with Destiny." Accessed: 1st September 2013 <http://www.svc.ac.in/files/TRYST%20WITH%20 DESTINY.pdf>.

Nehru, Jawaharlal. "Will and Testament." S. Gopal and Uma Iyengar N.D. (eds.) *The Essential Writings of Jawaharlal Nehru* (New Delhi: Oxford University Press, 2003).

———. *The Discovery of India* (1946) (Delhi: Oxford University Press, 1994).

Nelson, Micheller and Sharon Shavitt. "Horizontal and Vertical Individualism and Achievement Values: A Multimethod Examination of Denmark and the United States." *Journal of Cross-Cultural Psychology* 33.5 (2002).

Nesdale, Drew and Mikako Naito. "Individualism-Collectivism and the Attitudes to School Bullying of Japanese and Australian Students." *Journal of Cross-cultural Psychology* 36.5 (2005).

Nielsen, Kai. *Globalization and Justice* (America: Humanity Books, 2003).

Niyogi, Subhro. "Violence, not Ahimsa, integral to Indian culture: Upinder," *The Times of India,* ed. Kolkata, 28 Jan 2012, http://articles.timesofindia.indiatimes.com

O'Neil, L. Thomas. *Towards the Life Divine: Sri Aurobindo's Vision* (New Delhi: Manohar, 1979).

Olivelle, Patrick. "Preface." *Dharma: Studies in its Semantic, Cultural and Religious History*. Patrick Olivelle (ed.) (Delhi: Motilal Banarsidass Publishers, 2009).

Oommen, T.K. "Citizenship and National Identity in India: Towards a Feasible Linkage" T.K. Oommen (ed.) *Citizenship and National Identity: From Colonialism to Globalism* (New Delhi: Sage Publications, 1997).

Oren, Neta and Daniel Bar-Ta. "Ethos and Identity: Expressions and Changes in the Israeli Jewish Society," *Estudios de Psicología* 27.3 (2006).

Pali Text Society Translation. Series No. 45. *The Group of Discourses (Sutta-Nipata)* 2nd ed. (Great Britain: The Pali Text Society, 2006).

Palling, Bruce. *India: A Literary Companion* (London: John Murray, 1992).

Pandey, Vinay Kumar. "The Effect of Myth in the Novel of Raja Rao's *Kanthapura*," Jaydeep Sarangi (ed), *Raja Rao: The Master and His Moves* (New Delhi: Authors Press, 2007).

Panikkar, K.M. *The State and the Citizen* (Bombay: Asia Publishing House, 1956).

Parameswaran, Uma. "Shashi Tharoor." Emmanuel S. Nelson (ed.) *Writers of the Indian Diaspora: A Bibliographical Critical Source Book* (New Delhi: Rawat Publications, 2010).

———. *Writing the Diaspora: Essays on Culture and Identity* (New Delhi: Rawat Publications, 2007).

Parekh, Bhikhu. *Colonialism, Tradition and Reform: An Analysis of Gandhi's Political Discourse* (New Delhi: Sage Publications India Pvt Ltd, 1989).

Parmar, Himanshu. "The Indian Counter Narrative in Midnight's Children." *Language in India.* 11.11 (2011), Academic OneFile. Accessed: 27th June 2013 <http://go.galegroup.com>.

Pathak, Preeti S. "Itihas, History and Novel in *The Great Indian Novel*." Jaydipsinh K. Dodiya (ed.) *Perspectives on Indian English Fiction* (New Delhi: Sarup & Sons, 2006).

Paz, Octavio. *In Light of India* (United States of America: Rediff Books, 1998). <http://books.google.co.in>

Perera, L.P.N. *Sexuality in Ancient India: A Study Based on the Pali Vinayapitaka* (Colombo: The Postgraduate Institute of Pali and Buddhist Studies, 1993).

Pfaff, William. "Nationalism and Identity." *The Way: Contemporary Christian Spirituality*, January (1994).

Porunnedom, Jose. "Meeting of Two Laws: Influence of Western Missionaries on St. Thomas Christian Church." *Journal of St. Thomas Christians* 13.4 (2004).

Radhakrishnan, S. *Religion and Society* (London: George Allen and Unwin Ltd., 1947).

Rai, Lajpat. "Reform or Revival (1904)" Nalini Bhushan and Jay L. Garfield (ed.) *Indian Philosophy in English: From*

Renaissance to Independence (Oxford: Oxford University Press, 2011).

Raizada, Harish. "'*Train to Pakistan*': A Study in Crisis of Values", R.K. Dhavan (ed.) *Commonwealth Fiction*. Vol. 1 (New Delhi: Classical Publishing Company, 1988).

Ram, Jagjivan. "Casteism: Impediment to Democratic Socialism". Indira Gandhi Abinandan Samiti. *The Spirit of India*. Vol. II (New York: Asia Publishing House, 1976).

Ramana, P.S. *Message in Design: A Study of R.K. Narayan's Fiction* (New Delhi: Harman Publishing House, 1993).

Rao, Raja. "Foreward" in Kanthapura. 1983 (New Delhi: Oxford University Press, 2005).

Rasquinha, Dionysius. *Towards Wholeness from Brokenness: The Dalit Quest* (Delhi: ISPCK, 2013).

Reddiar, N. Subbu. "Emotional Integration and Ancient Tamil Literature." Indira Gandhi Abinandan Samiti, *The Spirit of India*. Vol. II (New York: Asia Publishing House, 1976).

Rig Veda, HYMN XC. *Puruṣa*. Ralph T.H. Griffith (trans.). 1896. Accessed: 5th May 2014. <http://www.sacred-texts.com/hin/rigveda/rv10090.htm>.

Rosen, Steven J. "Introduction." Steven J. Rosen (ed.) *Vaisnani: Women and the Worship of Krisha* (Delhi: Motilal Banarsidass Publishers, 1996).

Roy, Himadri. "Deconstructing Femininity: The Image of Indian Women During the Freedom Struggle in Kanthapura," Jaydeep Sarangi (ed.) *Raja Rao: The Master and His Moves* (New Delhi: Authors Press, 2007).

Roy, Rammohun. "The need of modern education." Ramachandra Guha (ed.) *Makers of Modern India* (New Delhi: Penguin Books, 2010).

Rushdie, Salman. "Introduction." *In Midnight's Children*, 1981 (London: Vintage Books, 2013).

Sachchidananda, "Integration of Tribes in Indian Society." Indira Gandhi Abinandan Samiti. *The Spirit of India*. Vol. II (New York: Asia Publishing House, 1976).

Sanker, Hithesh T.S. and Praveenlal Kuttichira. "Custody Deaths in Kerala: A Study from Post-mortem Data in Thrissur Medical College." *Economic & Political Weekly,* xlvii. 12 (2012).

Santis, Stefano De. *Nature and Man: The Hindu Perspective* Vol. 2 (Delhi: Sociecos & Dilip Kumar Publishers, 1995).

Sarangi, A.C. "Four Purusarthas and Their Role in Society." V.N. Jha (ed.) *Dharmasastra and Social Awareness* (Delhi: Indian Books Centre, 1996).

Satchidanandan, K. "Literature: Signing in Different Scripts." Hiranmay Karlekar (ed.) *Independent India: The First Fifty Years* (Delhi: Oxford University Press, 1998).

Saul, John S. *Decolonization and Empire: Contesting in Rhetoric and Reality of Resubordination in Southern Africa and Beyond* (New Delhi: Three Essays Collective, 2007).

Scharfe, Hartmut. "Artha." Sushil Mittal and Gene Thursby (ed.) *The Hindu World* (London: Routledge, 2004).

Schimmel, Annemaire. *Gabriel's Wing: A Study into the Religious Ideas of Sir Muhammad Iqbal* (Netherlands: E.J. Brills, 1963).

Scott, James C. *Domination and the Arts of Resistance: Hidden Transcripts* (New Haven: Yale University Press, 1990).

Sebastian, A.J. "Poor-Rich Divide in Aravind Adiga's *The White Tiger*". *Journal of Alternative Perspectives in the Social Sciences* 1.2 (2009). EBSCOhost Research Database. Accessed: 3rd August 2013 <http://ehis.ebscohost.com.ulm.idm.oclc.org/>.

Seeland, Klaus and Franz Schmithusen. *Man and Forest Series* (New Delhi: D.K. Printworld, 2002).

Sen, S. and J.K. Chopra, *Untouchable: Mulk Raj Anand* (New Delhi: Unique Publishers, 2007).

Sethi, Rumina. "Contesting Identities: Involvement and Resistance of Women in the Indian National Movement." *Journal of Gender Studies* 5.3 (1996).

Shah, Shalini. *Love, Eroticism and Female Sexuality in Classical Sanskrit Literature: Seventh-Thirteenth Centuries* (New Delhi: Manohar, 2009).

Shahare, Vasant A. "Theme, Title and Structure in Khushwant Singh's *Train to Pakistan* and Chaman Nahal's *Azadi*." *The Literacy Criterion* 25.2 (1990).

Sharma, R.S. *India's Ancient Past* (New Delhi: Oxford University Press, 2005).

Sharma, Shankar Dayal. "Indira Gandhi and the Congress." Indira Gandhi Abinandan Samiti. *The Spirit of India*. Vol. II (New York: Asia Publishing House, 1976).

Singh, Ajit K., Gaya Pandey, and Prabhat K. Singh. *Forest and Fribals in India* (New Delhi: B.K. Taneja, 1998).

Singh, Balmiki Prasad. *India's Culture: The State, the Arts, and Beyond* (India: Oxford University Press, 2011).

Singh, L.K. *Indian Cultural Heritage Perspective for Tourism* (Delhi: ISHA Books, 2008).

Singh, Manjit Inder. *The Critical Space: Studies in Literature, Theory, Nationalism and Diaspora* (New Delhi: National Publishing House, 2005).

Singh, N.K. *Not by Reason Alone: The Politics of Change* (New Delhi: Penguine Group, 2009).

Sivakumar, B. "Half of India's dalit population lives in 4 states." Web: 2nd May 2013. Accessed: 18th March 2014 <http://timesofindia.indiatimes.com/india/Half-of-Indias-dalit-population-lives-in-4-states/articleshow/19827757.cms>.

Sivaramkrishna, M. *Hindu View of Life: A Contemporary Perspective* (Bangalore: Dharmaram Publications, 2001).

Smith, Donald Eugene. *India as a Secular State* (1963) (New Jersey: Princeton Press, 1967).

Soh, Star and Frederick T.L. Leong. "Validity of vertical and horizontal individualism and collectivism in Singapore: Relationships with values and interests." *Journal of Cross-cultural Psychology* 33.1 (2002).

Srivastava, Neelam. *Secularism in the Postcolonial Indian Novel: National and Cosmopolitan Narratives in English,* 2007 (New York: Routledge, 2008).

———. "Languages of the nation in Salman Rushdie's Midnight's Children and Vikram Seth's A Suitable Boy." *ARIEL.* 36.1-2 (2005), Academic OneFile. Accessed: 22nd June 2013. <http://www.http://go.galegroup.com/>.

Su, John J. "Epic of Failure: Disappointment as Utopian Fantasy in *Midnight's Children.*" *Twentieth Century Literature* 47.4 (2001). Academic OneFile 29 June 2013. <http://go.galegroup.com>.

Tagore, Rabindranath. "Nationalism in India" (1917). Nalini Bhushan and Jay L. Garfield (eds.) *Indian Philosophy in English: From Renaissance to Independence* (Oxford: Oxford University Press, 2011).

———. "Nationalism." Fred Dallmayer and G.N. Deny (ed). *Between Tradition and Modernity: India's Search for Identity* (New Delhi: Sage Publications, 1998).

———. *Nationalism.* Ramachandra Guha (ed.) (New Delhi: Penguin Books, 2009).

Tank, N.D. "The Trauma of Partition in *Train to Pakistan* by Khushwant Singh and the Foreign Aggression and Its Impact on Indian Politics in *Shadow from Ladakh* By Bhabani Bhattacharya." Web page: 2011. Accessed: 1st June 2013 <www.shodhganga.inflibnet.ac.in/bitstream/10603/2301/.../07_chapter%202.pdf>

Tharoor, Shashi. *From Midnight to the Millennium* (India: Penguin Books, 1997).

———. *Nehru: The Invention of India.* 2003 (New Delhi: Penguin Books, 2007).

The Bhagavad Gita III.8. *Nitya Chaitanya Yati* (Tran.) (New Delhi: D.K. Printworld, 1993).

The Bhagavad Gita 7.9. Trans. O.P. Dwivedi "Dharmic Ecology" Christopher Key Chapple and Mary Evelyn Tucker (eds.), *Hinduism and Ecology* (Harvard: Harvard University Press, 2000).

The Collected Works of Mahatma Gandhi (New Delhi: The Publications divisions: Ministry of Information and broadcasting government of India, 1983).

The Kama Sutra of Vatsyayana. Richard Burton and F.F. Arbuthnot (Trans.) (Great Britain: Wordsworth Classics, 1996).

The Kurall, 32.317. "Tahtinen Unto," *Ahimsa: Non-Violence in Indian Tradition* (London: Rider and Company, 1976).

The Mahabharata, Uddyogaparva, 124, 34-38. Urmila Sharma and S.K. Sharma (Trans.) *Indian Political Thought* (New Delhi: Atlantic Publishers and Distributors, 1996).

Thomas, Cyriac. "Christian Contribution in Nation Building." *Journal of St. Thomas Christians* 14.1 (2003).

Tiwary, Tripti. "R.K. Narayan's Waiting for the Mahatma: A Reappraisal." *Indian Scholar* 3.2 (1981).

Varma, Pavan K. *Being India: The Truth about Why the Twenty-First Century will be India's* (New Delhi: Penguin Group, 2005).

Varshney, Ashutosh. "Editor's Preface." Ashutosh Varshney (ed.) *In The Indian Paradox: Essays in Indian Politics* (New Delhi: Sage Publications, 1989).

Vashi, Ashish. "Ahmedabad turned Akbar Veggie." *The Times of India,* Ahmedabad. 23 Nov. 2009. Accessed 2nd September 2012 <http://articles.timesofindia.indiatimes.com/2009-11-23/ahmedabad/28111782_1_mughal-emperor-akbar-jainism-architecture>.

Vatsyayan, Kapila. "Culture: The crafting of institutions" Hiranmay Karlekar (ed.), *Independent India: The First Fifty Years* (Delhi: Oxford University Press, 1998).

Vempeny, Bandhu Ishanands. "Western Secularism and Religion-Centered Indian Secularism: An Indian Alternative to Western Secularism." Antony Kalliath and Raj Irudaya (ed.) *Indian Secularism: A Theological Response* (Bangalore: Indian Theological Association, 2010).

Vishnu, Ashwini Kumar. "The God of Small Things: A Note on Roy's Sociological Imagination." Amar Nath Prasad and Bithika Dasgupta Sarkar (ed.) *Arundhati Roy: A Critical Elucidation* (New Delhi: Sarup Book Publishers, 2010).

Waller, Kathleen. "Redefinitions of India and Individuality in Adiga's *The White Tiger*." *Comparative Literature and Culture* 14.2 (2012) web: 2012. Accessed: 5th November 2013. <http://go.galegroup.com/>.

Weiner, Myron. "Preface." Ashutosh Varshney (ed.) *The Indian Paradox: Essays in Indian Politics* (New Delhi: Sage Publications, 1989).

William, Walsh. *R.K. Narayan: A Critical Appreciation* (Great Britain: University of Chicago Press, 1982).

Williams, Haydn Moore. *Studies in Modern Indian Fiction in English* (A Writers Workshop Publication, 1973).

Xaxa, Vani. "Globalization, Culturalism and Mass Media." *Women's Link* 15.2 April-June 2009.

Yoo, Boonghee. Naveen Donthu and Tomasz Lenartowicz. "Measuring Hofstede's Five Dimensions of Cultural Valuesat the Individual Level: Development and Validation of CVSCALE." *Journal of International Consumer Marketing* 23. Web: 1st May 2011. Accessed: 8th November 2013. <http://ehis.ebscohost.com.ulm.idm.oclc.org>.

"Dark India: Dalit in India Facts and Figures." Accessed: 18th March 2014. <http://darkindia.wordpress.com/dalit-in-india-facts-and-figures/>

"Is there something called Indianness?" Web page 30th January 2011, Accessed: 4th September 2011. <http://www.ghadar.in/gjh_html/?q=content/there-something-called-indianness>.

"Languages of India." Web page. *Wikipedia: The Free Encyclopedia*. Accessed: 28th August 2012. <http://en.wikipedia.org/wiki/Languages_of_India>.

"Now Tharoor's book under fire," *The Times of India*. 31 March, 2014. Kerala.

"Train to Pakistan 2007: Decolonization, Partition, and Identity in the Transnational Public Sphere." Accessed: 1st June 2013. <www.temple.edu/tempress/chapters_1800/1958_ch1>.

"What's in a name; 'India' and the 'Indian' Identity" Accessed: 3th September 2013. <http://vepa.us/dir8/identity.htm>